Marginal Conventions

Marginal Conventions:

Popular Culture, Mass Media and Social Deviance

edited by
Clinton R. Sanders

Bowling Green State University Popular Press
Bowling Green, Ohio 43403

In Memorium
Priscilla Kiehnle Warner
1952-1989

Contents

I
Introduction

'A Lot of People Like It':
The Relationship Between Deviance
and Popular Culture

Clinton R. Sanders

Introduction: Deviance, Popular Culture, and Power

The complex network of shared meanings we refer to as culture and the rules which derive from these meanings are the essence of social life (Geertz, 1973). Cultural artifacts and activities are based on shared understandings and rule-violation is a natural consequence of the existence of rules. The sources and consequences of both cultural products and rule-breaking are issues of significant concern in social scientific and everyday discussion. The essays included in this collection all focus on unconventional behavior and the groups, products, controversies, and themes which revolve around it.

Guided primarily by their vested interest in seeing society as an orderly structure bound together by shared norms, conventional sociologists typically have presented individual normative violations as, at worst, threats to a stable social order (eg., Merton, 1957: 131-194) or, at best, one mechanism by which the social system either undergoes necessary adaptive change or reinforces (through ritualized reaction to violations) the dominant social order (Durkheim, 1938). The major alternative perspective on deviance presents a very different picture. Rather than seeing deviance as an objective phenomenon—behavior is either deviant or not depending upon whether it conforms with or is in violation of social norms—the "labelling" or "social reaction" perspective presents deviance as largely a definitional issue. In this view, no behavior is intrinsically deviant. Instead, the "deviance" of an act depends on whether or not it is known to others and, consequently, whether or not it comes to be the focus of negative social reaction (Becker, 1963; Lemert, 1972; Schur, 1971). Like other forms of interaction, the deviance of an activity, therefore, depends upon the relative power of the actors and the situation in which the action takes place. Interpersonal violence, for example, is not inherently deviant. It is widely regarded as such when it is engaged in by those who do not possess the authority and fill the accepted roles (eg., law-enforcement officer, soldier, parent) for which violence is a legitimate component and it takes place in situations in which violence is conventionally deemed to be inappropriate. In short, deviance, from this

3

perspective, depends on *who engages* in the behavior, the *purpose* of the action, who becomes *aware* of the conduct, and the *situation* in which the behavior is carried out.[1]

Power has further relevance to this definitional/subjectivist perspective on deviance. Power insulates one from the reactive consequences of behavior which has the potential of being socially discrediting. The powerful actor can engage in rule-violating activities apart from situations in which he or she runs the risk of being observed and subsequently subjected to negative social reaction. Should knowledge of the discreditable behavior somehow slip out of the protective boundaries of privileged information control, however, those in positions of power typically possess the economic, political, legal, and interpersonal resources by which they can deflect or avoid negative repercussions.

Those in positions of control (elites, members of the "establishment," the "ruling-class," authorities, and so on) have, therefore, a distinct interest in shaping societal definitions of deviance. To the extent that social order exists, it rests upon the maintenance of a general consensus regarding good and bad behavior. The powerful have the most to gain from order and the most to lose from significant alterations in social patterns and understandings. For this reason elites consistently employ the considerable resources at their disposal to shape shared understandings of normality, dangerousness, acceptable behavior, legitimacy, immorality, and the myriad other definitional components of deviance and conventionality. Products commonly regarded as popular cultural—especially mass media fare—are of key importance in these efforts intended to maintain the status quo. Popular culture themes are consistently chosen and constructed by production "gate-keepers" so as to reinforce conventional norms and perspectives on reality. In other words, popular culture is, as many of the contributors to this volume emphasize, an eminently *political* phenomenon.

We come then to the second phenomenon which is the focus of this collection. Most simply, popular culture is regarded as made up of products which—as indicated in the quote by Irving Berlin[2] which provides part of the title of this piece—are consumed and (presumably) enjoyed by "a lot" of people. More specifically, popular culture is typically presented as consisting of materials and activities which are mass produced, acquired through some form of commercial exchange by members of a large and heterogeneous audience/consumer group, not intended solely for members of elite social segments, and characterized by formulaic/conventionalized form and content (Browne, 1983; Nye, 1970; Lewis, 1972: 2-4). Elitist critics of popular culture have tended to view these types of materials and activities with considerable distaste. Those who have employed a leftist political perspective (eg., Horkheimer and Adorno, 1972; Marcuse, 1966) have asserted that "mass culture" is created primarily for profit, borrows from and thereby trivializes "high culture," draws talented people away from the more worthy endeavor of creating elite products, and generates uncritical and passive consumers who are open to the wiles of totalitarian leaders. Conservative right-wing critics have tended to take a rather similar position. They have stressed the view of popular culture as presenting themes which are trivial, brutal or otherwise unworthy and as being a major factor causing the decline of the society's moral principles (see Rosenberg, 1964; Kaplan, 1972; Greenberg, 1972; cf., Markson and Lewis in this volume). These negative presentations of popular culture were particularly fashionable in the 1950s but died out somewhat during the 60s when elitist ire was redirected at the youth culture and its presumed advocacy of hedonism, nihilism, mysticism, and related "countercultural" orientations.

With the apparent decline of the youthful counterculture in the 70s, criticism of popular culture enjoyed something of a resurgence. Spearheaded by the religious right on the one hand and neomarxist analysts on the other, popular culture was again seen as the source of moral decay and/or the primary tool of the "ruling class" intent upon establishing authoritarian hegemony through the simplistic blandishments of mass produced "bread and circuses" which contain the ideological underpinnings of the current system (see Gitlin, 1979; Kellner, 1981; Goldman and Wilson, 1983; Dorfman, 1983).

These negative views of the simplistic form, banal content, and untoward social effects of popular culture have, in turn, been the ongoing focus of various counter-critiques by analysts with more pluralist or less judgmental orientations. Herbert Gans (1974) is the best-known advocate of this "populist" view of popular culture (cf., Barzun, 1956; White, 1964). Rather than decrying the supposed dangerous effects and mediocre content of contemporary culture, Gans and the other pluralist commentators present an image of society as composed of interdependent "taste publics" centered around specific cultural items and events. Members of taste publics—from elites attending the performance of a symphony orchestra to working class viewers of professional wrestling—*enjoy* the cultural forms they consume, *employ evaluative criteria* to differentiate "good" from "bad," and *use their knowledge* of the conventional elements of the materials to focus interaction and establish co-membership. The taste cultural items, in turn, *incorporate and reflect the values and interests* of the publics that consume them. The conventional view that culture is hierarchically ordered with materials consumed and activities enjoyed by the elites being of more value than those consumed and enjoyed by the less affluent is, therefore, simply a form of ethnocentrism reflecting the tastes of academics, members of the production world surrounding "fine" art, and other elites. The pluralist perspective emphasizes a separate-but-equal orientation toward contemporary culture and rejects the notion propounded by both conservative and leftist critics that popular culture degrades its consumers and the society in which it is situated. Popular culture should, according to pluralists, be the focus of serious attention because it is of intrinsic interest rather than because analysis can necessarily lead to a better understanding of the mechanisms by which cultural producers purposefully debase or manipulate members of the consuming public.[3]

The Process of Cultural Production

The pluralist perspective has provided a major grounding for the serious investigation of contemporary popular culture. To a significant degree it is at the core of the "production of culture" approach which examines the social process whereby cultural products are conceived, created, selected, evaluated, disseminated, chosen, and used. Like all social processes, those centered around cultural production are expedited by the fact that participants—from creators to consumers—share conventional knowledge which eases the collective action surrounding production and facilitates the evaluative communication between producers and consumers (Peterson, 1976; Becker, 1982; Sanders, 1982; Jensen, 1984).

It is here within the network of social interaction surrounding popular cultural production that we may see one of the key connections between deviance and popular culture. Driven largely by the ongoing problem of "commercial uncertainty"—creators and administrators of mainstream popular culture are not sure of the features that guarantee commercial success—popular culture tends to be characterized overwhelmingly by formulaic form and content. Producers decrease uncertainty by reproducing materials like those which have made money in the past (Hirsch, 1972). However, because key actors in the process—especially creators and consumers—value, at least, some degree of novelty, stylistic innovation is necessary. Innovative materials hold the promise of establishing newly successful formulae and innovative work allows popular culture creators to retain a creative self-definition. Culture administrators commonly display a conservative resistance to innovation, seeing it as a "deviant" threat to the established formulaic order (see Gitlin, 1983: 273-324; Kaplan, 1987; Cruz in this volume). In many cases the innovative creator must take steps to redefine the formula-violating materials as non-deviant through an overt "promotion" process (Lewis, 1986). This promotion of deviant/innovative cultural materials within the interaction system surrounding cultural production is analogous to the "educational" efforts which organized groups of social deviants (homosexuals, ex-mental patients, alcoholics, and so forth) direct at "the public" in order to attack widespread negative definitions and ease the weight of social reaction.

Deviance as a Popular Cultural Theme

In addition to the violation of stylistic conventions as a conflictual mechanism by which innovation takes place in the form and content of cultural products, rule-breaking is one of the favorite themes in contemporary popular culture. Deviance is an especially "hot topic" in the mass media (see Lyon, Crew, Cruz and Farnen in this volume). The general image of rule-breaking presented in the media is simplistic and stereotypic—deviance is atypical, pleasurably rewarding, and eventually results in the nonconformist suffering extraordinarily painful consequences. Most commonly, media deviants are presented as being driven by sickness, innate wickedness, weakness, or ignorance. Further, they are typically portrayed as not only acting abnormally, but also as *looking* like deviants. The rule-breaker's appearance reflects his or her moral status (Needleman and Weiner, 1976). Heroic characters who uphold the rules are attractive and ordinary citizens look ordinary while deviants are conventionally presented as ugly, misshapen, dirty, bizarrely costumed, atavistic, dark, and frightening (see Warner in this volume).

The physical and motivational atypicality of the media deviant and the obligatory conclusion in which the nonconformist pays for his or her deviant pleasure by suffering extraordinary pain point to what a number of analysts see as the major function of the presentation of deviance in the media and other popular culture products. Images of deviant behavior and the deviant actor provide object lessons which define and reinforce the consensual boundaries of social order. The normative order is legitimate, official agents of social control are necessary, rule-breaking is unusual, and violators are always punished for their misbehavior (see Wilkins, 1973; Young, 1973; Gerbner, 1978; Crew, Cruz, and Carveth in this volume). Recent discussions presenting a "constructionist" view of the media and its effects (eg., Gamson, 1988) stress similar ideas. Media messages are ideological constructs used by members of the audience to identify, interpret, and devise solutions for deviance and the other social "problems" which are the dominant focus of media attention.

Some Unanticipated Consequences of the Deviance Theme

It may be that popular cultural presentations of deviance work against the interest of those that have a major stake in maintaining conformity. Wilkins (1973), for example, observes that stereotypic displays of rule-breaking actually act to "amplify" deviance. To the extent that members of the media/popular culture audience see these materials as reflective of reality, the intense focus on deviance tends to increase public perceptions of the frequency and threat of rule-breaking. Consequently, heightened negative perceptions of nonconformity within the public generate more rigorous social reaction. In turn, rather than convincing deviants of the error of their violative ways, increased social reaction acts to further isolate deviants from "normals" thereby decreasing the likelihood that they will climb back onto the normative straight and narrow (see Crew and Farnen in this volume).

Most of the ways in which analysts see the negative social consequences of popular cultural presentations of deviance are considerably more straightforward than that provided by the amplification notion. Most common views of the relationship between portrayals of deviance and "real life" rule-breaking posit a more or less direct causal connection. Cultural consumers who are routinely bombarded with fictional accounts of "anti-social" (ie., "anti-status quo") behavior will take those presentations and model their own actions after them. Bolstered by the findings generated by a massive body of experimental studies, advocates of this rather simplistic behaviorist image of human behavior have mounted organized attempts to "clean up the airwaves" or ban other popular cultural materials which they see as causing the supposed increase in immoral or misanthropic activities. The efforts of groups opposed to media violence (see Lyon in this volume), "lewd" rock and roll lyrics (see Markson in this volume), and the graphic erotic depictions contained in "pornography" (Dworkin, 1981; Lederer, 1980) reflect this understanding of the social impact of the presentation of deviance in popular cultural materials.[4]

Taste Publics and Deviant Subcultures

The highly social nature of both deviance and popular cultural production/consumption points to yet another linkage between the two phenomena. As emphasized in the pluralist view of popular culture, social groups form around specific cultural products and devise a considerable body of evaluative information about the central conventions which characterize the focal materials or activities. These "taste publics" are, in essence, *subcultures* which are generated by the mutual leisure interests and shared problems of the members (see Arnold, 1970). Similarly, subcultural groups adhere around activities conventionally regarded as deviant and are the focus of negative social reaction. Deviant subcultures provide a variety of services for their members. Within them participants may acquire the materials and knowledge which are essential to successfully pursuing the disvalued activities. These groups also incorporate and share values and definitions of reality which members use to understand themselves, the behaviors for which they are condemned, and the larger society which is the source of negative definitions and overt social reaction. Deviant subcultures are protective social phenomena—they offer group support, provide information about protective techniques, and supply positive definitions useful as alternatives to the negative labels conferred by conventional agents of social control (see Sutherland and Cressey, 1978: 77-97). Not infrequently, these informal groups develop a more formally organized core which directs collective efforts intended to encourage a redefinition of the condemned behavior thereby easing the pressure of negative social reaction.

Taste groups surrounding popular cultural phenomena function similarly for their adherents. They provide direct or mediated social contexts in which evaluative conventions are communicated, pleasurable interactions with like-minded individuals can take place, and access to the cultural items around which the taste public revolves is available. Although the materials and activities constituting taste cultures are rarely subjected to the same degree of negative social reaction as are the unconventional activities which provide the organizational focus of deviant subcultures, taste publics—like organized groups of deviants—do act as sources of innovation. Popular culture administrators and creators commonly borrow from taste cultures in their search for new styles and products. This form of "bottom-up" innovation is especially apparent in the areas of fashion, popular music, dance, "fine" art, and colloquial language (see Hirschman, 1981; Castleman, 1982; Levine, 1988; Sanders, 1989).

For the deviant social group as well as the taste public, this process of education, innovation, and borrowing can have both positive and negative consequences. A major pleasurable aspect of membership in subcultures is the exclusivity and unconventionality of involvement with the core phenomenon—be it illegal drug use or zydeco music (see Lewis, 1988; Stern and Friesen in this volume). Although cultural and behavioral difference commonly has negative aspects—especially for those involved in illegal activities—involvement with unconventional tastes and knowledge provides feelings of uniqueness and separation from the rigid blandness of the mainstream. When ad executives begin to wear long hair, Pat Boone records a song by Little Richard, established politicians sport tattoos, or insurance agents smoke marijuana, these activities, styles, and products lose their raw impact and their power to symbolize "hipness" is significantly reduced. Of course, for those individuals whose tastes and behaviors are especially discrediting and who are consistently subjected to inconvenient social reaction, the legitimation which comes from "educating" the public about the lack of threat posed by a particular lifestyle or consumption activity offers considerable advantage (see Sanders, 1989: 25-35 and Stenross in this volume).

Deviance within Cultural Production Worlds

A final connection between deviance and popular culture is seen in those situations where salient norms are violated by participants in the social worlds surrounding cultural creation. One obvious example of this type of rule-breaking is seen in those cases in which higher-ups in the hierarchy of the production world overtly victimize those with less status. The sexual exploitation of the "casting couch" in theatrical or film production (Morris, 1987) or the theft of a subordinate's ideas or products are two examples of common, but formally condemned, activities in the social networks surrounding cultural production.

The construction of "news" by newsworkers is an issue of rule-breaking within popular culture organizations which has been the focus of contemporary concern. Widespread ethical expectations held by the media public center around the basic "facticity" of news stories. When newsworkers fabricate or initiate events and present them as being independent newsworthy occurrences, the public commonly views this as being a significant violation of the expectations constraining news reporting. There is, of course, some flexibility in expectations depending on the media organ in which the fraudulent news story is presented. Purposeful misrepresentation of events reported in the *New York Times* or on the CBS Evening News is an issue of considerable concern (Eason, 1988). Fanciful stories constructed out of the thin air and presented as fact in *The National Enquirer* or other "check-out counter" tabloids are defined as quasi-fiction by all but those readers with the most tenuous connection to consensual reality. These popular culture products are the focus of negative social reaction only when they claim to present facts about public figures who feel themselves to be slandered and initiate legal proceedings (see Ressner, 1988).[5]

Conclusion

The papers presented in this anthology cohere around three interconnected themes. In general, deviance is not seen as an "objective" attribute of behavior. Instead, whether an activity is regarded as deviance and the person who participates in it is regarded as a deviant depends on a complex process of social definition. The status of the actor, the situational context in which the activity occurs, the visibility of the behavior, and the degree of social consensus which surrounds the rules which are violated are key factors shaping definitions of deviance and subsequent social reaction.

The vested interest of those in positions of power in maintaining the established social order by controlling salient definitions of deviance is another theme underlying these essays. By shaping the form and content of popular cultural products—especially messages disseminated through the mass media—the powerful (the "State," the "ruling-class," the "establishment," and so forth) construct the larger reality which provides the foundation of social action and reaction. Our experience with popular culture products provides us with information about the "reality" of AIDS, rock and roll, immoral behavior by film stars, televised violence, gun collectors, and political terrorism and the dangers inherent within them. The controllers of cultural production self-servingly direct reactions to deviance by shaping how it is consensually understood.

Finally, involvement with a marginal or disvalued activity or product entails certain social risks. Popular cultural taste groups and deviant subcultures revolve around the shared interests and knowledge of their members. Cultural publics and subcultures provide access to valued activities and objects, contact with like-minded others, protective insulation from negative judgments and actions of "outsiders," and an evaluative typology members can use to maintain positive understandings of themselves and the social objects to which they and their fellows are committed.

Notes

[1]The act of swallowing an amphetamine tablet, for example, is "conforming" if it is done by a soldier in a front-line position, under the supervision of a physician, in order to achieve the alertness demanded by the immediate battle situation. On the other hand, when engaged in by a teenager, the same act of drug ingestion is "deviant" (at least in the view of parents, police, guidance counselors, and other powerful actors intent upon controlling teenagers) especially when it takes place at a party and is intended to enhance the "fun" of the recreational experience (Young, 1973).

[2]Irving Berlin is reputed to have stated that, "Popular music is popular because a lot of people like it."

[3]Viewing popular culture from a pluralist perspective does not necessarily require that the analyst reject the notion that cultural materials may have socially untoward effects or that they are, not uncommonly, purposefully constructed so as to reflect and reinforce the interest of elites. The sizeable literature on the construction of "news," for example, provides considerable evidence that this cultural product is consciously chosen and shaped by powerful "media gatekeepers" so as to present a particular, status quo maintaining, image of the ongoing "reality" of current events (see Gans, 1979; Altheide, 1976, 1985; Schlesinger, 1978; Cohen and Young, 1973; Stein, 1974; Herman and Chomsky, 1988). These effects are, however, limited by the selectivity exercised by cultural consumers in the forms and content of the materials they consume, their interpretive activities premised on pre-existing beliefs, and the central importance of immediate co-interactants in shaping the attitudes and opinions held by social actors (Klapper, 1960; Bauer, 1963).

[4]For cogent counter-arguments to this modeling view see Tong, 1987; Caught Looking, Inc., 1988; Pattison, 1988; Markson in this volume.

[5]Constructed events presented as factual sometimes do have significant social impact even when the media creators do not intend the public to interpret them as being anything but realistic fiction. The widespread panic generated by the broadcast of "The War of the Worlds" by Orson Welles and the Mercury Theater (Cantril, 1940) and the similar reaction to a Swedish radio broadcast reputedly carrying the story of a nuclear accident (Rosengren, et al, 1978) are examples of social reaction to "unintentional" media deviance.

Bibliography

Altheide, D. (1976) *Creating Reality: How TV News Distorts Events*, Beverly Hills: Sage.
———. (1985) *Media Power*, Beverly Hills, CA: Sage.
Arnold, D. (1970) *The Sociology of Subcultures*, Berkeley: Glendessary.
Barzun, J. (1956) *Popular Music in America*, New York: Doubleday.
Bauer, R. (1963) "The Obstinate Audience," *The American Psychologist* 18: 319-328.
Becker, H. (1963) *Outsiders*, New York: Free Press.
———. (1982) *Art Worlds*, Berkeley: University of California Press.
Browne, R. (1983) "Popular Culture—New Notes Toward a Definition," in C. Geist and J. Nachbar (eds.), *The Popular Culture Reader* (third edition), Bowling Green, OH: Popular Press, pp. 13-20.
Cantril, H. (1940) *The Invasion From Mars*, Princeton: Princeton University Press.
Castleman, C. (1982) *Getting Up*, Cambridge: MIT Press.
Caught Looking, Inc. (1988) *Caught Looking: Feminism, Pornography and Censorship*, Seattle: Real Comet Press.
Cohen, S. and J. Young (eds.) (1973) *The Manufacture of News*, Beverly Hills: Sage.
Dorfman, A. (1983) *The Empire's Old Clothes*, New York: Pantheon.
Durkheim, E. (1938) *The Rules of Sociological Method* (8th edition), Glencoe, IL: Free Press.
Dworkin, A. (1981) *Pornography: Men Possessing Women*, New York: Perigee.
Eason, D. (1988) "On Journalistic Authority: The Janet Cooke Scandal," in J. Carey (ed.), *Media, Myths, and Narratives: Television and the Press*, Newbury Park, CA: Sage, pp. 205-227.

12   Marginal Conventions

Gamson, W. (1988) "A Constructionist Approach to Mass Media and Public Opinion," *Symbolic Interaction* 11 (2): 161-174.

Gans, H. (1974) *Popular Culture and High Culture*, New York: Basic Books.

———— (1979) *Deciding What's News*, New York: Pantheon.

Geertz, C. (1973) *The Interpretation of Cultures*, New York: Basic Books.

Gerbner, G. (1978) "Deviance and Power: Symbolic Functions of 'Drug Abuse'," in C. Winick (ed.), *Deviance and Mass Media*, Beverly Hills, CA: Sage, pp. 13-30.

Gitlin, T. (1979) "Prime Time Ideology: The Hegemonic Process in Television Entertainment," *Social Problems* 26 (3): 251-266.

———— (1983) *Inside Prime Time*, New York: Pantheon.

Goldman, R. and J. Wilson (1983) "Appearance and Essence: The Commodity Form Revealed in Perfume Advertisements," in S. McNall (ed.), *Current Perspectives in Social Theory*, Vol. 4, Greenwich, CT: JAI Press, pp. 119-142.

Greenberg, C. (1972) "Avante-Garde and Kitsch," in J. Hall and B. Ulanov (eds.), *Modern Culture and the Arts*, New York: McGraw-Hill, pp. 147-163.

Herman, E. and N. Chomsky (1988) *Manufacturing Consent*, New York: Pantheon.

Hirsch, P. (1972) "Processing Fads and Fashions: An Organization-Set Analysis of Cultural Industry Systems," *American Journal of Sociology* 77: 639-659.

Hirschman, E. (1981) "Retailing and the Production of Popular Culture," in R. Stampfl and E. Hirschman (eds.), *Theory in Retailing: Traditional and Non-traditional Sources*, Chicago: American Marketing Association, pp. 71-83.

Horkheimer, M. and T. Adorno (1972) *Dialectic of Enlightenment*, New York: Seabury.

Jensen, J. (1984) "An Interpretive Approach to Culture Production," in W. Rowland, Jr. and B. Watkins (eds.), *Interpreting Television: Current Research Perspectives*, Newbury Park, CA: Sage, pp. 98-118.

Kaplan, A. (1972) "The Aesthetics of the Popular Arts," in J. Hall and B. Ulanov (eds.), *Modern Culture and the Arts*, New York: McGraw-Hill, pp. 48-62.

Kaplan, E. A. (1987) *Rocking Around the Clock*, New York: Methuen.

Kellner, D. (1981) "Network Television and American Society," *Theory and Society* 10 (1): 31-62.

Klapper, J. (1960) *The Effects of Mass Communication*, New York: Free Press.

Lederer, L. (ed.) (1980) *Take Back the Night: Women on Pornography*, New York: William Morrow.

Lemert, E., (1972) *Human Deviance, Social Problems, and Social Control* (second edition), Englewood Cliffs, NJ: Prentice-Hall.

Levine, L. (1988) *Highbrow/Lowbrow: The Emergence of Cultural Hierarchy in America*, Cambridge: Harvard University Press.

Lewis, G. (ed.) (1972) *Side-Saddle on the Golden Calf*, Pacific Palisades, CA: Goodyear.

———— (1986) "Uncertain Truths: The Promotion of Popular Culture," *Journal of Popular Culture* 20 (3): 31-44.

Lewis, J. (1988) "Punks in L.A.: It's Kiss or Kill, *Journal of Popular Culture* 22 (2): 87-97.

Marcuse, H. (1966) *One Dimensional Man*, Boston: Beacon.

Merton, R. (1957) *Social Theory and Social Structure*, Glencoe, IL: Free Press.

Morris, L. (1987) "Beyond the Casting Couch: Actors and Directors Feeling Each Other Out," paper presented at the meetings of the Midwest Sociological Association, Chicago (April).

Needleman, B. and N. Weiner (1976) "Heroes and Villains in Art," *Society* 14: 35-39.

Nye, R. (1970) *The Unembarrassed Muse*, New York: Dial.

Pattison, R. (1988) "The Mean Machine?," *The Nation*, August 13/20, pp. 140-142.

Peterson, R. (1976) "The Production of Culture: A Prolegomenon," *American Behavioral Scientist* 19 (July): 669-684.

Ressner, J. (1988) "Enquiring Minds," *Rolling Stone*, June 30, pp. 53ff.

Rosenberg, B. (1964) "Mass Culture in America," in B. Rosenberg and D.M. White (eds), *Mass Culture*, New York: Free Press, pp. 3-12.

Rosengren, K., et al (1978) "The Barseback Panic: A Case of Media Deviance," in C. Winick (ed.), *Deviance and Mass Media*, Beverly Hills, CA: Sage, pp. 131-149.

Sanders, C. (1982) "Structural and Interactional Features of Popular Culture Production: An Introduction to the Production of Culture Perspective," *Journal of Popular Culture* 16 (2): 66-74.

———— (1989) *Customizing the Body: The Art and Culture of Tattooing*, Philadelphia: Temple University Press.

Schlesinger, P. (1978) *Putting Reality Together*, London: Methuen.

Schur, E. (1971) *Labeling Deviant Behavior*, New York: Harper Row.

Stein, M. (1974) *Shaping the News*, New York: Washington Square.

Sutherland, E. and D. Cressey (1978) *Criminology* (tenth edition), Philadelphia: Lippincott.

Tong, R. (1987) "Women, Pornography, and the Law," *Academe*, September/October, pp. 15-22.

White, D. (1964) "Mass Culture in America: Another Point of View," in B. Rosenberg and D. M. White (eds.), *Mass Culture*, New York: Free Press, pp. 13-21.

Wilkins, L. (1973) "Information and the Definition of Deviance," in S. Cohen and J. Young (eds.), *The Manufacture of News*, Beverly Hills, CA: Sage, pp. 22-27.

Young, J. (1973) "The Myth of the Drug Taker in the Mass Media," in S. Cohen and J. Young (eds.), *The Manufacture of News*, Beverly Hills, CA: Sage, pp. 314-322.

II
Social Reactions to
Popular Cultural Deviance

Introduction

When popular cultural phenomena come to be regarded as deviant—especially by social actors who exercise significant amounts of power—they become the focus of collective reaction. The two papers in this section deal with examples of social movements forming around definedly problematic cultural worlds and products.

Jerry Lewis presents an historical incident in which the allegedly deviant behavior of a well-known film star—Fatty Arbuckle—acted as a symbolic representation of what was widely regarded as the immoral lifestyle of those involved in the Hollywood film industry. Public figures were and are considered to be models and their violation of cherished norms—recreational use of illegal drugs, sexual exploits, criminal involvements, and so forth—are commonly regarded as especially troublesome, particularly because young people are presumed to emulate their behavior. Despite the fact that Arbuckle was, as Lewis points out, "falsely accused" of the acts which became the focus of legal proceeding, he became a convenient target. His career was seriously affected and the incident was used to generate as social movement directed at "cleaning up" film content and the subculture surrounding film making.

Stephen Markson discusses a contemporary example of "moral panic." In this case, the form and content of the popular cultural product—rock and roll—are simplistically presented by influential figures who have ready access to the mass media as being the major cause of the various forms of typical teenage behavior of which adults disapprove. As Markson emphasizes, the "rock and roll menace" provides a widely appealing "quasi-theory" to explain why young people, in the view of their parents, dress so outlandishly, fail to obey parental commands, have sex, experiment with certain drugs, and otherwise act to irritate adults. Since the "rock and roll makes kids go bad" quasi-theory encapsulates the cause and related appropriate means of solving the "problem," it deflects attention away from much more relevant issues such as the oppressive status of youth and the conflict built into the parent/child relationship which adults are loath to acknowledge and examine.

17

Comedy and Deviance:
The Fatty Arbuckle Case*

Jerry M. Lewis
Assisted by
Linda Powell

Introduction

Popular culture in American society has often been considered a cause of social problems. Popular culture content presented to the society via the mass media has been perceived as causing social problems in two ways. First its content, music, pictures and words, have been seen as the direct cause of social problems. Some have suggested, for example, that the words of rock music may be the stimulus for drug use among young people. Second, the personal lives of popular culture personalities have been seen as a cause of social problems, even when the content generated by the personalities is seen as harmless.

The Fatty Arbuckle case is probably the first clear example of this dimension in the history of American popular culture. In the pages that follow, I look at the Arbuckle Case using Neil J. Smelser's (1962) model of collective behavior. His model, derived from the ideas of Talcott Parsons, argues that a variety of collective behavior including panic, hysteria, hostile outbursts, and social movements can be explained with a few key ideas. Using five determinants combined with subdeterminants, the model allows the analyst to look at phenomena as value-added. That is, each determinant describes concrete entities that contribute "value" to the eventual collective behavior episode. This model has been used to study a variety of subjects ranging from student riots to soccer hooliganism. But to my knowledge, it has never been used to study social movements focusing on popular culture.

The first determinant is *structural conduciveness* and refers to societal conditions that are necessary, but not sufficient, for the rise of a social movement. The analyst must decide whether the movement is a value-oriented or norm-oriented movement. I propose that the response to the Fatty Arbuckle case was a norm-oriented movement because people attempted to protect or create new norms rather than calling for a fundamental modification of norms with new values. Smelser further argues that social movements

*I wish to thank Raymond Adamek, Diane L. Lewis, and Linda Powell for their help on this research.

18

are facilitated if people have access to legitimate channels for expressing grievances and these people have the ability to communicate with each other.

The next determinant is *structural strain* particularly at the level of norms and values. For Smelser strain at the normative level refers primarily to issues of social integration. The *generalized belief* in a norm oriented movement has two components. First, there is a diagnosis of the forces causing the strain and, second, there are proposals for solving the problem. These components become agreed upon and shared by leaders and members of the protesting groups.

Mobilization for action is the determinant which classifies behavior by the use of several subdeterminants including leadership, initial and derived phases, success or failure of strategies and tactics and the institutionalization of the movement. *Social control* is the final determinant and refers to the response of the social control authorities to the movement. In particular, it looks at whether the authorities do what the movement wants them to do.

Methodology

The data for this study are drawn primarily from secondary sources. The major one is David Yallop's (1976) *The Day the Laughter Stopped*. Yallop provides a detailed account of Arbuckle's life before, during, and after the trial. It relies on actual transcripts of the court proceedings. There is an excellent bibliography of books about film in the 1920s. However, his book has to be carefully used as he rarely provides citations for his direct quotes other than trial transcripts.

Yallop is an English film critic. His book was widely and, for the most part, favorably reviewed. The *New York Times* (Lingeman, 1976) said that the book was, "a fascinating work of film history, which catches the social currents of the times." The reviewer praises the fact that the book was based, in part, on court transcripts thought lost, as well as interviews with surviving principals. *Publisher's Weekly* (1976) describes it as "meticulously researched." However, the *New Statesman* (French, 1976) while noting the value of the newly discovered material from the court transcripts expresses concern over Yallop's "Dreyfusard" tendencies to totally vindicate Arbuckle.

I have used the *New York Times* and *Variety* as a check on Yallop's work. *The Times* carried at least one Arbuckle article, six on the front page, from September 11 to October 1, 1921. It continued to report the Arbuckle case until its conclusion.[1]

The Arbuckle Case[2]

Roscoe "Fatty" Arbuckle had become well-known to the public by 1916 through his involvement in the antic films of the Keystone Kops. Paramount saw so much potential in him that he was offered a contract which gave him total control over his pictures and an income of one million dollars per year—the first contract ever of this magnitude.

On September 5, 1921, Labor Day, an impromptu party was held in Arbuckle's suite at the St. Francis Hotel in San Francisco. At this party, liquor although illegal at the time, was consumed freely. Many people came and went, the party lasted for most of the day. Sometime during the party, Virginia Rappe, an actress, became ill. She had been nauseous, complained of abdominal pains, and had lost consciousness. After various "home" remedies, including immersion in ice water, were attempted without success, the house doctor was summoned.[3] He concluded that she had had too much to drink. Although her condition did not improve, no further medical attention was given for some time.

By the time she was taken to a hospital (September 8), it was too late. She died September 9 of peritonitis caused by a ruptured urinary bladder, possibly a victim of medical malpractice. Arbuckle had returned to Los Angeles by the time he heard of her death. He returned to San Francisco, where he was arrested and charged with murder on the basis of a complaint by Maude Delmont, a guest at the party. Delmont accused Arbuckle of sexually assaulting Virginia Rappe and thus causing her death. Ms. Delmont never testified at the trial because her story was too full of holes and her character questionable.

Regardless of Delmont's motivation, the charge was made. The evidence was insufficient for an indictment for murder, however, and the charge was reduced to manslaughter. If public interest had not been so aroused by Ms. Delmont's accusations and other rumors, it is quite possible that no charge would have been filed. The facts later emerged that Arbuckle was not alone with the victim more than ten minutes, that she was fully clothed and showed no signs of attack, and that she suffered from chronic bladder problems. Still it took three trials to acquit Arbuckle. For all practical purposes, Fatty Arbuckle's career was over. As Buster Keaton said, "all of the laughter stopped." Hollywood's first major comedy star would wait over a decade before he could entertain in films again.

Analysis

This analysis based on Smelser's model of collective behavior focuses on a period of time from September 5, 1921 to November 14, 1921 looking particularly at the groups attacking Fatty Arbuckle and the American film industry. I begin with the first determinant in Smelser's model, *structural conduciveness.*

Structural conduciveness refers to conditions that allow for collective behavior. These include, first, the premise that Arbuckle should be removed from films rather than the notion that the American film industry needed significant change. Second, the idea that his opponents had legitimate channels for protest. Third, there were mechanisms for the opponents to communicate with each other.

Almost immediately four elements became central to the protest, the press, ministers, women's groups, and theatre owners. The press, as represented by San Francisco and Los Angeles papers, began to attack Arbuckle soon after the death of Virginia Rappe was announced.

The attack on Arbuckle was led by two Hearst papers, the Los Angeles and San Francisco *Examiner,* through their stories and editorials. But other groups entered the fray. Ministers spoke from their pulpits, women's groups organized town meetings, and theatre owners banned Arbuckle's films.

The focus of the protest was on Arbuckle. The complaining groups used legitimate channels rather than developing new ones. For example, the press used its pages through news stories and editorials while women's groups worked through town meetings. Theatre owners contributed by banning Arbuckle's films. No new structures emerged at this time. Lastly, primarily through the press and public meetings, the various complaining groups were able to develop an awareness of each other. The stage was set for *structural strain* which refers to a tension or disequilibrium in the social system.

The opponents perceived a tension between Arbuckle's comedic lifestyle and his alleged deviant off-screen lifestyle. We have a fascinating situation where on-screen content is perceived as potentially or actually harmful because of the alleged deviant behavior of the actor who presented the content. Indeed, it makes no difference that the actor (in this case Fatty Arbuckle) was never convicted of a crime. In the 1920s, the suggestion of a possible crime was enough to bring the call for censorship.

The issue of immorality in Hollywood has been raised before the Arbuckle case, particularly in the Mary Pickford—Douglas Fairbanks marriage which took place within a month after Pickford's divorce. But even this event was not clear cut, for Pickford had been planning to divorce her husband anyway. The Arbuckle case gave critics and reformers a clear target.

The Arbuckle case became a metaphor for the more general concern that lifestyles of the movie community had to be considered in relation to the content of any film. The norm was clear. Only "good" people could make comedies. The moral panic had begun. This idea is examined in the section on mobilization for action.

The idea of a *generalized belief* is that the views of the complaining groups can be identified by the analyst in terms of identifying the causes of problems and solutions for them.

Arbuckle's misfortune gave critics and reformers a clear issue. A woman had died because of a "deviant" act by a major film star. A minister commented, "The motion picture is poisoning the mind of the youth of America." *(New York Times:* September 14, 1921, p. 3)

The judge at the preliminary hearing recognized that Arbuckle was being punished for more than an illegal act.

This is an important case. We are not trying Roscoe Arbuckle alone...Actually, in a large sense, we are trying our present day morals, our present social conditions, our present day looseness of thought and lack of social balance (*New York Times*: September 29, 1921, p. 2).

The St. Louis Dispatch wrote on September 13, 1921 (p. 1)

For several years the motion picture industry has been a bone of contention. The business community has supported it—for it brought the city millions of dollars annually. The "home folks" element and the "natives" have denounced it, claiming Hollywood where the motion (picture) people have centered was a hotbed of immorality.

On the same day, the *New York Times* (September 13, 1921, p. 1) commented, "An actor or actress with a questionable reputation might be acceptable in a sophisticated drama, but not in a simple, frolicsome comedy that will be watched by thousands of young people and children." The mayor of Philadelphia noted that the showing of Arbuckle pictures at this time would tend to offend "public morals" (*New York Times*, September 14, 1921, p. 2).

The fourth determinant, *mobilization for action*, is examined in terms of leadership, real and derived phases, success and future of specific tactics and the institutionalization of the movement.

The leadership against Arbuckle came from the four groups including the press, ministers, women's organizations, and theatre owners.

The Hearst papers led the charge. They printed stories that were untrue or contained partial truths. For example, one story described how Rappe accused Arbuckle of harming her. This turned out to be completely false. Much has been written about Hearst, the model for Orson Welles' *Citizen Kane*, but it does seem that the Hearst papers were unfair. Indeed, Yallop (1976, p. 138) describes them as "criminally unresponsible." He (Yallop, 1976, p.138) writes about Arbuckle and Hearst that Hearst was:

...later able to boast that he sold more newspapers reporting the Arbuckle case than he had since America entered the First World War (or as Buster Keaton overheard him say, since the Lusitania went down). His ruthlessness in boosting circulation was to have a significant effect on Arbuckle's fate, so it is worth pausing here to describe the man behind the press.

Ministers, women's organizations, and theatre owners also attacked Arbuckle. Ministers used their pulpits. On Sunday, September 18, 1921, two weeks after the party, the clergy focused on Arbuckle. *Variety* (9/23/21, p. 46) writes, "The Arbuckle case has aroused a deep feeling against the entire profession [film making]. Sermons against picture people were preached from practically every pulpit last Sunday." For example, a minister in a church across the bay from San Francisco, in Oakland, said (Yallop, 1976, p. 150):

Honors we seek are the honors of the world. We too often make the mistake of bowing to some man in the world who may be a great star. Like Arbuckle. As far as his condition is concerned, if he is guilty as alleged, he should receive a court trial and justice be meted out to him.

If a moral leader goes down, it is a moral crash, but if a man foremost in lines of entertainment that can be capitalized and commercialized goes down, man loses nothing.

The shame of it all is that good people like you make possible the continuance of such a man before the public.

Women's groups in many cities took up the crusade against Arbuckle. One of the most powerful was the Women's Vigilant Committee of San Francisco. Its activities included town meetings, letter writing, lobbying officials, and monitoring hearings and trials. Yallop describes the Committee's program during a meeting with the Chief of Police of San Francisco, Daniel O'Brien. Yallop (1976, p. 183) writes:

On Wednesday, while the coroner's jury was deliberating, O'Brien addressed them: "It makes no difference whether Arbuckle is just a laborer, a film star or king of the South Sea Islands, he will be prosecuted the same as any other man." He got a standing ovation, and the women began to chant, "Punish Arbuckle. Punish Arbuckle."

Speaker after speaker went to the rostrum at the Women's Vigilant Committee meeting. It appeared that Roscoe had personally outraged every woman in San Francisco. From among several hundred applicants, eighteen women were selected to attend Arbuckle's trial in a body and "give moral support to the women witnesses who are called upon to give testimony;" this was done "in the interests of justice." One of the members proposed a resolution condemning Arbuckle, but the president of the Women's Vigilant Committee, Dr. Mariana Bertola, dissuaded the meeting from passing it, because to do so "might affect the qualifications of any of us who may be called to serve on a jury to try Arbuckle." The implications were clear, the resolution withdrawn.

Lastly, theatre owners took up the challenge of Arbuckle. They had the power to stop showing Arbuckle's films which were generally very successful (Telotte, 1988, p. 173). Newspapers reported that the ban of showing Arbuckle's films was, for the most part, voluntary. It was often supported by city officials.

The banning of his films by theatre owners began almost immediately after Arbuckle's involvement in the party became known. It started in Los Angeles when the largest theatre owner, Sid Grauman, stopped showing "Gasoline Gus" on September 11, 1921 just six days after the Labor Day party. The same response seemed to happen all over the United States particularly in the large cities. The New York Times (9/13/21, p. 2) wrote:

The movement to banish Arbuckle films from the screen began, apparently, in California and reports from other sections of the country indicate that within a week there would be very few showing "Fatty" Arbuckle here [New York City] or elsewhere.

Why was all this happening? The concept of "moral panic" (Cohen, 1972) seems useful here. Stanley Cohen, an English sociologist, describes a moral panic as a situation where societies define a "condition, episode, person or group, as a threat to societal values and interests" (Cohen 1972, p. 1). He gives particular power to the media's role in spreading the moral panic through a process of what he calls deviance amplification. The media set the agenda for discourse by identifying who the "folk devils" are at any time in society.

The Arbuckle case appears to be a classic case of moral panic. The Hearst papers were fanning the fires of moral outrage aided and abetted by ministers and women's clubs. Arbuckle was being defined as a folk devil by all sides. But why? What caused this moral panic? Three reasons seem plausible. First, there is the persona of Fatty Arbuckle himself. Arbuckle was wealthy and successful. But he was not like the typical film goer at 266 pounds. Telotte (1988, p. 173) writes, "Then too, he simply looked different, his very size distinguished him from the other, usually slightly built, silent comedians, and furnished a comic springboard for his interactions with smaller players in his films." Second, Arbuckle represented a medium that was increasing in power. He became the focal point for those who feared the power of theatre film. Therefore, the producers of comedic material had to be pure because of their power. Third, where there is smoke there is fire. Even with the lack of criminal or civil convictions, some reasonable people assumed that something bad happened at the party. Thus, these factors, combined with the media and the lobbying efforts of ministers and women's club, fueled the moral panic of turning Fatty Arbuckle into a folk devil.

The initial stage of the movement was the response of the complaining groups to the death of Rappe and Arbuckle's possible involvement in it. The derived phase was the monitoring of the legal activities by the various groups, particularly the press and the Women's Committee. The L.A. *Examiner* on September 17, 1921 listed four possibilities for Arbuckle (Yallop, 1976, p. 189):

1. Murder in the first degree without recommendation by the jury calls for the death penalty.
2. Conviction on the charge of murder in the first degree with a recommendation by the jury, carries life imprisonment.
3. A verdict of murder in the second degree means an indeterminate sentence of one year to life imprisonment.
4. A verdict of manslaughter is punishable by imprisonment from one to ten years.

But as Yallop (1976, p. 189) notes, the paper missed a fifth possibility—"acquittal." Women's clubs, particularly the Women's Committee, put pressure on the authorities through monitoring of hearings and trials. These groups made sure that several of their representatives were present whenever open court activities were being conducted in the Arbuckle case. The main strategy was the punishment of Arbuckle and the primary tactic was getting him indicted and convicted for murder. The massive outcry encouraged authorities to bring Arbuckle rapidly to trial. It also suppressed any pro-Arbuckle activities which, beyond those of family and a few famous friends, were muted. The friends that supported him included Stan Laurel, Oliver Hardy, Jimmy Durante, and of course, Buster Keaton.[4]

The power of the complaining groups in both the initial and derived phases was apparent from the speed with which officials reacted. Harold Kelly, secretary of the grand jury, attributes the indictment to the protesters:

So many women's clubs and private individuals interested in the moral welfare of the city have demanded an investigation, that I will present their demands to the jury (*New York Times*, September 11, 1921, p. 1).

Lastly, there is the question of whether the movement continued after the problem had been solved. Was there a permanent Arbuckle or film monitoring group established out of the four complaining groups of the press, ministers, women's clubs, and theatre owners? The answer seems to be no. However, when Hays lifted the ban on Arbuckle in December, 1922 the groups protested Arbuckle's attempts to resume film acting. But, in general, it's safe to say that no established group emerged out of the conflict.

Social control is crucial to Smelser's approach. The question that is central is how social control authorities respond to the complaining groups. In particular, are the complaining groups satisfied with the response of the authorities or do they see it as inappropriate or inadequate? It is clear that the complaining groups were satisfied with the response of the authorities. The speed with which matters went to trial, as well as the fact of bringing Arbuckle to trial three times, certainly indicated that the authorities were trying for a conviction. Even though he was never convicted, the complaining groups got some satisfaction. His career was ruined. He had been punished.[5]

Conclusions

This paper has analyzed the case of Fatty Arbuckle, Hollywood's first million dollar movie star. Using ideas developed from Smelser's model, the study found that the response to Arbuckle was a norm oriented movement that could be understood as a moral panic. The analysis is based on secondary sources, primarily David Yallop's *The Day the Laughter Stopped* and the *New York Times*.

I have argued that most of the conditions proposed by Smelser's model were met in the Arbuckle case. Structural conduciveness was indicated by legitimate channels of protest, particularly the press and public meetings. Structural strain was interpreted as the perceived disjuncture between Fatty Arbuckle's on-screen life as a clown and his off-screen "sexual" activities. It was argued that the Arbuckle case became a metaphor for more general concerns about Hollywood lifestyles in the 1920s.

The generalized belief was that on-screen behavior had to be congruent with off-screen activities and this was clearly not the case for Arbuckle. For mobilization for action several activities were described including editorials by the Hearst papers, sermons by ministers, speeches from women's organizations leaders and bans by theater owners. Social control was seen as minimal because those involved in mobilization got what they wanted while using legitimate channels of protest.

With the Smelser approach I have taken a general social movement model and applied it to a specific case. This approach seems to work. However, further research needs to be done to determine the value of Smelser's model. In particular, scholars need to examine situations of scandal in other time periods where social movements developed in reaction to popular film stars. For example, the case of Ingrid Bergman (Damico, 1975) would be interesting to study. An alternative would be to investigate a sex scandal that did not generate a norm-oriented social movement. For example, the Roman Polanski case in 1977 should have generated some social movement activity but it appears not to have done so.

Notes

[1]Another book by Gerald Fine (1971) is available to scholars. Fine's book is based on interviews with Arbuckle's first wife, Minta Durfee. It is loaded with subjective impressions, hypothetical meanderings, and an account of Arbuckle's early life. Basically it is a novel.

[2]This narrative, as well as the material in Figure 1, was prepared by my research assistant, Linda Powell.

[3]It was one of these home remedies that caused Arbuckle so much trouble. He placed ice cubes on Rappe's genitalia in an effort to awaken her (New York Times, 9/22/21, p. 8). This story eventually became falsely known as the "coke bottle" incident with Arbuckle using the bottle to assault Rappe. There is absolutely no proof to support this story.

[4]Keaton proved to be an extraordinary friend. He was the main financial support for Arbuckle for the remainder of Fatty's life (Dardis, 1979: 83-84).

[5]A ban on the Fatty Arbuckle films still exists in England according to Harold Messing's (1978) valuable article on the impact of the Arbuckle case on film director's contracts.

Figure 1
Chronology of Roscoe "Fatty" Arbuckle's Life

1887	Born on a farm in Kansas; shortly after, family moved to California
1895	Began acting in local traveling shows
1909	Acted in first movie, continued live performances
1910	Married Minta Durfee on stage
1913	Became involved with Keystone Films
1916	Well-known to public; picked

		up by Paramount with unique contract
		allowing him a free hand in his films
1919		Paramount signed him for $3 million contract
1920		Prohibition Amendment passed
1921	Sept. 5	Party at St. Francis Hotel, San Francisco
	Sept. 9	Virginia Rappe dies
	Sept. 11	Arbuckle charged with murder on basis of Maude Delmont's accusations
	Nov. 14—	First trial: charge-manslaughter; verdict—10 not guilty,
	Dec. 4	2 guilty
1922	Jan. 11—	Second trial: 2 not guilty,
	Feb. 3	10 guilty
	Jan.	Hays appointed "watchdog" of the industry
	Feb.	William Desmond Taylor murder
	Mar. 13—	Third trial: acquittal
	Apr. 12	
	Apr. 18	Hays bans Arbuckle from films
	Dec. 22	Hays lifts ban on Arbuckle
1923		Arbuckle makes live appearances and directs, but public outcry prohibits acting
1925		Divorced Minta, married Doris Deane; still unemployable as screen actor
1928		Divorced Doris Deane
1932		Married Addie McPhail; resumed acting in films
1933	Jun. 29	Died in his sleep after party celebrating the completion of his first new films

Bibliography

Books and Articles

Cohen, Stanley (1972) *Folk, Devils and Moral Panics.* London: MacGibbon and Kee.

Damico, James (1975) "Ingrid from Lorraine to Stromboli: Analyzing the Public's Perception of a Film Star," *Journal of Popular Film,* Vol. IV (1): pp. 3-19.

Dardis, Tom (1979) *Keaton The Man Who Wouldn't Lie Down.* New York: Charles Scribner's Sons.

Fine, Gerald (1971) *Roscoe "Fatty" Arbuckle.* Published by author.

Messing, Harold (1978) "The Arbuckle Clause: Are You Morally Fit to Direct Your Picture?" *Action,* March/April, 1978, pp. 11-12.

Smelser, Neil J. (1962) *Theory of Collective Behavior.* New York: The Free Press.

Telotte, J.P. (1988) "Arbuckle Escapes: The Pattern of Fatty Arbuckle's Comedy," *Journal of Popular Film and Television,* Vol. 15 (Winter) 4: pp. 172-179.

Yallop, David (1976) *The Day the Laughter Stopped.* New York: St. Martin's Press.

Newspapers

French, Philip (1976) "Star Struck." *New Statesman* (October 8, 1976) p. 485.

Lingeman, Richard R. (1976) "The Ordeal of Fatty Arbuckle." *New York Times* (August 27, 1976) p. C-17.

New York Times
  September 11—October 1, 1921
  April 19, 1922
  December 21-23, 1922
  December 26, 1922
  January 5, 1923
  January 8, 1923
  January 31, 1923
  February 1, 1923
Publisher's Weekly—1976
St. Louis Dispatch
  September 13, 1921
Washington Post
  December 22, 1922

Claims-Making, Quasi-Theories, and the Social Construction of the Rock 'n' Roll Menace

Stephen L. Markson

I am appreciative of the funding for this project provided by the University of Hartford Humanities Center.

> Some contend that rock and roll is bad for the body and
> bad for the soul
> bad for the heart, bad for the mind
> bad for the deaf and bad for the blind

Introduction: The Rock 'n' Roll Rating Controversy

While Lowell George of the 1970s band Little Feat assuredly wrote those lines with tongue in cheek, the sentiments aptly convey a point of view that others take more seriously. That rock should be suspect of malevolent intent and dangerous impact is neither new nor startling. Attempts to censor or prohibit rock are a familiar refrain, dating virtually to its origins in the 1950s Black rhythm and blues. Songs by Little Richard, Chuck Berry, Fats Domino and others had to be cleansed and sanitized in "Pat Boonized" cover versions before distribution to a mass audience was deemed appropriate.[1]

During the past decade, presumably as a component of increased concern for the moral welfare of youth, rock has been targeted even more vociferously. Recently, the Nevada Supreme Court decided that a lawsuit could proceed against the heavy metal band Judas Priest. The suit seeks damages against the band alleging that their 1978 album "Stained Class" instigated the suicide attempts of two young men who had listened to the album for six consecutive hours. A similar lawsuit implicating Ozzy Osbourne's "Suicide Solution" in a suicide was not heard when a Los Angeles Superior Court ruled that the song was entitled to first amendment protection. In August 1987, a Los Angeles judge denied prosecution's motion for a retrial after Jello Biafra, former lead singer of the San Francisco punk band The Dead Kennedys, and Michael Bonanno, their manager, were acquitted of charges of distributing harmful material to minors. The allegedly pornographic product was The Dead Kennedy's third album "Frankenchrist" which contained a poster of an H. R. Giger painting. The painting, "Landscape #20: Where Are We Coming From?", depicted nine disembodied genital sex acts of a

29

color and texture resembling armadillo skin. A sticker on the album cover read: "The inside foldout to this record cover is a work of art by H. R. Giger that some people may find shocking, repulsive or offensive. Life can sometimes be that way." It is clear that the battle over rock 'n' roll continues to be waged.

At the center of the controversy has been the *Parents' Music Resource Center* (PMRC). Cofounded by Susan Baker, Tipper Gore, Pamela Howar, Sally Nevius and Ethelynn Stuckey in May 1985, the stated purpose of the organization is to educate parents and consumers about the explicit and violent lyrical content of some popular music. However, with a number of wives of Washington D.C. "politicos" exerting their influence, the group quickly moved beyond their stated role as an information clearinghouse and consumer interest group. The PMRC publication the *Rock Music Report* identified five persistent and objectionable themes promoted by rock 'n' roll:

1. Rebellion
2. Substance Abuse
3. Sexual Promiscuity and Perversion
4. Violence
5. Occult

Their efforts, aimed at the *Recording Industry Association of America* (RIAA), implied that either the RIAA should regulate their own industry with specific warning labels affixed to offending albums or legislation to restrain the industry might be forthcoming. As it was unlikely that any legislation could survive a constitutional challenge, a form of self-censorship seemed the best outcome the PMRC could realistically expect. After considerable lobbying and information gathering hearings in the Senate, an agreement was reached calling for a generic, nonspecific label ("Parents' Advisory: Explicit Lyrics") to be affixed to the backs of albums deemed by the individual record companies to warrant such a label. Neither the PMRC, RIAA, nor the interested artists were entirely satisfied with the compromises and sporadic compliance that followed the agreement. However, the "rock 'n' roll threat" to American youth had undoubtedly received a stamp of political legitimation and was now to be regarded as a "social problem."

Rock and the Symbolization of Teenage Rebellion

Of all the forms of popular culture, rock speaks most pointedly to teens. While television and movies are shared with the adult world, rock music is virtually the exclusive property of the young. To most parents it remains the "great noisy unknown." (Pareles, 1988) Furthermore, rock has always maintained a powerful association with adolescent resistance to adult authority. Lull argues that...

music serves to legitimize an opposition that speaks to the concerns of adolescents. It portrays cultural alternatives to the values and lifestyles of the dominant culture that are so thoroughly represented in the popular media and the home, neighborhood, work and school environments. Rock introduces themes that are ignored, refuted or downplayed by "mainstream" institutions of social control. (Lull, 1985:367)

Rock 'n' roll embodies popular culture, the larger category of which it is a part, quite well. It is "unofficial" culture, the culture of the non-elite, designed for mass consumption and entertainment. Not surprisingly rock is also targeted for the criticisms aimed more generally at popular culture—that it is profit-driven and divorced from a higher aesthetic, thematically simple, technically uncomplicated, repetitive, formulaic, and ultimately not beneficial to its audience.

But rock is also a special category within the broader realm of popular culture. It is that aspect of popular culture most pointedly oriented to youth. Rock is undeniably the music of youth and consequently is also targeted for the criticisms aimed more generally at youth, especially teens. In the 1950s, the relatively new concepts of "teenager" and "juvenile delinquent" appeared simultaneously on our symbolic landscape. They were often used interchangeably and freely associated in the media. The message seemed to suggest that without careful parental vigilance the teen would become the delinquent. Films such as *Blackboard Jungle, Rebel Without a Cause* and *The Wild Ones* blurred the distinction between the good and bad teen implying that all teens lacked an internal moral code and therefore needed external control and discipline.

While our views of teen culture may have become somewhat less rigidly stereotyped and compartmentalized over the ensuing thirty years, there remain some strikingly similar themes in current fears about so-called "porn rock"—fears revolving around youthful resistance to adult authority and discipline. Foucault (1977) used the term "disciplinization" in referring to overt attempts to control youth within the institutional settings of family and school. Rock emerged as part of the resistance to such disciplinization as a music of opposition to the enforcement of mainstream values.

Conservatives of the Reagan era have had a rather busy moral agenda. Following attacks on sex and drugs, it was perhaps inevitable that rock 'n' roll, the last sin in the "hedonistic trinity" of "sex, drugs and rock 'n' roll" would also be targeted for the "just say no" bandwagon. We are seemingly in the throes of what can be termed a "moral panic." Moral panics describe controversies over the location of normative boundaries between the "respectable" and the "deviant." Historical accounts of past episodes of moral panic involving fears of prostitution, alcohol, and abortion reveal that when moral concerns take on political dimensions, sexuality (especially the sexuality of young people) is commonly employed as a symbol of disorder and diminished social control. Sexuality can become a potent cultural metaphor for social disorder and chaos. Furthermore, rock and sexuality are inextricably entwined... "Rock", writes Karen Durbin (Frith, 1981:239), "provided women with a channel for asserting their sexuality without apologies and without having to pretty up every passion with the traditionally feminine desire for true love and marriage." Rock 'n' roll, whether as a symbol of social disorder or as a vehicle of resistance to adult authority, can become a highly charged political resource.

When I indicate that rock can be a political resource, I am echoing the conception of politics advanced by political scientist Murray Edelman. In *The Symbolic Uses of Politics* (1964) and *Politics as Symbolic Action* (1971), he argues that politics does not really begin with mass emotions or policy preferences—the roots to which it is often traced. Rather, it is the cognitive structures through which people receive and process information in order to construct a worldview that are most fundamental to the political process. Political battles are waged and political power is often exercised within the realm of culture, as attempts to control or limit access to the ideas and products of culture are in reality attempts to shape people's beliefs about the social world. Dominant groups as well as those who aspire to dominant status seek to acquire and maintain power by influencing how people define reality—its possibilities and constraints as well as its current configuration. This process, facilitated by the manipulation of symbols of all sorts, is central to explaining why and how certain conditions and situations in society come to be defined as "social problems," while others do not attain such legitimate status.

Claims-Making, Quasi-Theories and the Construction of Social Problems

The social constructionist perspective on social problems significantly reshaped the contours of sociological discourse on the topic. Social problems, it is argued, should not be conceptualized as static, objective conditions; but as the negotiated products of a series of collective definitions. Blumer cautions that...

to attribute social problems to presumed structural strains, upsets in the equilibrium of the social system, dysfunctions, breakdowns of social norms, or deviations from social conformity, is to unwittingly transfer to a suppositious social structure what belongs to the process of collective definition. (Blumer 1971:306)

Consequently those who have sought to locate social problems purely in objective conditions that are intrinsically harmful to the society have overlooked this process of collective definition. It is the *process* that determines which social problems arise, whether they attain the status of legitimate concern, how they are shaped and defined in discussion, and how they come to be addressed in official policy. The "careers" of such issues as poverty, racial and gender-based inequality, and environmental concerns vividly demonstrate that it is the emerging perspective on an issue, rather than its objective makeup, that ultimately determines its fate as a high priority problem or a non-issue absent from the public agenda. While this definition of the problem emerges from the interplay of a number of factors including efforts of interest groups, media attention, how media "frame" their coverage, citizen activism, political endorsements, etc., the aspect of the process most germane to this argument about the rock lyrics controversy concerns what Spector and Kitsuse (1977) refer to as "claims-making activities."

In "claims-making activities" interest groups attempt to:

1. assert the existence of a particular condition, situation or state of affairs in which human action is causally implicated.

2. define the asserted conditions as offensive, harmful, undesirable or otherwise problematic to the society and amenable to corrective human action.

3. stimulate public scrutiny of the condition from the point of view advanced by the claims-makers.

Claims-making, while central to the development of a definition of the problem, usually proceeds in a fashion that in no way approximates a rational, objective, or truth-seeking enterprise. In fact, the explanatory process is decidedly non-scientific and has been described by Hewitt and Hall (1973) as "quasi-theorizing." While positivistic theorizing traditionally identifies some effect and then proceeds to seek its causes, quasi-theorizing is apt to reverse this process—to settle on a cause *before* identifying an effect and then to structure how the problem is to be defined in terms of the agreed upon solution. Quasi-theories, then, are collective constructions of reality that:

1. assert simple, intuitively-pleasing solutions to problems that may be complex, vague, or ill-defined,

2. construct the "reality" of the problem around the acceptable solution,

3. assure that the problem becomes both comprehensible and soluble, thereby masking aspects of the problem we prefer not to acknowledge.

Consequently, unlike "scientific" theories, quasi-theories are under no pressure to be consistent with the relevant empirical data because their primary purpose is less oriented to valid explanation than to support a wish to see a problem in a particular fashion irrespective of the evidence. Fritz and Altheide (1987), while they do not discuss quasi-theories in their analysis, certainly allude to their internal logic in their account of the social construction of the missing children problem. The seductive appeal of quasi-theory logic played a pivotal role in the process through which media imagery catapulted an issue to national prominence. As we were beseeched with pictures of missing children on milk cartons and grocery bags, with docudramas and exposés on child molesters and pornographers, the objective character of the issue was lost in a flood of menacing images. The reality of the issue as defined by empirical data—that the vast majority of missing children have either voluntarily left home or have been taken by a parent on the losing side of a custody battle—became a rather dull footnote to an engrossing novel.

The conceptualization of missing children as innocents being emperilled by perverts lurking in dark alleys is not only better copy it is consistent with quasi-theory logic. If we must confront the fact that children are in jeopardy, then we would rather blame clearly identified villains than indict through much more complex logic the entire family institution in contemporary American society. Blaming, as one parent put it, "sick, sadistic monsters who roam our country at random" serves to displace our anxiety and obscure aspects of a problem we wish to ignore. The recently renewed furor over the lyrics of some rock songs has been ignited by an almost identical set of concerns. Those who argue that AC/DC stands for "Anti Christ/Devil's Children," that KISS stands for "Kids in Satan's Service," as have PMRC supporters, do indeed seem to fear monsters. However, these monsters may be even more menacing than those behind the missing children phenomenon. As they have been portrayed by anti-rock crusaders, these monsters are capable of surreptitiously entering the minds of unsuspecting adolescents through the medium of rock music.

The Rock 'n' Roll Threat as Quasi-Theory

At the heart of the claims-making activities of the PMRC have been what might best be termed "anecdotal atrocity tales" of murder, suicide, and sexual mayhem in which it is imputed that rock lyrics were instigating or contributory factors. Best and Horiuchi (1985) and Brunvand (1981) use the concept "urban legend" to describe the stories that circulate in response to public demands for explanations of bizarre or frightening events that reputedly have occurred. Such socially constructed accounts bear striking similarities to many of the rock horror stories alluded to by the PMRC. The allegations that suicides and suicide attempts can be instigated by the lyrics and music of Judas Priest and Ozzie Osbourne play a key role in the claims-making process whether or not they are ultimately substantiated. The fate of a claim is not merely a function of the objective validity of the evidence it brings forth. On the contrary, the symbolic character of the imagery that the claim projects—its ability to contextualize an issue within fears and anxieties that are already prevalent—better explains why some claims are more successful than others. An effectively framed quasi-theory easily masks the logical inconsistencies that would be its undoing were it subjected to a more systematic analysis.

While disturbing and often frightening, the atrocity tales of the anti-rock crusade are, at best, a very flimsy evidenciary base. Exposure to media messages can certainly affect our attitudes and perhaps even our behavior in some instances. But the established normative order remains an attenuating factor that limits media impact concerning serious challenges to fundamental values and moral conventions. Few would question the persuasive power of media to reinforce already accepted cultural norms or to activate normatively sanctioned behavior. However, media impact studies do not indicate that many people can be moved to traverse established normative boundaries by virtue of their exposure to media messages. It is indeed a bizarre leap of logic to equate being convinced to vote for a particular candidate or buy a particular brand of product with being moved to take your own life. When the PMRC quotes from Motley Crue's "Live Wire": "I'll either break her face/or take down her legs/Get my ways at will/Go for the throat/Never let loose/Goin' in for the kill," they've exposed that the lyrics are vulgar. They've not however proven, as one of the atrocity tales charges, that these lyrics inspired a forcible rape or murder. The atrocity tales have become numerous as the medium of the music video to some extent lifted the veil of secrecy surrounding the "great noisy unknown."

MTV has taken rock performers and songs previously known by perhaps a small group of fans (and certainly not many parents), beamed them into living rooms across the country and greatly increased their public visibility. And the lyrics, dress, stage demeanor, (heavy makeup, chrome studs, leather handcuffs) indeed, the overall look of some heavy metal performers, do seem likely to generate parental ire with their apparent celebration of values and lifestyles that are deviant by conventional standards. However, a rational consideration of the claims of detrimental impact through exposure (called "secondary child abuse" by one critic) produces scant support. Certainly the claims are exaggerated and empirically unsubstantiated.

Two major themes emerge from a survey of recent research on rock lyrics and lyrical cognition. The initial finding is that there is sparse, limited comprehension of song messages through lyrics. Consistent with most previous studies, Rosenbaum and Prinsky (1987) report that no more than 25% of adolescent respondents are able to accurately interpret lyrics even when choosing for interpretation their own favorite songs. This finding not only reinforces the conclusions of earlier studies, but is not as surprising as some observers think it to be. Songs are not regarded as "texts" to be studied and analyzed. They are not cognitively monitored for maximum comprehension as they are used as background noise to provide a setting for other activities in which beat and sound are much more relevant than words and imagery. Furthermore, it is rather difficult, even if it was the lyricist's intention, to tell much of a story in approximately two minutes and 250 words with many of the lyrics garbled and unintelligible in their delivery. Desmond (1987), focusing on cognitive research on memory and the processing of auditory information, also argues a minimal effects model. While he does suggest that music videos, dealing with visual as well as verbal coding, do add some learning potential, his conclusion is that "given the accumulating evidence regarding media and cognition, there is little reason to believe that rock music has some special ability to facilitate learning from its lyrics." (Desmond, 1987:282)

The second major finding of research on popular music (Denisoff and Levine, 1971; Edwards and Singletary, 1984; Gantz, 1977; Rosenbaum and Prinsky, 1987) about which there is little disagreement concerns which themes and topics are most often presented. The themes that the PMRC finds objectionable (rebellion, drugs, violence, and sex) are not only rarely understood by listeners, they are rarely pursued by the lyricists in the first place. Such themes are clearly the exception rather than the rule in the overall rock genre where some variation of "ain't love a bitch" seems to predominate thematically in any representative sample of songs. So there is precious little in the way of "hard" evidence to suggest a powerful negative impact on youths from their exposure to rock. But this inconsistency between PMRC claims and findings at variance with their claims is unsurprising during the entrepreneurial stages of moral controversies over the location of normative boundaries between the "respectable" and the "deviant."

The rules or moral boundary lines that define our shared conceptions of deviant behavior categories are invariably the product of someone's initiative. Moral entrepreneurs, as they are termed by Becker (1963), find symbols of disorder to be potent political resources in their efforts to move moral boundaries. Whether that symbol is alcohol (Gusfield, 1963), abortion (Markson, 1982; Luker, 1984), or rock 'n' roll, its imagery and representational power are essential to the success of the political enterprise. Symbols, when effectively employed, can bolster the tenuous claims of claims-making and mask the illogical leaps of faith of quasi-theorizing.

These ideas do much to explain why PMRC claims can fly in the face of contradictory evidence and greatly exaggerate the objective threat posed by the putative problem they identify. The attack on so-called "porn rock" should be interpreted as an exercise in quasi-theorizing rather than an objective, truth-seeking endeavor, since it represents an effort to assert a simple, clear-cut, and intuitively pleasing answer around which one can reconstruct the reality of a more complex and vexing problem. The themes that the PMRC imputes to rock music (rebellion, drug abuse, sexual promiscuity, violence) can be reconceptualized and considered from a different perspective. If these themes are viewed *not* as a litany of the sins of rock 'n' roll, but as the principal adult fears of youthful deviance, a revised interpretation begins to surface. The list speaks to very real parental anxieties—the nagging anxiety that teens will rebel against authority, use drugs, be sexually active lest there be constant parental vigilance to contain those tendencies. It is quite appealing and convenient to assert that each of those problematic outcomes basically shares a common cause and hence a single solution.

To the extent that PMRC claims can causally link rock music to their list of evil-doings, an immensely serviceable quasi-theory is created. It is implied, if not asserted, that the elimination of the pernicious influence of rock 'n' roll will begin to restore traditional morality as it curtails teen violence, drug use, and sexual experimentation. The benefits of this quasi-theory can be summarized as follows:

1. A complex, deeply troubling set of circumstances that does, in fact, exist—some teens do abuse drugs, engage in violence, commit suicide, etc.—has been neatly reduced to a single "proto-problem".

2. When this "proto-problem" incorporates the deleterious influence of rock 'n' roll into its explanatory model, a clear attribution of blame is fixed upon those purveyors of "porn rock." "Good folks" are absolved of any responsibility or complicity, for as we successfully fix blame on others we deflect it from ourselves (in the same fashion as blaming sexual perverts for the missing children problem absolves the family system).

3. Rock music and performers are exceptionally attractive targets for such righteous indignation. It is certainly intuitively pleasing even if not empirically accurate, to find fault in an unregulated and highly visible industry that does indeed pander to the fantasies of youth culture. Clearly, these performers who openly flaunt conventional authority as the stereotyped embodiment of parental nightmares of children gone wild, do at least seem to be guilty of something.

Conclusion: "Sticks and Stones May Break My Bones..."

"Down and Dirty" by Quiet Riot— *QR III* (Pasha Records, a division of and distributed by CBS)

> She's a dancin' girl
> Who brings out the heat
> Inside all the men
> She knows how to move

"Damage, Inc." by Metallica— *Master of Puppets*
(Elektra/Asylum Records, a division of Warner Communication)

> Dealing out the agony within
> Charging hard and no one's gonna give in
> Living on you knees, conformity
> Or dying on your feet for honesty.

Quiet Riot and Metallica are two groups whose explicit lyrics have especially troubled anti-rock crusaders. However, while some might question their taste, they are ultimately far less threatening to the values of a free society than those who would seek to limit their freedom of expression. Their lyrics clearly deal with extreme emotions and explosive imagery. In fact, what most heavy metal bands deliver to their audiences are shock, speed, fury, vulgarity, and high decibel, authority-baiting thrills—no doubt designed to shatter the sensibilities, if not the eardrums, of the adult world. But in that regard, they may be providing a needed outlet for the pent-up frustrations that are a natural part of growing up. When rock 'n' roll disturbs parents, it is fulfilling a function for which it is expressly designed. Rock *should* disturb parents for this is undoubtedly one of its intents.[2] But beyond the intent to shake up parents and other authority figures, this form of rock tackles some issues that mainstream pop and rock avoid. Danger, brutality, and violence are generally not represented in the droned monotony of top forty music. However, there is a long tradition in artistic expression that has always sought to explore, often in exaggerated form, the bleakest and most frightening aspects of existence. Pareles points out:

it's not the job of any performer to be a babysitter or a peer counselor or a role model, but speed-metal bands strike a chord with millions of teenagers because they reflect what's on their minds—and the songs tell them they are not alone. (Pareles, 1988)

Frank Zappa, pointing out at a congressional hearing that it should remain a parent's responsibility, and not the state's, to monitor what his child should be exposed to, said: "a buzzsaw blade between the guy's legs on the album cover is a pretty good indication that this record may not be for little Johnny." Certainly a warning label affixed to the album would appear superfluous in this example. But it would only be superfluous if the anti-rock crusade were engaged in an instrumental, rational effort within the political process of problem solving. On the other hand, if the issue of record labeling is seen as symbolic rather than instrumental, as a quasi-theory of the rock 'n' roll threat, then the question of whether the labeling is superfluous becomes a moot point. The success of moral crusades is not measured purely in instrumental terms as a rational calculation of wins and losses.

The claims-making activities of the PMRC aptly display the often hidden symbolic dimension of politics. Participants can in association with others who share their values reaffirm the legitimacy, if not the dominance, of traditionally defined morality. And irrespective of the success or failure of their enterprise, supporters can share in the collective identity of the organization as an embattled outpost of decency in a war over the moral welfare of American youth.

While the specific issue that spawned this particular campaign will likely recede from significance and diminish in urgency (as it already seems to be doing), the underlying moral tensions will not similarly recede nor diminish. Consequently, although the arena in which the battle is waged may shift, the politics of cultural prohibition will likely remain a fixture in American political life for quite some time to come. Our understanding of that political process has been enhanced by the insights of the social constructionist perspective on social problems. Claims-making activities play a pivotal role in the rise and fall of the countless issues that reach the public agenda. However, the determinant of which claims ultimately resonate with the power to move the political structure is not merely a measure of the authenticity of those claims. It is rather the imagery and symbolism that the claims evoke which will determine the fate of the issues they represent. Since that imagery is often a product of the quasi-theories that support claims-making, they merit more attention than they generally receive in sociological analyses of social problems.

Notes

[1]On the Ed Sullivan show, Elvis Presley and his suggestive pelvic thrusts were shown only from the waist up. The Rolling Stones in their first Sullivan appearance had to sing let's spend "some time" together rather than let's spend "the night"

together. The Kingston Trio recording *Greenback Dollar* had the word "damn" excised from the lyrics before it could receive airplay. The F.C.C. investigated the record *Louie Louie* by the Kingsmen, convinced that it was "dirty." After studying it frontwards, backwards, and at varying tempos, it was pronounced "unintelligible at any speed." This state of affairs was obviously recognized by Peter, Paul and Mary who sang in *I Dig Rock 'n' Roll Music* "and if I really say it, the radio won't play it, unless I lay it between the lines."

[2]I am quite sure that when I was a teenager if my parents didn't express their displeasure with what was being blasted from my stereo, my enjoyment of it would have been drastically curtailed. And when, on rare occasions, they grudgingly approved of a selection ("that's not as bad as the trash you usually listen to"), the particular non-offending record would be swiftly dispatched to the back of my record bin on the logic that if they could actually tolerate it, it couldn't be very good anyway.

Bibliography

Becker, H. (1963) Outsiders, New York: The Free Press.

Best, J. and G.T. Horiuchi (1985) "The razor blade in the apple: the social construction of urban legends." Social Problems 32 (5):488-499.

Blumer, H. (1971) "Social Problems as collective behavior." Social Problems 18:298-306.

Brunvand, J. (1981) The Vanishing Hitchhiker. New York: Norton.

Corn, R. (1987) "The F.C.C. cleans up the airways." The Nation 5 December:679-680.

Denisoff, S. and M. Levine (1971) "The popular protest song: the case of eve of destruction." Public Opinion Quarterly 35:117-122.

Desmond, R. (1987) "Adolescents and music lyrics: a cognitive perspective." Communication Quarterly 35:276-285.

Edelman, M. (1971) Politics as Symbolic Action. Illinois: University of Illinois Press.

———— (1964) The Symbolic Uses of Politics. Illinois: University of Illinois Press.

Edwards, E. and M. Singletary (1984) "Mass media images in popular music." Popular Music and Society 9:17-26.

Foucault, M. (1977) Discipline and Punish. New York: Vintage Books.

Frith, S. (1981) Sound Effects. New York: Pantheon Books.

Fritz, N. and D. Altheide (1987) "The mass media and the social construction of the missing children problem." Sociological Quarterly 28 (4): 473-492.

Gantz, W. (1977) "Gratifications and expectations associated with popular music among adolescents." Popular Music and Society 4:14-22.

Gusfield, J. (1963) Symbolic Crusade. Illinois: University of Illinois Press.

Hewitt, J. (1984) Self and Society (third edition). Boston, MA: Allyn and Bacon.

Hewitt, J. and P. Hall (1973) "Social problems, problematic situations, and quasi theories." American Sociological Review 38:367-374.

Hirsch, P. (1971) "Sociological approaches to the popular music phenomenon." American Behavioral Scientist 14:371-388.

Luker, K. (1984) Abortion and the Politics of Motherhood. Berkeley, CA: University of California Press.

Lull, J. (1985) "On the communicative properties of music." Communication Research 12 (3):363-372.

Markson, S. (1982) "Normative boundaries and abortion policy." pp. 21-33 in M. Lewis (ed.) Research in Social Problems and Public Policy, Vol. 2 CT:JAI Press.

Markson, S. and R. Rosenthal (1986) "Music as ideology." Presented at the annual meetings of the Popular Culture Association.

Nathanson, C. (1987) "Private behavior as a public problem: continuity and change in social movements." Presented at the annual meetings of the Eastern Sociological Society.

Pareles, J. (1988) "Speed metal: extreme, yes; evil no" New York Times 25 September.

_____ (1985) "Should rock lyrics be sanitized." New York Times 13 October.

Rosenbaum, J. and L. Prinsky (1987) "Sex, violence and rock 'n' roll: youth's perceptions of popular music." Popular Music and Society 11 (2): 79-89.

Spector, M. and J. Kitsuse (1977) Constructing Social Problems. Menlo Park, CA: Cummings Publishing Company.

Stefanac, S. (1986) "Rock, roll and repression." Maximum Rock and Roll (September): 18-27.

Wishnia, S. (1987) "Rockin' with the first amendment." The Nation 24 October: 444-446.

III
Popular Culture and
Deviant "Taste Publics"

Introduction

Social groups form around materials and activities of interest or concern to group members. Within the context of these collectivities, expectations, modes of evaluation, values, lore, and other important items of information are communicated and reinforced. The subculture also acts as a setting in which interactants can gain recognition and status. In general, the more one knows about the various conventions surrounding the focal phenomenon and the more directly involved one is in the production, evaluation, and dissemination of the cultural materials or practices, the higher one's status within the subculture.

When the cultural phenomenon is negatively defined by a social audience of significant size and whose members possess significant resources, those who are interested or participate in the phenomenon become the objects of unwanted and troublesome attention. Members of the conventional audience typically see the focal activities or materials as harming those who are involved in them and/or as constituting a threat to the larger social order in which they have a vested interest. Consequently, those involved in the disvalued cultural phenomenon are not only drawn together by their shared interests, they are also pushed together by the conventional social reaction directed at them by others who usually justify their persecution by telling unconventional participants that they are "doing it for their (the deviant taste public's members') own good."

The papers in this section present research into taste groups surrounding activities and products that enjoy some degree of questionable repute in conventional social circles. Carrie Stern provides an account of some of the central issues which arise as ballroom dancers who are, in essence, rented by clients as partners engage in this interesting form of service work. "Taxi-dancing" acquired its deviant reputation in the 1920s when it came to be seen as closely connected to prostitution. In addition, this type of service work has the potential for discrediting those involved because it entails the worker's touching the client's body for pay without the legitimating protection of some type of official license such as that held by medical doctors or even hairdressers. One of the major problems for taxi dancers, then, is to structure their interactions with their clientele in ways which "disavow" the definitions of deviance which some clients and many members of conventional society carry with them into their encounters with the dancers. Client control is the central problem. Taxi dancers must ongoingly structure

43

their presentations of self so that they "make the client look good" while, at the same time, fending off unwanted sexual advances.

Barbara Stenross presents three interrelated taste publics cohering around involvement with a symbolically and functionally controversial cultural product—the gun. Recognizing the distaste with which many members of the larger public regard firearms, "gun avocationists"—those who collect guns or use them to kill animals or ventilate targets—construct and present "dignifying rationales" whereby they can disavow their deviant reputation, legitimate their hobbies, and deflect negative social reaction. In short, hunters emphasize their "respect" for wildlife, shooters maintain their activity teaches self control, and gun collectors present their practice as being a harmless— if somewhat eccentric—hobby.

Bruce Friesen's discussion of the taste public surrounding "heavy metal" music touches on some of the issues previously discussed by Markson. A major degree of the pleasure "head bangers" derive from their musical taste culture comes from the "dis-taste" it generates in their parents and other "straight" adults. For heavy metal fans, then, the music is a source of intrinsic pleasure while symbolically setting aficionados apart as members of a cohesive group characterized by its uniqueness and love for unconventional excitement. This latter "function" is encountered in many, if not most, socially disvalued activities—the power and pleasure of deviance derives from its symbolic "nose thumbing" in the face of mainstream tastes and sensibilities.

Selling the Dancer:
Client/Dancer Interaction in Modern Taxi-Dancing

Carrie Stern

In 1982, a few years after the closing of the last taxi-dance hall in New York,[1] Albert Ginsberg who had recently purchased Roseland Dance City decided to bring taxi-dancing, dime-a-dance partners, back to Roseland Dance City, long New York City's premiere dance palace. Ginsberg said " 'We had a feeling it would go over—you know things like that run in cycles.' " (Ferretti, 1982:B4). So, a new mini-age of taxi-dancing, partners for hire, began one day a week at Roseland.

Historically taxi-dancers were considered immoral women by the reformers of the nineteen-teens and twenties both because they participated with strangers in an activity generally reserved for established couples and because some engaged in various forms of prostitution. In their hey-day of the 1920s, taxi-dancers were generally very young, some only 15 despite laws to the contrary. They were hired primarily for their looks and, at times, their willingness to engage in "obscene dancing."[2] Taxi-dancing was their primary mode of support, providing a better and more interesting means of earning an income than being a clerk, secretary, or laborer. However, it was generally a short-term job, most young woman either marrying or turning to other forms of work after a few years. A few taxi-dancers—but many fewer than the reformers of the period would have us believe—turned to prostitution, utilizing the job to obtain money and/or goods and services in exchange for sexual favors. It was this practice, combined with the reputation of the thés tango of the 1920s as a place for gigolos to pick up women, that created the unflattering image of dancing partners for hire that exists today, even among dancers within the ballroom world itself.

Modern taxi-dancers differ in many ways from those of the 1920s.[3] They now include both men and women of mixed class and ethnicity. In addition they are older than historical taxi-dancers, tend to be educated, and taxi-dancing is not their major source of support. Eight individuals, three men and five women, were my primary informants for this study.[4]

Modern taxi-dancers are primarily performers and teachers within the social dance setting of the ballroom subculture. Despite the views of outsiders, including uninitiated ballroom dancers, within their own subculture the taxi-dancers activity is not only acceptable but provides an important service. In this paper I want to explore how these dancers who are essentially

45

independent entrepreneurs within Roseland's structure, market themselves, their skill as dancers, and perhaps more importantly their image. I also want to ask how this performance then affects the client/dancer relationship.

Selling the Dancer

Taxi-dancing, like waitressing or flight attending, is a service occupation. What is the service that the taxi-dancer sells? It has several components but the primary three are to a) perform as a technically competent partner; b) to "look good," thereby enhancing your partner; and c) to teach new steps, dips, proper ways to turn, and styling.

The taxi-dancers begin by using their personality to sell their services. Their "smile...[becomes] a commercialized lure (Mills 1956:183)," as they join what Mills calls a "personality market." The interactions of taxi-dancer and client are direct and often ongoing in nature and thus more likely to have a personalized content.

In order to facilitate a relationship between client and dancer, most dancers arrange ahead of time to spend a certain amount of time with an individual client. In their terms they "book" them. Officially, the dancers are forbidden by the management to "book" because it makes them unavailable to other customers. There are, however, two major advantages for the taxi-dancer to "booking." First, though "booking" does make the dancers unavailable to a larger pool of clients, it allows them to protect themselves from less desirable customers, to control their clientele. Secondly, the financial advantages of arranged bookings are so great that most dancers find it worth their while despite the management's rule. The taxi-dancer's salary is minimum wage plus a $1 per dance.[5] Due to the length of the dances, however, the maximum one can earn without "booking" ahead is approximately thirteen dollars per hour in dance tickets. An hour booking, however, earns one twenty-five to thirty dollars. In either case the dancers may be tipped in addition.

Booking does have some disadvantages. It allows the client to "exert various kinds of pressures on the worker including [the withdrawal] of his patronage and the conferring of it on some others" (Becker, 1968:82). In addition the client may assume rights to feelings and displays that are not always comfortable for the dancer. This discomfort is supposedly eased by the singular commitment of client to an individual dancer and by the tips with which, as is true of a number of lower-status service occupations, the client attempts to assure the dancer's involvement. Tips today, though not as grandiose as formerly, come in the form of cash, restaurant script, birthday and holiday gifts, flowers, and food. The women clients particularly love to cook for the dancers.[6]

Like the taxi-dancers of the 1920s, modern taxi-dancers are not allowed to solicit customers, i.e. to verbally offer to dance with someone for pay, but they need to attract clients in order to work. As business people they are selling their wares in a competitive market. Erving Goffman (1976), writing about print advertising, points out that the limitations of the medium require that a whole story be told within a small space and with limited text. Similarly the taxi-dancer's wares must be sold initially without language and judged only by the quality of both the dancing and the performance of the dance.

"The task of any advertiser is to favorably dispose viewers to his product, his means, by and large, to show a sparkling version of that product in the context of glamorous events" (Goffman, 1976:26). Taxi-dancers advertise by performing on the dance floor in order to attract and maintain a clientele. One means of advertising is to attract attention by the manner in which you dance. A good example of this occurred one evening when one dancer began doing a little dance of her own near the tables where the taxi-dancers wait for customers. It was a way of killing boredom and frustration but, more importantly, it was a way of advertising her availability as a partner.

Invariably I was told that one of the things that draws a particular customer to a particular dancer is how the dancer appears on the floor. A lot of customers look for someone "who can be 'flashy' on the floor with them." Two of the female dancers are particularly aware of this. One wears clothes that she feels show her off, she says "I'm flairy, so people notice me." The key to the other dancer's success is that she "always looks like she's having fun no matter who she's dancing with." In contrast to these two dancers, another woman (who is probably one of the better dancers) "doesn't show off her dancing [and therefore] she doesn't get as many customers" as she might if she were more showy.

The male taxi-dancers are equally conscious of their image on the floor. Where the females wear flashy clothes it is the tux's the men wear that immediately sets them apart from the crowd. Female taxi-dancers must respond to whatever mood their client/partner sets up. The male dancers on the other hand are responsible for creating that mood for their clients. Though generally not as flashy as the women, the men cultivate a variety of images—debonair, attentive, funny—each of which attracts a different type of woman. One dancer has done his own informal survey as to why his clients chose him as their partner. He sums up their responses by saying, "Personal style is what attracts a customer to you. It's important to pay attention to the woman you're dancing with," to act as if for that moment she is more important than anything else. Clearly then, one must first be a performer capable of playing many roles, as well as a competent dancer, in order to be a successful taxi-dancer.

This performative aspect of the taxi-dancer's job is one of its major attractions. As I indicated earlier, the taxi-dancers perform differently with each partner. Those clients that want to use their time to concentrate on learning spend each dance during their "booked" period working on new steps, dips, techniques, etc. In this case the taxi-dancers function as private teachers and the emphasis at that moment is not particularly on looking good.[7] Many clients, however, are interested in the pleasure of just dancing with an excellent performer, in the ability of an accomplished partner to make them look good creating their own version of Fred Astaire and Ginger

Rogers. The dancer's job is to make this dream come true. For the men this means anticipating their partner's desires in terms of a style of dancing. It may mean leading a less accomplished partner through a series of turns and dips in order to create the feeling of a certain danced image, at times having to control the dancing of a much larger partner. The female taxi-dancers, in turn, have to respond to the lead of their partner no matter how unclear or overly vigorous that lead may be. Some male partners love to lead their partner through a dizzying array of spins, dips, and lifts. A few clients even stop dancing at times in order to admire their partner who continues to dance alone.

The taxi-dancers do not necessarily dislike this part of their job. Dancing, by its nature, is always a performative activity, an activity that has an autoerotic component which is pleasing to the participant, while the outward manifestation is pleasing to the observer. For many ballroom dancers, not just taxi-dancers, a big part of the pleasure of dancing is in being watched. One female taxi-dancer finds that on the dance floor she is less inhibited than she ever imagined she could be. "Dancing is like a dream come true," she says, "I feel like the heavenly dancer, or the girl who walks on water." However, in addition to the personal pleasure to be found in the act of dancing in public, for taxi-dancers this performative element becomes crucial. Ultimately, as hired professional dancers, the taxi-dancers are being paid for always looking good so their clients look good, thereby satisfying their clients performative desires.

The "Face Engagement"

Taxi-dancers and their clients are involved in a mutual activity that Goffman calls a "face engagement," two or more partners engaged in a "single mutual activity entailing preferential communication rights" (Goffman, 1963:89). A face engagement can last anywhere from the three minutes of a dance to an entire evening. Once the engagement is made and opened, generally at the beginning of dancing, the shared definition of the situation comes to include degrees of mutual considerateness and sympathy. A lack of attention amounts to a breach of that commitment (Goffman, 1963:90 & 96).

A male dancer expressed feelings of friendship toward his long-term clients. "When [I] first dance with someone there is generally not much additional physical contact. [I] stand by [them] but don't touch [them]. But as you get to know someone over a period of time you get to be friends. It seems strange to just drop away and leave the warmness that is established." Another dancer feels that this is part of being a professional. You almost need to be over qualified as a dancer at Roseland, he says, in order to focus "on what you're really doing...expressing something nice and helping other people experience the same thing." This caring and friendship, whether genuine or in appearances only, is another means by which the taxi-dancers keep their clients involved with them. The more a taxi-dancer can care about his or her customer the better he or she is likely to be at the job. The mutual commitment involved in dancing together regularly helps develop the bond between clients and dancers which stems from learning a great deal about each other's personal lives. One woman has also come to feel that the client she has had the longest is almost a friend, in part because she knows many things about his personal and work life.

One method by which the taxi-dancers express this caring while binding the clients to them is by tacitly agreeing to enter into a type of fantasy world with them. This world is primarily comprised of images from the movies; Fred Astaire and Ginger Rogers and *Saturday Night Fever* are two of the major influences. The clothing that many of Roseland's clients wear— cocktail and disco dresses for the women, and color coordinated shirts, ties, handkerchiefs and an occasional boutonniere for the men—are clear evidence of the fantasy they are trying to create. A female taxi-dancer sums up this fantasy world by saying, "You get to dress up like Ginger Rogers for the night," and the dancing can make her forget her problems for the six hours of work. This combination of costume and ballroom movement, particularly its dramatic aspects such as dips, turns and lifts, help create the ballroom fantasy.

Part of this fantasy may be an unspoken and unacted upon flirtation. Many of the customers desire this and it also can be pleasing to some of the dancers. One taxi-dancer says that she likes the idea that "maybe I'm someone's fantasy, I want to be. It's a flirtation thing but there's no harm done." Another dancer dances regularly with a married man whom she does not think is interested in an affair. He simply likes the excitement of the flirtation. In many cases the husbands or wives of clients know about the taxi-dancers and some occasionally come to Roseland to meet them. One couple comes to Roseland together and both dance with taxi-dancers. In this way the dancing itself becomes a performance of a fantasy relationship that is other than the real one between client and dancer.

The married dancers think that being married probably makes flirtation a little safer for them. One says she does not get a lot of passes made at her, probably because most of the clients know both that she is married and her husband is in the room. However, her marital status also complicates her interaction with her clients. The presence of her husband makes her feel uncomfortable holding a client's hand between dances or standing with her arm around his waist as many of the male and female dancers do. Yet, despite her claims to feeling uncomfortable with the flirtatious aspects of the job, when you watch her dance she is one of the most vivacious and flirtatious of the dancers on the floor. The needs and desires of the clients, and the inherent possibilities for flirtation in ballroom dancing, override her more conservative feelings of what is proper.

A few of the women dancers are less comfortable with the physicality of the job that is not directly connected to dancing; it disturbs their sense of "real self," that sort-of "inner jewel that remains [ones] unique possession" (Hochschild 1986). The problem, says one woman, is that "You can't separate yourself from the situation....In some ways you have to let [the clients] into your life." Her inner self is threatened by the intimacy that is required by the face-engagement that is necessary in dancing, and by an ongoing relationship with certain clients that seems to require a peculiar type of intimacy that is necessary to taxi-dancing. This threat to the inner self becomes even more prevalent because of the flirtation that is so much a part of successful partner dancing, but which some clients misinterpret.

There are, therefore, two opposing forces working in the face engagements the taxi-dancers experience. On the one hand there is an openness that allows the taxi-dancers to perform their job well, on the other a closing off that is necessary for self-preservation. Goffman says that a society reconciles these two forces by a type of gentlemen's agreement. The dancer is under an obligation to respond to potential invitations, while clients are "under obligation to stay their desires" (1963:106). These forces are generally at work in all couple dance situations even if neither is a partner for hire. The majority of the taxi-dancer's clients, no matter what their fantasies, keep to this agreement and typically protect their taxi-dance partners. The dancers are then able to reciprocate with warmth and friendliness unprecedented in a normal couple dance situation between relative strangers. One client says of the dancers, " 'They're a joy to be with. They're energetic and exciting and all it costs is paper. What the heck is wrong with that? I'm at the stage when you get aches and pains and the girls make me look good' " (Ferretti, 1982:B4). Another customer found that after his wife died " 'The kids [dancers] kept me going. They're my friends, and I'll go down any street to say so' " (Ferretti, 1982:B4).

Some of the taxi-dancers, primarily males, may agree to escort a client to an evening of dancing at Roseland, to a party, or to another ballroom. One taxi-dancer even accompanied a woman, for pay, to a wedding as her guest. This sort of activity *seems* to fall just short of being a gigolo; outsiders assume that dancers also provide sexual favors.[8] However, one male dancer responded to my question about this by saying "No, gigolos make $200 per hour, I only make $25 for dancing." As far as I could ascertain dancing is the sole extent of any of the dancers' services.

Mills believes that friendliness of the sort found between taxi-dancers and their clients or any service worker is insincere (1956:282). Because the relationship between the taxi-dancers and their clients is so on-going and, in many ways intimate, with some clients the initial insincerity of the dancer does disappear eventually. However, there is always a distancing, and for some clients the false smile remains and allows dancers to protect their "real self," which is pushed further inside.

It seems then that the nature of the "friendship" between the dancers and clients varies depending on the needs and personality of the individual dancers. "Kindness and friendliness become aspects of personalized service or of public relations...rationalized to further the sale of something...'The successful person thus makes an instrument of his own appearance and personality' " (Mills 1956:182). Some taxi-dancers are able to use techniques similar to acting to more fully enter into a relationship with the client.

As in acting, the taxi-dancer creates a character which needs to be believed, but unlike acting, that character is not other than self. It is a representation of self which is sold in the market. Others are less comfortable doing this. Unfortunately, even if they are fine dancers the inability to enter into a character, a certain spirit, makes them less successful as taxi-dancers. All the taxi-dancers, however, draw two lines around their performance. One line allows a few clients to enter a more personal and caring sphere; the other line protects their "real self." The more natural a dancer's "performance" seems, i.e. the more disguised their feelings, the more successful the dancer is at his or her job of enhancing others.[9]

Deviance

It is the performative aspect, the selling of an appearance of oneself, that leads outsiders to see taxi-dancing as a deviant occupation. Our culture has a complicated relationship with those who sell the appearance of self such as actors, models, and prostitutes. All these jobs entail some skill in manipulating appearance and manner. We assume that people who look and perform in a sensual way must also have fantastic sex lives. For many it is not conceivable that certain types of performers can sell looks and skill without sex.[10]

The taxi-dancers themselves reflect this social view. For some their backgrounds and work lives are such that their friends, clients, and co-workers would be shocked to know about their dance careers.[11] One woman had never accepted a tip prior to dancing at Roseland, and at first it made her "feel cheap." Another says many of the people he knows never reveal that they were once ballroom teachers, much less taxi-dancers, because this could stigmatize them in the "straight" world.

Much of this lies in the attitudes of conventional members of western society towards dancing in general and ballroom dancing in particular. To the outside world actions such as accompanying a woman to a wedding as a paid dancing partner, standing on a dance floor hugging a client, and the very act of dancing as a paid partner are shocking and the desire to do so deviant.[12] Within the dance subculture, however, many things are so normalized that they are no longer even noticed.[13]

Howard Becker says that "Social roles are the creation of specific social groups" (Becker, 1968:15). Therefore, what one individual considers deviant can become acceptable and normal to another. Because deviance is conventionally defined as an infraction against the rules of a group, there are several possible layers of deviance in ballroom and taxi-dancing. Drawing on conventional ideas of deportment and proper behavior, the rules for where, when, and with whom one may dance are still rigidly set. Society at large sees a person who is paid for dancing with another as deviant. Within the rules of the ballroom subculture, couple dancing is, of course, the norm. Dancing for pay, however, is still seen by many as a peculiar—if not a deviant and questionable—thing to do. Yet within the still smaller world of ballroom performers, teachers, and their clients, such behavior is totally acceptable and above board. In their eyes deviance is flouting the gentlemen's agreement that is expected to be observed in such face engagements, or entirely stepping outside the "professional" client-worker relationship.

There are some clients who are looking for something more sexual than mild flirtation, who hold taxi-dancers too close or press them for dates after work. Even the men occasionally get passes made at them. The dancers say that some clients think that "because they've hired you it's their right to grab your ass and rub against you." Taxi-dancers are supposed to be able to "handle" the customers when this situation arises.[14] They learn to do this only through experience on the dance floor. The management will protect the taxi-dancers only in extreme situations by removing an overly amorous client from the room. The expectation seems to be that the dancers "must try and *feel* and *act* [italics mine] as if propositions and such physical attentions are a sign of my attractiveness and your sexiness (Hochschild, 1986:94)." The dancers are supposed to suppress their feelings that "such behavior is intrusive or demeaning, (Hochschild 1986:94)" as some clients and outsiders feel that they "asked for it" when they accepted their fee.

The taxi-dancers seem to manage their feelings about this type of behavior through conversation about their clients; gossiping about their lives, joking and teasing about their failings, pretensions and skill.[15] They warn each other about various clients peculiarities, and point out whom to avoid altogether. The less desirable clients are left to those taxi-dancers that are not part of the inner core, and as the "break-ins" for new dancers.

Taxi-dancing seemingly puts men in a sexually subservient role generally reserved for women. Still, the men retain more power in the situation than do the women. This may in part be connected to the fact that, despite the growing presence of men in service occupations (male waiters, stewards, etc.), men in general tend to be involved less in service work than are women. The outside jobs of the male taxi-dancers—radio announcer, psychiatrist, and real estate agent—are of higher status than are the jobs of the female—bookkeeper, secretary, and store clerk. This makes the men more aware of their power in general and gives even those who really need the income a more casual approach to the job. Although no dancer can officially refuse a dance, the men can lead so badly that a particular client will never purchase them again. A woman is more at the mercy of how her partner leads since it is harder to control a dance as the follower. In addition women clients are less likely than men to direct either anger or sexual advances at the dancer.

Conclusion

It seems then that there is a direct correlation among the relationship established between the dancer and the client, the performance of the dance, and the marketing of the dancer's skills. This correlation grows from the fact that the dancers, as service workers, are involved in a complicated process of performing their "self" by exposing a selected aspect of it for the purpose of attracting customers and maintaining a clientele. At the same time, they must hide and protect that "self" in order to maintain their integrity. This performance seems to have three major parts; an appearance of caring, the creation of a fantasy world, and the actual performance of the dances. The dancer's skill at all components of the performance serves to bind the client to him or her, while advertising the individual performer to other potential customers. Both elements boost the dancer's financial gain. The requirement of the larger performance—maintaining a clientele—leads to behavior which is viewed by the outside world as deviant. But to insiders it is simply the way one earns a living.

The dancers, through costume, performative skills, and specialized forms of acting, tie customers to themselves. Customers' suspension of disbelief allows them to enter the fantasy world the dancers help create while generally observing a "gentlemen's agreement" not to step beyond certain limits. The relationship between dancer and client is based on this suspension of disbelief. Ultimately, the clients are paying for a fantasy world that exists only in certain types of couple dancing.

Notes

[1] The Tango Palace

[2] "Obscene dancing" generally means couple dancing which is extremely close and at times includes partners grinding their hips together. At times the intention to give the male partner an erection or even bring him to orgasm was explicitly stated.

[3] I began my research on modern taxi-dancing in February of 1987 by attending Roseland on a Thursday afternoon between 4 and 10 p.m., the only time the taxi-dancers work. The taxi-dancers turned out to be a very mixed group. In addition to the presence of both men and women, modern taxi-dancers are older, tend to be educated, and taxi-dancing is not their major source of support.

The backgrounds of the eight respondents in this study are also varied. One woman works in a health food store and is the mother of six children. In her teens she was often the Lindy champion of Astoria Park. Another woman is originally from Bagdad. As a child she performed belly dancing for parties at her parents house. She was trained to teach by the Astaire studios who changed her name. Today she works as a bookkeeper and continues to work towards becoming a Royal Academy of Dance examiner, a five part process. A degree in modern dance from Cal Arts began yet another female taxi-dancers career. In 1983 she won the Harvest Moon Ball Lindy championship with ex-Savoy dancer George Lloyd. She is the only one of the taxi-dancers I interviewed who supports herself entirely through her dancing. Another woman is an executive secretary who has coached a number of Harvest Moon Ball contestants, including a married couple who are now taxi-dancers. The woman of that couple is a kindergarten teacher on Long Island and her husband is a psychotherapist in Manhattan. They finished second in the Harvest Moon Ball hustle competition for three years before moving on to teaching and small scale performances.

One of the men is a real estate agent who figured dancing would be a good way to meet women. He signed up for lessons at Fred Astaire's where he eventually became a teacher. Dancing helped support him through college. Another man is, a radio broadcaster and actor. He began dancing when he was given a gift of 25 free lessons at an Arthur Murray studio in 1958. His dancing landed him a role in *Saturday Night Fever* as the heroines first dance partner.

Other taxi-dancers have worked as a choreographer and teacher on a cruise ship, a medical technician, and an assistant professor of psychology at a local university. One is a writer who used his experiences as the basis of a play, *Taxi-dancer,* currently in it's first readings.

[4]I want to thank Nevart ("Belina") Babaian, Margaret Batiuchok, Dwight Carter, Roy Cheverie, Joel and Pam Greenspan, Judy Petardi, Penny Perucha and "Jacquline" for the many hours they spent with me, answering my questions, discussing their thoughts and feelings and even teaching me to dance a little. Their willingness to share their experiences are what made this study possible.

[5]Formerly taxi-dancers received half of $.10 per dance.

[6]Clyde B. Vedder reports the following types of support received by taxi-dancers in the 1930s and 1940s. "One patron may furnish the cement for a foundation for a house, another may put on the roof another install the electric wiring, furniture and other supplies. Patrons may donate hundreds of dollars worth of labor or material for the home of a taxi-dancer. During World War II rationed items were seldom a problem to the taxi-dancer. One patron had butter flown out to Los Angeles from his farm in Iowa for his favorite taxi-dancer. Taxi-dancers get customers to co-sign checking accounts, one makes the down payment, and another pays the rent" (1954).

[7]In fact there are some private dance teachers who do meet their students at Roseland and get paid for an hour of dancing just as do the taxi-dancers.

[8]There are gigolos at Roseland according to the regulars, but they bring their long-term clients there, and they do not solicit on the premises.

[9]One female dancer, however, does not see her job in this way. She sees herself as a teacher and sees her job as helping the person to dance better, not to look flashy and, in that way, enhance a partners ego.

[10]I believe that the tabloids feed this propensity through their "reporting."

[11]The shocked reaction to the idea that certain types of people would work at a job such as taxi-dancing is even true of some people involved in the ballroom subculture. The husband of a USBA champion and dance studio owner, asked one couple "What would you want to do that for?" "To pay for the lessons we take here" the woman replied.

[12]In Cathy Peiss' excellent book *Cheap Amusements* she points out that much that was viewed as deviant by the reformers of the first part of this century, groups like New York City's Committee of Fourteen and Fifteen, was simply a lack of understanding on the part of the observers as to the nature of certain types of cultural differences.

[13]Nanette J. Davis in her work on prostitutes, and Howard Becker in his work on drug users and musicians found that members of a subculture found ways of justifying and thus normalizing their activities. Often this happens through association with older members of the culture, a sort-of "everybody does it" justification.

[14]These problems are not exclusive to the taxi-dancer's job. A novice female in a ballroom dance setting is particularly prone to the attentions of men who want more than a dance. The dancer must also learn to "handle" male customers, either through refusing to dance with certain people, or by being able to keep strongly back from their partner. This is also a judgment call, some men simply lead closer than others and mean no harm. This can be difficult for the novice to distinguish, but should not be for the taxi-dancer.

[15]In an interview with stewardesses Hochschild was told that talking about clients to other workers is not an acceptable method for dealing with feelings about them as it may make the worker more angry. For the taxi-dancer it is imperative to discuss clients as it is one means by which members of the group can protect each other.

Bibliography

Becker, H.S. (1982) *Art Worlds*. Berkeley: University of California Press.

_____ (1968) *Outsiders: Studies in the Sociology of Deviance*. New York: The Free Press.

Beeman, W.O. (1986) "Freedom to Choose: Symbols and Values in American Advertising." *Symbolizing America*. Lincoln: University of Nebraska Press 52-65.

Cottle, T.J. (1966) "Social Class and Social Dancing." *The Sociological Quarterly*, spring 7:2.

Cressey, P.G. (1969 [1932]) *The Taxi-Dance Hall: A Sociological Study in Commercialized Recreation and City Life*. Montclair: Patterson Smith.

Davis, N.J. (1985). "Becoming a Prostitute." *Down to Earth Sociology*. New York: The Free Press 171-179.

English, B. (1982) "Where are the Dancers?: At Roseland, where it takes two—and a dollar—to tango." *Daily News*, Manhattan, 22 March 1&3.

Ferretti, F. (1982) "Taxi dancing takes a new turn at Roseland." *New York Times*, Style, 27 August PB4.

Garmaise, F. (1985) "Dancers for money: Vintage chic at Roseland." *The Village Voice*, 23 July.

Geist, W.E. (1984) "About New York: At Roseland no longer ten cents a dance." *New York Times*, Metropolitan Report, 28 April.

Goffman, E. (1963) *Behavior in Public Places*. New York: The Free Press.

_____ (1976) *Gender Advertisements*. New York: Harper and Row.

_____ (1959) *The Presentation of Self in Everybody Life*. Garden City: Doubleday Anchor Books.

Hickey, B. (1986) "In the mood for Roseland." *American Way*, 15 April, 19:8, 52-56.

Hochschild, A.R. (1983) *The Managed Heart: Commercialization of Human Feeling*. Berkeley: University of California Press.

Mills, C.W. (1956) *White Collar: The American Middle Classes*. New York: Oxford University Press.

Unpublished manuscripts of the Committee of 14 and 15, holdings of the New York Public Library Research Library.

Vedder, Clyde B. (1954) "Decline of the Taxi Dance Hall." *Sociology and Social Research*, July-August, 38:6, 387-391.

Video tape: David Susskind Show 1982-83 season.

Video tapes: Taxi-dancer shows "Roseland Follies" and "The History of Dance", plus some miscellaneous footage.

Wylie, Lou. (1933) "Dance Hall Lady." *American Mercury*, July, 29, 269-274.

Turning Vices into Virtues:
The Dignifying Accounts of Gun Avocationists*

Barbara Stenross

Hunters, target shooters, and gun collectors use guns as props (Goffman, 1959) to support valued leisure activities and identities. Yet gun enthusiasts face disapproval from many Americans. Urban Americans who did not grow up around guns tend to associate guns with violence and crime. Hence, they may question the motivations of people who use guns "for fun."

People who act in ways others consider deviant often develop accounts (Lyman and Scott, 1970) to excuse (Sykes and Matza, 1957) or justify (Mitchell, 1983) their behavior. In-depth interviews revealed that gun enthusiasts create justifying accounts that *dignify* the very aspects of their activities that others devalue. Thus, hunters are criticized as cold-blooded killers, but view their activity as teaching them respect for life. They regard themselves as conservationists who assist wildlife through herd thinning, paying fees that support research and habitat preservation, and the non-wasteful use of game animals for food. Shooters reverse their public image as aggressive and violence-prone. They stress their activity as a source of calmness, discipline, and self-control. And gun collectors play with the conventional image of collectors as "nutty." They poke fun at their "craziness," showing how their infatuation with guns and collecting makes them harmless, not dangerous.

Hughes (1971:344) argued long ago that low status workers may use the charisma associated with dirty work to give their work honor. This paper suggests that members of stigmatized avocational groups may pursue a similar strategy. In dealing with outsiders' negative images, they can turn public vices into private virtues.[1]

Hunters: Hunting Teaches Respect For Life

In early American history, people hunted as a way to put meat on the table (Tonso, 1982). Today, many nonhunters see hunting as blood-thirsty and barbaric. Hunters turn this criticism around: they argue that hunting teaches them respect for life.

*This research was supported in part by a grant from the University Research Council of the University of North Carolina at Chapel Hill. I thank Jeanne Brooks for research assistance and Sherryl Kleinman for helpful comments on earlier drafts.

We might expect hunters to avoid discussing hunting as "killing." Instead, the hunters confronted the matter of killing directly. One hunter who felt I was skirting the issue challenged me on it:

I was wondering why you didn't ask me, "How can you *shoot* them [game animals]?"

Hunters do not mind discussing hunting as killing because they believe that all meat-eating humans are predators. As one hunter put it, "in order for us to survive, some [species] must die." Yet hunters complain that critics ignore this uncomfortable fact. In the words of a professor who hunted deer, "critics are far happier to let *others* kill their meat and wrap it in saran wrap." In contrast, hunters believe that they confront death and life directly and honestly. A graduate student who grew up in Colorado explained that (ethical) hunters "have a sense of the significance of what [they] are doing." He added:

After all, you are killing something, and that should be cause for some reflection.

Hunters feel that ethical hunters follow rules that acknowledge and teach them respect for life. One such rule is not to let any part of a game animal go to waste. A young hunter who worked as a conservation officer said:

When I shoot, I'll keep the horns, use all the meat, get it packaged, and tan the hide. Do it myself. There's less waste when I shoot a deer than when a cow is butchered.

The hunters felt that it was immoral to hunt for "trophies" (notable body parts of the male of the species) without also consuming the animal as meat. A "big game" hunter who hunted on three continents and wished to bag one of every big game animal described how he learned to prepare and eat everything he killed:

I killed a wild turkey in the spring—people said you can't eat that turkey after it's been out eating in a field of wild onions, but we dressed it out. We had a game dinner. We had rattlesnake, groundhogs, that turkey—wound up with no meat on the bone.

Revealing the importance hunters attach to the "no waste" rule, one hunter joked that he hoped he never had to "shoot another guy" because he would hate to have to "clean him and eat him." Another hunter disliked squirrel meat; he decided to stick to hunting deer.

Hunters feel it is unethical to prolong an animal's suffering. Hence, they view it as a point of honor to kill an animal "quickly and cleanly." A small businessman who hunted on private lands explained:

Since that [killing] is part of it, I feel my responsibility to them. If I decide to take that animal, I like to take it as quickly and cleanly as I can.

Hunters also honor those who can get a deer or a "good bag" using bow and arrow and older, simpler guns, especially black powder pistol and muzzleloader. These methods demand greater skill and hence, give wildlife a greater opportunity to escape. Hunters disidentify with those who "blast away" or resort to "overkill:"

There are a lot of different kinds of hunters out there. Some are people who, by God, want to kill something, anything. They [use a gun] that can shoot everything for a mile in any direction.

Although the hunters criticized some hunters and hunting practices, hunters feel that most hunters are friends of wildlife, not their enemies. Hunters argue that the main threats to wildlife populations are loss of habitat, pollution, and automobiles, not hunters. They point out that hunting fees pay for wildlife and conservation programs:

If it weren't for hunters and fishers, there wouldn't be any more wildlife. We protect them, feed them when necessary. Hunters pay resources for disease research. If we didn't pay for that, who'd pick up the tab?

* * *

I've run into people all the time who say I shouldn't kill animals. I try to explain that buying a hunting license *supports* wildlife. It provides revenues. That the deer are overpopulated and disease sets in. If it weren't for the licenses, there wouldn't be any.

One hunter said that he often told critics who "really loved" animals to "buy a license and just not use it." Other hunters had joined organizations such as Ducks Unlimited that simultaneously support hunting and conservation (see also Hummel, 1983).

Many people dislike hunting because they see it as cold-blooded killing. Instead, hunters argue that hunting can give honor to life. Hunters reflect upon the drama of hunting as containing the universal riddle of life and death:

[In seeing deer out of season,] I sometimes wonder, what happens when the moment of truth arrives? Their attitude is the same as mine.

Hunters view their own experience with the natural world as more honest than the abstracted romanticism of their urban critics.

Shooters: Shooting Teaches Self-Control

Shooters identify themselves as athletes and view their guns as sports equipment (Hummel, 1985). Nevertheless, they face criticism from outsiders who regard their guns as weapons and see their sport as combat practice. A physician said:

If it's my day off, people might ask if I play golf. Well, I don't play golf, I shoot. People ask me, "Shoot what?" That upsets their world. Shoot what! Most people don't understand that it can be a sport. People play golf—no explanation needed. I have to explain everything.

Shooters respond by developing a counter-perspective: they view shooting as a source of calmness, discipline, and self-control.

Competitive shooters learn to be good shots, but they do not see themselves as combatants, Rather, shooters feel they are *less* likely to perpetrate violence with their guns than those who have less shooting experience. Shooters believe their training makes them more aware of the damage a gun can do and hence, more careful about handling guns than ordinary protection owners who may purchase a gun but not learn to handle it safely. Competitive shooters become furious when they recall safety lapses. A pistol competitor who shot for the National Guard said:

Competitive shooters get real mad if you risk a shooting accident. That's probably the only thing that makes shooters angry. That, and people who think that you don't have a right to go out and shoot. Put them in the same category.

Safety is such a great concern among shooters that members of the local pistol club said they tested prospective members on safety procedures before allowing them to join.

Shooters feel that match competition teaches not only safety, but also self-control. Shooters describe target practice as "physical and mental exercise." A medical examiner who competed in pistol and rifle matches explained how the shooter's view of guns contradicts the image of power and violence portrayed in the national media (see also Bayloff, 1988):

I try not to look at firearms as weapons or a means of power. I have not introduced these ideas to my kids. TV does a good job of that. Firearms function as more a mental exercise.

Shooters emphasize that the mental concentration required in match competition demands and produces a calm personality. A police chief who competed in matches "up and down the eastern seaboard" described the "typical shooter" as "low-key" and "square-away." He described fellow shooters as "very controlled people."

I've never seen a hyper person be a good shooter, doesn't fit that way. You can't go out there with a lackadaisical, nonchalant approach. Some people *can't* master that, the sport of firearm shooting.

A physician who enjoyed competing in benchrest rifle, in which one tries to "put five shots through a single hole," said that the stress and concentration of match competition "washes your mind." He believed that the world would be a calmer place if fewer people attended football games and more joined him at the firing range:

Matches are a wonderful experience. I've never seen anybody arguing with anybody. I wish more people who go to football games were shooters. They would learn a lot.

Another shooter, a college student who planned to enter the seminary, compared the effect of shooting to meditation:

I enjoy shooting. It requires control, calmness, steadiness. It's like meditation. I do *not* see myself as a combatant.

Finally, shooters believe that the "more proficient you get with firearms, the less likely you are to use them." Competitors who worked as police officers argued that they were less hasty about pulling or firing their guns than officers with less training who were less proficient:

If you are real proficient, you can wait longer, know that you have lethal force you can use, can strike where you want to.

One police officer felt that even the standard practical police course (P.P.C.) that officers shoot is too stylized and formalized to prepare them to use a gun defensively:

I was beginning to get into law enforcement and P.P.C. was too stylized to be training for the job. It would not pay for me to play games.

This officer took up combat (sometimes called practical) shooting instead. Yet he felt that even combat shooting prepared him to use restraint, not use his gun as an assault weapon:

Firearm competition puts you under a stress that is impossible to duplicate. If you do well, it breeds confidence. If you have a confident bearing, you may not draw your weapon. With less confidence, you could use a weapon more quickly.

Competitive shooters believe that shooting teaches calmness and self-control. By using guns a lot, shooters feel they become experts on gun safety and non-violence.

Collectors: Crazy Enough to be Harmless

Outsiders may fear that gun collectors are crazy people whose paranoia leads them to assemble dangerous arsenals. Collectors turn this criticism around, claiming they are indeed crazy, but in a harmless way: their fanaticism for firearms causes them to salt away dozens of special guns they do not shoot.

Gun collectors own many guns. Most of the North Carolina collectors owned at least 30 guns and four owned one hundred or more. Yet the collectors disclaimed having an interest in "any and all" of the guns that are "out there." Rather, collectors value particular guns that meet exacting standards for beauty, historical interest, or craftsmanship (see also Tonso, 1982; Olmsted, 1988). As one collector put it,

Unless it was used during World War II, for example, or it's in mint condition, a collector doesn't want it. It *has no value.*

Some collectors "reach back to hold onto the past." They collect historically significant guns of good "enough quality to last all this time." Others collect guns that incorporate particular design features (e.g. side-by-side shotguns; European "predecessors to cartridge arms") or that they regard as works of art (e.g. antique inlaid pistols; limited edition engraved commemorative guns.)

Collectors may be seen as "crazy" about guns. Yet collectors defuse the negative image of the gun "fanatic" by stressing an important irony: gun collectors are fanatic enough to collect the "same gun" over and over and to never *use* the guns that they collect (see also Tonso, 1982). By emphasizing a "theme" for their collection (Tonso, 1982), many collectors end up collecting multiple instances of the "same gun:"

Years ago I collected Lugers. I had 120, 130 in all, all contract models. They all look alike (laugh).

* * *

I collect Colt single action armies, made from the same mold from 1873 to 1980.

Moreover, collectors resist firing their firearms. Collectors of antique guns do not fire their collection guns for fear it will reduce their quality:

Condition is everything with antiques. I don't shoot them. Old ones *will* shoot, but it goes against the condition.

Collectors of modern guns do not even "open" their guns, but keep them locked away, closed and unloaded, in their original boxes:

I *never* shoot them. The trade thing is "NIB"—new in the box. It loses value if it's not in the original container and that container is not in original condition.

Gun collectors believe that only *they* are crazy enough to lock away dozens of guns they have never fired:

Of the 200 or so guns I have, I shoot maybe three or four of them. The rest are sitting in boxes, probably rusting (laugh).

Gun collectors also play with the common image of collectors as "nutty" by portraying their passion for collecting as an amusing personality quirk, not a mania. Several collectors laughed that collecting things seemed to "run in the family." A physician who collected commemorative items of all kinds laughed that his mother "could never buy less than three of anything." He blamed his "condition" on an "accrual gene." Another collector who owned more than 100 guns and 500 hats laughed that his 5-year-old son had inherited his craziness:

You know my son had a battery collection, all kinds, all sizes, he had them all categorized. Then he wanted to collect locks, so I gave one to him and one to Erin [daughter]. In two days he had Erin's, too, and the key. I think it must be inherited!

When I asked another collector if he collected anything besides guns, he laughed that the chair he was sitting on was a collector's item, and that the room was furnished with valuable antiques.

Gun collectors acknowledge that non-collectors might regard them as potential "gun crazies." They incorporate this notion of craziness into their perspective, but strip it of its dangerous connotations. They argue that among gun owners, only they are crazy enough to keep dozens of the same firearms sitting in boxes.

Discussion and Conclusion

People who enjoy activities that others devalue may deal with stigmatization by developing collective "dignifying rationalizations" (Hughes, 1971:341). Unlike "techniques of neutralization" (Sykes and Matza, 1957), which excuse actors from personal liability for deviant behavior, dignifying accounts redefine the devalued activities as honorable. Ironically, participants may use the most devalued aspects of their activities as "raw material" to construct these dignifying accounts.

Hunters, gun collectors, and competitive shooters counteract others' negative definitions with dignifying accounts. In each case, members reverse conventional wisdom. Portrayed as cold-blooded killers, hunters perceive their activity as teaching them respect for life. Seen as combatants, shooters emphasize their calmness and non-violence. And feared as potential "gun crazies," gun collectors joke about their "fanaticism" as proof that they are harmless. Thus, the gun enthusiasts parlay publicly-perceived vices into privately-held virtues.

How common are dignifying rationalizations among those who share the gun enthusiasts' commitment to some activity as "serious leisure" (Stebbins, 1982)? Because hunters, shooters and gun collectors "play" at activities that cause others' emotional pain, they may have greater cause to develop justifying accounts than other hobbyists such as anglers, coin collectors, or runners. Yet in the "protestant ethicalist" (Wilson, 1981) American culture, people who take their leisure seriously may always be regarded as somewhat deviant. Laughing that one is indeed a "little crazy" (as did the gun collectors) may be a common defense among the seriously leisured. Only further research, however, can tell us whether other avocationists feel the same need as the hunters and shooters to elevate stigmatized activities into noble pursuits.

Note

[1]This paper is based on in-depth interviews with 43 hunters, target shooters and gun collectors residing in central and eastern North Carolina. Gun owners are often wary of discussing their interest in guns with academics and other outsiders. To obtain interviews, then, I relied mainly on the method of snowball sampling. I gained the trust of two gun enthusiasts who then introduced me to others. In addition, I advertised for respondents in two local newspapers and interviewed the proprietors of 7 local gunshops and sporting goods stores. Among those contacted, there were no refusals to participate.

The gun recreationists varied in age from the early twenties to early seventies and worked in a variety of occupations, but with a concentration in professional and technical fields (e.g., engineer, welder, physician, dentist, attorney). The hunters were more diverse in their occupational and class backgrounds than the collectors or competitive shooters, whose avocations may require a larger financial investment. All of the respondents were white; only two were female (one hunter, one shooter). Categorizing respondents by their most important leisure interest, I interviewed 14 gun collectors, 17 competitive shooters and 12 hunters.

I used a grounded theory approach (Glaser and Strauss, 1967) to discover the meanings of hunting, shooting and gun collecting to the gun enthusiasts. In interviews that lasted about 90 minutes, I asked respondents how they became interested in their gun sport or hobby, how they used guns, and with whom they associated. I took detailed field notes during the interviews (as much verbatim as possible), then transcribed the interviews for analysis.

Bibliography

Bayloff, E. (1988) "Popular and media images of firearms in American culture." Paper presented at the Annual Meetings of the Popular Culture Association, New Orleans, March 26.

Glaser, B. and A. Strauss (1967) The Discovery of Grounded Theory. Chicago: Aldine.

Goffman, E. (1959) The Presentation of Self in Everyday Life. Garden City, New York: Doubleday.

Hughes, E. (1971) The Sociological Eye: Selected Papers. Chicago: Aldine.

Hummel, R. (1983) "Hunting and fishing, sports of millions, neglected subjects for the sociology of sport." Human Dimensions Newsletter 2, 3: 10-15. (1985) "Anatomy of a wargame: target shooting in three cultures." J. of Sport Behavior 8: 131-143.

Lyman, S. and M. Scott (1970) "Accounts," pp. 111-143 in S. Lyman and M. Scott (eds.) A Sociology of the Absurd. New York: Appleton-Century-Crofts.

Mitchell, R. (1983) Mountain Experience: The Psychology and Sociology of Adventure. Chicago: University of Chicago Press.

Olmsted, A. (1988) "Morally controversial leisure: the social world of gun collectors." Symbolic Interaction 11: 277-287.

Stebbins, R. (1982) "Serious leisure: a conceptual statement." Pacific Sociological Review 25: 251-272.

Sykes, G. and D. Matza (1957) "Techniques of Neutralization: A theory of delinquency." American Sociological Review 22: 664-670.

Tonso, W. (1982) Gun and Society: The Social and Existential Roots of the American Attachment to Firearms. Washington, D.C.: University Press.

Wilson, R. (1981) "The courage to be leisured." Social Forces 60: 282-303.

Powerlessness in Adolescence:
Exploiting Heavy Metal Listeners[1]

Bruce K. Friesen

In his classic study on adolescence, James Coleman (1961) suggested that the development of the secondary school system in industrial society, particularly in the post World War II years, produced the age and geographical segregation that provided a breeding ground for a distinctive youth subculture. Popular music was viewed by Coleman as an expression of this adolescent subculture which provided a catalyst necessary to unite young people, and allow them the ideological freedom to develop a collective identity of their own.

Empirical research conducted since Coleman's analysis has failed to substantiate the existence of thematic homogeneity in popular music. In fact, since the 1960s popular music has consistently grown more diverse in terms of the increasing number of styles and genres of music that receive radio airplay (Anderson et. al., 1980; Tanner, 1981; Hirsch, 1971). Since adolescents increasingly identify each other in terms of what type of music they listen to (Chapman and Williams, 1976:61), popular music today creates the conditions where several subcultures may consequently develop in response to this musical diversity. Etzkorn (1976:20) summarizes by saying:

Within delimited social contexts certain musical forms become clearly associated with specific social groups, and are practiced within them to the exclusion of alternatives. These specific musical forms are socially learned and transmitted within delimited social groups in ways comparable to those characteristic for other values and certain non-material cultural practices. Group-specific socialization practices offer a key to the analysis of the maintenance of specific musical culture.

This elaboration of musical genres has led to the identification of some musical styles as deviant. One style of music frequently identified as deviant is most often referred to as "heavy metal."[2] The subcultural activity surrounding the consumption of heavy metal music is frequently associated with the more "seedy" side of humanity. *The Economist* (1985:25), for example, described heavy metal as:

...a raw, loud and violent type of music. Its excesses are justly notorious—Mr. Blackie Lawless, a singer with a band called Wasp [sic], abuses a semi-naked girl on stage while wearing a chainsaw codpiece. A violent attitude to sex is often taken in the lyrics; an extreme example is 'Eat me alive' by Judas Priest, which is alleged to deal with forced sex at gunpoint.

Such "allegations" perpetuated by the rock music press and other moral entrepreneurial agents allow the "deviant" label to be applied continually to the heavy metal genre of music. Heavy metal, then, provides an interesting case study in the relationship between popular culture and deviance.

The heightened media attention on heavy metal facilitates the application of a deviant label to this genre of music. However, labeling heavy metal as such does not negate the possibility that values promulgated in the heavy metal subculture are "truly" deviant; in the sense that they differ from those of mainstream society.

Adolescent Subcultures and Deviance

In general, adolescents and their subcultures have been labeled in negative ways. They have been portrayed as rebellious, immoral, unappreciative, irresponsible, and rude (Rice, 1981; Barr, 1971; Drane, 1973; Feigelson, 1970; Gerzon, 1970). Yet most empirical studies concerned with normal adolescents indicate that the majority are not rebellious, not politically active, not resistant to the values of their parents, not at the mercy of their emotions, nor even in turmoil (Adelson, 1979, pp. 33ff). In a recent major survey which surveyed 3,600 Canadian youth, Bibby and Posterski (1985:23-24) concluded:

We do not mean to minimize the potential of youth minorities to have a cultural and political impact on our societies. However, we would underscore the fact that even in this period of such publicized societal disaffection on the part of youth, the values and related lifestyles of the majority of young people were largely untouched....Our survey has found that those terminal and instrumental values deemed most important by adult Canadians are also held by a solid majority of young people.

If adolescents generally support values that are congruent with those of mainstream society, why then are their subcultures labeled deviant? Georg Simmel (1955) offers some insight. Simmel's work (restated by Coser, 1964) suggests that deviance and the conflict it engenders performs positively in society in at least five interrelated ways.[3] First, when no external enemies exist, deviants exposed within the society can be used as scapegoats, serving to unify the general populace who do not deviate in the same manner. Secondly, since deviants are viewed by society at large with disgust and contempt, it adds a dimension of security and stability to the identity of the conformers, who perceive themselves to be morally superior and somewhat self-righteous. Kai Erikson (1966) argued that this distinction is, in fact, an essential need of society. Behaviors will continually be redefined as deviant in order to fill the need of having someone inferior with whom to compare.

Thirdly, assuming one can make the distinction between "healthy" and "harmful" deviance, non-conformity can serve as an early warning signal that something is wrong with the social system, and can help the society avoid potentially larger faults that could cause more damage at a later time. Both Simmel and Coser reinforced the idea that deviance in a society is healthy unless it attempts to seriously undermine the basic fabric of society.

Fourthly, the social change that is encouraged by certain forms of deviance may begin a process of progress and adaptation to new and largely acceptable norms and values in a given social system. Certain people in the past who were labeled deviant (such as Ghandi or Martin Luther King) encouraged social change in a fashion that is presently evaluated as positive.

Finally, assuming that certain behaviors can actually "let off steam," minor forms of deviant behavior may lead to fewer problems for society in the long run, since pent up frustration and aggression can be expressed in smaller rather than larger deviant behaviors. Prohibition was abolished partly due to this philosophy, since government leaders were willing to accept certain social consequences of legal alcohol consumption more readily than the problems of "bootlegging," organized crime and the like.

In other words, society increases its solidarity as certain social groups are labeled deviant. On the one hand, adolescents appear to be an intimidating group to label since they have numerous resources at their disposal. Adolescents are highly idealistic, have an abundance of energy and a surplus of free time. Yet despite these advantages, adolescents remain one of the most powerless groups in society. They are largely unsophisticated, and lack the knowledge or tact necessary to defend themselves effectively against any moral type of attack. Their dependency upon authority is crippling, since any attempt at criticizing the status quo is quickly quelled by parents who lean towards a more conservative viewpoint. In addition to this economic and emotional dependency, adolescents' lives are heavily regulated by teachers and the secondary school system. Elaborate control systems are maintained to ensure conformity to time schedules, attendance, and the like. And, in addition to these structural confines, most adolescents are in a crisis period of life, attempting to build their own self-esteem and make career decisions instead of trying to ward off moral attacks. Because many of them are likewise barred from obtaining more powerful positions in society (i.e. those that drop out of school are largely determined to fill only blue-collar positions), adolescents remain a relatively powerless group within society, and have frequently found themselves or their cultures to be the focus of a moral entrepreneurial attack. By labeling those who listen to heavy metal as deviant, then, society continues to function successfully.

At the same time, adolescents who choose to involve themselves with heavy metal also benefit from this relationship. Because many people are fearful of or intimidated by deviant groups, adolescents so labeled acquire status and power through these means. Heavy metal adherents experience power when they observe others stepping into stores or walking to the other side of the street to avoid a confrontation. This is a power applied only at the interactive (as opposed to structural) level, but it is an attractive and desirable status given adolescents' otherwise powerless position in society.

While heavy metal participants welcome the "deviant" stigma, most resent the "delinquent" label which often accompanies an application of the former. Headbangers recognize the term "deviant" as connoting "different," and the term "delinquent" as implying "criminal." While the criminal element is a part of the heavy metal scene, most of the participants do not take part in it.

Aspects of Heavy Metal Culture

To investigate this relationship, research was undertaken to find to what extent and in what ways the heavy metal subculture "deviates" from mainstream society.[4] While observing various activities and interactions in the scene it became apparent that certain things are highly valued among heavy metal adherents.

Music

Heavy metal enthusiasts maintain that music is a big part of their lives. This is consistent with recent findings: Bibby and Posterski (1985:33) found that some 90 percent of teenagers indicated that they listen to music "very often." Next to friendship, music was noted to be the greatest source of personal enjoyment. It appears that the high value heavy metal enthusiasts place upon music is something they have in common with other adolescents.

Along with the high level of enjoyment that headbangers receive from listening to their type of music, a keen defensiveness exists as well. In many cases heavy metal adherents displayed a strong dislike towards those who criticized their music on moral or aesthetical grounds. One female adherent commented:

I have a couple of friends that I said, "Here, I'll put on some [heavy metal] ballads for you," and they said, "no, it will hurt my ears," as if it's going to corrupt them or something. Shit, I mean, even Bruce Cockburn [easy-listening artist] swears in his songs. If there's a few harsh words in metal, what's the difference?

Reactions by adherents to others' dislike for heavy metal music range from relativism ("each to his own") to acts of antagonism. Turning up a stereo in a public place after someone has voiced criticism is often cited as a favorite antagonistic reaction.

Existential Pleasures

While studying the heavy metal subculture it became obvious that many topics of conversation center on various types of existential pleasures. These pleasures are in contrast to the long-term goals of "normal" society that involve deferred gratification. Getting drunk, driving fast, "doing" drugs, having sex and "partying" are examples of existential pleasures. Getting a university degree, saving up for retirement and taking yearly vacations are examples of deferred gratification. Over half of the conversations among headbangers deal favorably with existential pleasures. Bibby and Posterski (1985:19) found that almost six in ten young people desired a "life of excitement," but that excitement "took a back seat" to more conservative values of companionship and love. Similar values were expressed by heavy metal adherents. Matza and Sykes (1961:715) have also pointed out that "the values of a leisure class seem to lie behind much delinquent activity." When engaging in leisure activities, members of mainstream society also adopt values that appear to conflict with those values held at other times. Leisure participants may express a rejection of the work ethic, and may engage in conspicuous consumption of material goods and existential luxuries. For members of society in general, the transition between work and leisure value-systems is not seen as contradictory.

Headbangers also make a sharp distinction between work and leisure time. Older participants are better able to articulate this difference than are younger headbangers, but by high school the majority of heavy metal adherents identify their involvement in the subculture as a leisure activity (although some of the activity is carried out during school hours). Thompson (1969) suggests that "deviant" leisure pastimes were viewed by employers in the past as a potential disrupter of productivity because they act as a "counterthesis" to work. In the heavy metal scene, however, participants are quite able to differentiate between necessary duties in the "outside" world, and enjoyable activities engaged in apart from work or classroom. Leisure activities are purposely selected to provide a break from the routine of the week.

Further qualifications need to be made regarding existential pleasures. Most of the talk in the scene dealing with deviant activities is never put into action. There is frequent talk about having sex with a stranger of the opposite sex, for example, but the vast majority of participants leave the scene with the same friends with which they enter. This expression of deviant fantasies appears to be an accepted "rhetoric of deviance" among heavy metal adherents. When questioned about the practice, participants describe such discussions as a verbal exercise of venting frustrations. By describing such fictitious adventures, headbangers reaffirm to themselves and others their commitment to the leisure values of the subculture. Such discussions are also cathartic, in that they reduce high frustration levels caused by the discrepancy between what participants want to have happen and what really occurs.

A certain amount of illegal activity does take place in the scene, particularly in the form of soft drug consumption or purchasing (eg. marijuana, hashish, hashish oil). However, because observation of the heavy metal subculture was made almost exclusively at places of leisure, it is likely that observations of such activities were more numerous than would have been recorded when observing heavy metal adherents at other times. Adolescents and young adults are generally the heaviest users of marijuana, and non-students (i.e. high school dropouts) use marijuana more often than students (Stebbins, 1988:150). It is likely that such illegal activity is carried out to the same degree in other adolescent leisure subcultures as well (see Chambliss, 1973). This fact was emphasized by one adherent:

We are no more delinquent than anybody else. Preppies and all others drink as much as we do, do as many drugs, and have as much of the criminal element in their kind as we do in ours. As a matter of fact, I know a few thiefs [sic], and their favorite type of music is Top 40, not heavy metal.

Short-Term Job Preparation

For those listeners highly involved in promoting heavy metal music, the desire to be close to the music business often dictates the amount and type of education they seek. Most career positions in the music business (such as sound engineer or audio technician) require short-term training courses that many committed listeners involve themselves in. This is not to say that adherents of heavy metal are determined by their association with the music to limit their education. Rather, serious heavy metal adherents are more likely to want jobs that require such education.

Gender Expectations

One of the most distinctive aspects of the heavy metal subculture is the different expectations which exist for males and females. Males and females conform to these expectations in order to be evaluated as "cool" or "alright." Failure to conform to such expectations results in a range of sanctions; from a ridiculing of the behavior or person to ostracism from the group. For the most part, males conform to extremely rigid roles. Males are expected to emulate certain characteristics (eg., aggressiveness, independence) in their image, demeanor and argot, and are also expected to practice behaviors that disassociate them from anything feminine. Females, on the other hand, are allowed the option at times to display certain male qualities in addition to female characteristics.[5]

One obvious characteristic expected from males in the setting is "toughness" or "ruggedness." Toughness is expressed in the gait of many participants, wearing leather studded arm or wristbands, and walking with arms and legs slightly spread to make one look larger than normal. Toughness is also demonstrated by the lack of physical intimacy between males. Males come in contact with each other only through carefully mediated symbolic actions of support; such as a gentle punch on the shoulder, a special handshake where one person's hand clasps the other person's thumb, or a hand held high in the air while an approaching male does the same, slapping hands as they meet (a "high five"). Any other physical contact, even suggested, is negatively viewed. One headbanger, for example, relayed a story of a homosexual proposition on the street:

That's as bad as Grady jumping in this car, he's hitch-hiking and this car drove down the side of the road. Jumps in, buddy in a big Cadillac, and he says, [effeminate voice]: "Where're you going?" Grady, six foot four, right? Looks down at this guy, [deep bass voice] "I'm going down the street to get some gas." [effeminate voice] "Uh, do you mind if we stop around the corner a little bit? I've never had anybody as big as you before." And Grady just put his head through the window on that side; just nailed him; just cold-cocked him on the side of the face. Pushed his head right through the window on the other side. "You flaming faggot," he says, "stop this car."

Stories such as these, whether true or concocted, stress the behaviors expected of males.

Other observed traits of males included aggressiveness, independence, and desire for non-commital (i.e. self-oriented) sexual relations. While male traits are viewed by males and females more positively than female traits, females are evaluated by males in the setting more by physical appearance than expected behaviors. Participants commented in interviews:

Male 1: "Metal girls are sexy. They get dressed up in the shortest skirt, and they usually have long legs...

Male 2: And they usually wear the tightest spandex.

Male 3: But they're not always sexy; they're more wild.

Male 1: No they're not always sexy; they're more of a wild creation that is tolerable and acceptable, right? Little old ladies look at them and go "Little slut," but Dad goes "Oooh."

Male 3: Yeah, and swerves the car.

[Laughter]

The males in the setting also agree that "chicks" are there not because they enjoy the music, but because they want to "get a guy." The "pure" male motivation of being involved with the music for its own sake enables them to accord women a position of lower status. Since the heavy metal subculture is organized (however loosely) around a genre of music, appreciation of the music is the central value of the subculture. As one participant put it:

Male 1: They [females] like the musicians, whereas the guys like the music.

Male 2: But that's what the women are there for [to get a guy], it carries on the teen idol bit but for metal.

Male 3: That's chauvinistic.

Male 2: Okay, it's chauvinistic, but that's what I see, you know, like the girls at the Helix concert all backstage.

Male 1: Yeah, but girls are girls.

Male 2: Okay, girls are girls.

The distinct masculine identity in heavy metal is also reinforced by the recognition that few women listen to "thrash" metal; an extremely fast and aggressive form of heavy metal music little known outside of the subculture.

Male 1: Women don't like a lot of thrash. They don't like a lot of the intensity. They like a lot more mainstream stuff. It's all guys. You go to a thrash show and you'll be looking at about a 90 percent male turnout.

Male 2: But if you go to a show like Ratt you'll be looking at about 75 percent women.

These types of distinctions made by males reinforce masculine character traits that distinguish them from females.

While females are socialized into accepting these gender distinctions, it appears that they often downplay them through their own interpretations of their involvement in the scene. Females explain such differences in terms of individual tastes rather than male or female differences. For example, one female commented:

I don't like all of that thrash stuff, I don't know what it is, but it just doesn't turn me on. I'm sure that there are other chicks that enjoy the stuff, but it's just not for me.

Because of the stigma that is attached to getting involved in the scene for reasons other than music, females likewise tend to practice a certain amount of role distancing to try to demonstrate their "pure" attraction to the music. However, such role distance behavior is also evaluated on a personal rather than social level. One female commented:

Like, a few friends of mine who are working in bands or whatever, for them to turn around and say, "Oh fuck, the groupies are here again," like, I have to laugh you know, but then I kind of have to go "Don't fucking think that of ME," you know, because that's the last thing I want thought of myself... But some of them chicks with the lace around the ankles and the spandex and chains, like THOSE chicks, look at THEM.

While male adherents to heavy metal tend to emphasize the differences between the sexes, then, females tend to downplay them. This may be due, in part, to the stigma generally associated with female gender traits. These inconsistencies are not radically different than those of traditional society. In some cases gender presentations seem to be an extreme but logical extension of society's traditional gender expectations. What appears to be deviant is not the values, but the symbols that are used to express such values. Long hair on males, for example, is viewed in traditional society as effeminate or iconoclastic rather than masculine. Within the heavy metal subculture, however, long hair is a symbol of freedom, autonomy and, at times, virility for the male. These are values traditionally associated with masculine behavior (Chafetz, 1974; Freudiger and Almquist, 1978; Thaxton and Jaret, 1985). While these symbols seem somewhat extreme at times (eg. a "dog collar" worn by a male with 8 inch spikes sticking out of it), it should be remembered that the majority of adherents are adolescents. Adolescents are not confined by conventional social statuses and careers that demand a certain attire be worn. In society, adoption of such traditional symbols are socially accepted as presenting masculinity or femininity in proper ways.

In the heavy metal subculture it is the symbols rather than the values that deviate from mainstream society.

The Views of Key Insiders

Interesting insights were also gleaned by conducting in-depth interviews with heavy metal participants. Heavy metal adherents recognize the successful attempts of the media and others to label their music and subculture as both deviant and delinquent.

> Male 3: I'll tell you one thing. Any shit happens between four preppies and one headbanger and the headbanger will come out the big loser with the cops and everything...You even see it downtown in the arcades and everything...Preppies never got harrassed...The jock preps and those guys, they got enough money they're fuckin' around with more drugs than the headbangers are. You go in there, the cop sees the headbanger—"open up your cigarette package" [to check for marijuana cigarettes or "joints"]—that kind of shit.

Some adherents to heavy metal are drawn to the music because of it's distinctiveness; it helps to give them a feeling of individuality. Soon, they are labeled deviant by dint of their association with the heavy metal subculture. For others the deviant identity is acquired through "hassles" with police and other established groups in society, and their attempts to label headbangers as such.

It is not unusual, then, to find headbangers (particularly males) identifying themselves as deviant.

> Interviewer: Do you view yourselves as deviant?
> [Pause, then laughter]
> Male 2: YES! To sum it up from a song from Metallica, "Am I evil?"
> [several say at the same time] "Yes, I fucking am!"
> [laughter].

However, the large majority of headbangers do not accept the delinquent label that entrepreneurs also attempt to apply.

> Interviewer: Do you view yourselves as delinquent?
> Male 1: No.
> Male 4: No.
> Male 2: No.
> Interviewer: Do you think there are some people that listen to metal that are delinquent?
> Male 2: Sure, but there are people who listen to Wham! [mainstream group] who are delinquent too.
> Male 1: And there's people who listen to country music too who kill people all the time. Music, I don't think, has any bearing on a person's brain, or what they do, or how they function.

Heavy Metal Re-examined

This empirical examination of the world of heavy metal presents a look into an adolescent subculture traditionally perceived as deviant. Data gathered through field research has produced evidence to indicate that the activity surrounding heavy metal is indeed subcultural, and that participants share a collective definition of the scene they share. But a close examination of the values in the scene reveal that heavy metal participants do not adhere to values that are contrary to those of society. While the symbols used to express such values do indeed deviate from traditionally accepted means of symbolic communication, the implied messages are similar to those espoused in conventional society.

The stigmatization of the heavy metal subculture as deviant, then, is a classic example of the labeling process. In an attempt to develop an individual identity or acquire personal power, many adolescents involve themselves in a subculture perceived to be deviant. While this stigmatization can result in a change of status to "deviant," such a change is not always permanent. Many adherents to heavy metal never get involved beyond the most popularized versions of the music or dress. After oppressive structural constraints of parents, home or school are left behind (through graduation from high school, for example), heavy metal musical preferences are often replaced by an interest in more mainstream styles of music. Still, others develop a sincere appreciation for the aesthetics of heavy metal music, and continue consuming the music even after high school. Several older participants confessed that their interest in heavy metal music had become a secret past-time which they hid from co-workers for fear of ridicule or ostracism.

There are two important societal advantages to labeling adolescents in general, and heavy metal adherents in particular, as deviant. The first advantage is that it is a status that is removed simply with the passage of time. As adolescents grow older they are perceived to "grow out of" their deviant ways; the preference for heavy metal music is either abandoned or concealed. Members of society do not attribute this change in musical tastes to the removal of the structural constraints adolescents experience. Rather, the general public interprets this transition in moral terms. Those who renounce their interest in heavy metal are viewed as former delinquents who have since discovered the error of their ways. Societal members then gain a permanent group to stigmatize as deviant without forcing any one person to live with the consequences of that label for life.

The second advantage of labeling adherents to heavy metal deviant is that the basis of this labeling at first appears to be classless. While there is evidence to indicate that adolescents from blue collar homes may become more involved in heavy metal than others (Tanner, 1981; Brake, 1985), identifying deviants on the basic of musical preference tends to confound the class issue and helps ensure that a "false class consciousness" is maintained.

In the past, ethnic groups, homosexuals, the handicapped, and women have been among the favorite minorities in society to label deviant, in that a separate set of distinctive behaviors were expected from each group. With the growing concern over human rights legislation, however, moral entrepreneurs must be much more careful in stigmatizing such groups publicly in order to avoid legal prosecution. Adolescents still remain one group that is not protected by law against such discrimination. From a purely functional standpoint, the continuation of this practice may indeed aid society through the positive ways in which deviance can function. On the other hand, one may choose to take issue with the seemingly arbitrary way that powerless social groups are differentiated. These groups suffer humiliation and ostracism because a deviant label is applied to them for the purpose of the common social good. Where adolescents who have chosen to listen to heavy metal are concerned, this appears to be the case.

Notes

[1]This paper reports on part of the findings of a larger study (Friesen, 1986). I would like to thank Dr. Robert A. Stebbins for his helpful comments on this paper.

[2]While punk music could also be considered a "deviant" style of music, the political nature of the punk movement has generally appealed to young adults more than adolescents.

[3]These five functions are summarized in James Teevan, ed. (1982:69).

[4]To develop a grounded theory around the research question, participant observation was used for data collection (Becker, 1970; Lofland, 1971). A quantitative content analysis of the lyrics of two-hundred eighty two heavy metal songs was also conducted. The reader may consult the larger study for further information regarding the content analysis.

A heavy metal adherent or "headbanger" (as they are inclined to define themselves) was operationally defined as a person who had: 1) a tendency to select heavy metal as his or her favorite type of music; and 2) a propensity to define himself or herself as a "headbanger." Field research was carried out between July 1985 and July 1986 in Calgary, Alberta, Canada; a city with a population in excess of 600,000. The heavy metal scene was entered a total of 57 times and included concert arenas, nightclubs, a cable television station, musician's union concert hall, a band practice room, junior high and high school buildings, and home parties. Informal interviews were conducted with 43 different participants in the scene, 29 of whom were male. To conclude the research, semi-formal interviews were conducted with six informants heavily involved in the heavy metal subculture.

[5]For example, "aggressiveness" was an expected and desired characteristic of females when males viewed them in the erotic role. The behavior was seen as appropriate as long as it was oriented to the satisfaction of the male (i.e. other-oriented) rather than the female (i.e. self-oriented). At times females were expected to threaten or even engage in physical violence if another female threatened to "make a play" for a boyfriend or male companion. Such activity demonstrated commitment and faithfulness to the male; values which are traditional in nature.

Bibliography

Adelson, J. (1979) "Adolescence and the Generation Gap." Psychology Today 12:9:33ff.

Anderson, Bruce, Peter Hesbacher, Peter K. Etzkorn and R. Serge Denisoff (1980) "Hit Record Trends, 1940-1977." Journal of Communications 30:2:31-43.

Barr, R.D. (1971) "Today's Youth: Cluttered Values and Troubled Dreams." pp. 11-25 in Barr, R.D., ed. Values and Youth. Washington, D.C.: National Council for the Social Studies.

Becker, Howard S. (1963) Outsiders: Studies in the Sociology of Deviance. New York: Free Press of Glencoe.

Bibby, R.W. and D.C. Posterski (1985) The Emerging Generation: An Inside Look at Canada's Teenagers. Toronto: Irwin Publishing.

Brake, Michael. (1985) Comparative Youth Culture. London: Routledge & Kegan Paul.

Chafetz, Janet S. (1974) Masculine/Feminine or Human? Ill.: F.E. Peacock Publishing Inc.

Chambliss, William J. (1973) "The Saints and the Roughnecks." Society 11:1:24-31.

Chapman, Antony J. and Alan R. Williams (1976) "Prestige Effects and Aesthetic Experiences: Adolescents' Reactions to Music." British Journal of Social and Clinical Psychology 15:61-72.

Coleman, James S. (1961) The Adolescent Society. New York: Free Press.

Coser, Lewis A. (1964) The Functions of Social Conflict. Ill: Free Press.

Drane, J.A. (1973) A New American Reformation. New York: Philosophical Library.

The Economist (1985) "Obscene But Not Heard?" 296 (August 17):25.

Erikson, Kai (1966) Wayward Puritans. New York: Wiley and Sons.

Etzkorn, K. Peter (1976) "Manufacturing Music." Society 14:1:19-23.

Fiegelson, N. (1970) The Underground Revolution. New York: Funk and Wagnalls.

Freudiger, Patricia and E. Almquist (1978) "Male and Female Roles in the Lyrics of Three Genres of Contemporary Music." Sex Roles 4:1:51-65.

Friesen, Bruce K. (1986) Labelling Youth Cultures Deviant: Traditional Gender Roles in Heavy Metal. Unpublished Master's Thesis, Sociology, University of Calgary.

Gerzon, M. (1970) The Whole World is Watching. New York: Paperback Library.

Gold, Raymond L. (1958) "Roles in Sociological Field Observations." Social Forces 36:217-223.

Hirsch, Paul M. (1971) "Sociological Approaches to the Pop Music Phenomenon." American Behavioral Scientist 14:371-388.

Lofland, John (1971) Analyzing Social Settings. Belmont, Calif.: Wadsworth Publishing.

Matza, David and Gresham M. Sykes (1961) "Juvenile Delinquency and Subterranean Values." American Sociological Review 26:712-719.

McCall, G. and J. Simmons (1969) Issues in Participant Observation. Don Mills, Ont.: Addison-Wesley.

Rice, F. Philip (1981) The Adolescent. Boston: Allyn and Bacon Inc.

Schatzman, L. and A. Strauss (1973) Field Research. Toronto: Prentice-Hall.

Simmel, Georg (1955) Conflict: The Web of Group-Affiliations. Translated by

Reinhard Bendix. New York: Free Press.

Stebbins, Robert A. (1988) Deviance: Tolerable Differences. Scarborough, Ont.: McGraw-Hill Ryerson.

Tanner, Julian (1981) "Pop Music and Peer Groups: A Study of Canadian High School Students' Responses to Pop Music." Canadian Review of Sociology and Anthropology 18:1:1-13.

Teevan, James, ed. (1982) Introduction to Sociology: A Canadian Focus. Scarborough, Ont.: Prentice-Hall Canada Inc.

Thaxton, Lynn and Charles Jaret (1985) "Singers and Stereotypes: The Image of Female Recording Artists." Sociological Inquiry 55:3:239-263.

Thompson, E.P. (1969) "Time, Work Discipline and Industrial Capitalism." Past and Present 38:12-34.

IV
Media Content and Deviance

Introduction

Mass media programming is a major popular cultural product. With some 98 percent of American households having at least one television set (more households than have indoor plumbing), TV is the dominant mechanism of cultural dissemination. Deviant behavior is the most common phenomenon presented on television. For both informational and entertainment programming (a distinction which is often difficult to make), deviance provides "media managers" with the opportunity to present dramatic action and moral lessons while allowing viewers to vicariously involve themselves with the linked pleasures of rule-breaking and the status quo enhancing display of its eventual painful consequences. As we have seen in previous examples of the linkage between deviance and popular culture, media depictions of misbehavior generate considerable social conflict. They are (rather simplistically) perceived to be a cause of the violation of widely shared normative proscriptions in "real life." However, as a number of the papers in this section suggest, media portrayals of deviance can reasonably be seen as having the effect of supporting the established social order rather than tearing it down through the offering of "bad" examples after which audience members model their own behavior. How, and to what effect, the mass media (principally TV) present deviance is the theme around which the discussions in this section revolve.

Rod Carveth looks at the rise of Acquired Immune Deficiency Syndrome (AIDS) as an issue in TV entertainment programming. His main point is that television is the prime source of "definitions of reality" held by Americans. The ways in which moral issues are presented are directly supportive of the normative status quo and the commercial interests of media industries. In focusing on AIDS as the punishment for sexual promiscuity, homosexuality, commercial sex, and drug use, TV sets a conventional moral agenda while "symbolically annihilating" AIDS victims.

Russell Farnen's paper deals with the interplay between the media and "terrorism." He maintains that this relationship is symbiotic. News workers and managers need terrorist activities to provide dramatic action while groups that employ violence to achieve the social changes they desire need media coverage to publicize their cause. Established interests look for the reinforcement of legitimate authority while terrorists seek to demonstrate and spread social dissatisfaction. Farnen ends his paper with a discussion of some of the key policy implications of this media-terrorism symbiosis.

81

Priscilla Warner presents the results of a qualitative content analysis of children's cartoons. She argues that conventional depictions of "evil-doers" are shaped by factors and interests built into the cultural production apparatus. For example, cartoon villains are presented using a simplistic and clearly identifiable appearance code because the material is directed at children, cartoon segments are relatively short, and producers are interested in enhancing the commercial success of secondary products (toys, games, etc.) based on the cartoon characters. The implied etiology of deviance is correspondingly simplified as the villains' physically ugliness is connected to the biological/innate sources of their evil. Children's cartoons provide the vehicle for basic, "pro-social," moral lessons—deviance is unusual, unappealing, and eventually results in punishment dealt out by established and cooperative social groups.

Keith Crew's paper presents a similar picture of the structure and content of, and implied messages within, TV police dramas. Although more structurally complex than children's cartoons, cop shows offer a conventionalized view of criminal deviance as a dangerous threat to the social order perpetrated largely by psychopathic individuals. As a somewhat more sophisticated morality play, crime shows do present apparent criticisms of established institutions. The legal system is inept, business leaders and politicians are driven by greed and hunger for personal power to violate the law, and bureaucracy is a rigid and incompetent mode of social organization. This decontextualized critique of the status quo sets the stage for the central lesson. Society's salvation rests in the hands of competent individual heroes unfettered by considerations of due process. Their violations of established regulations are justifiable means of enhancing the larger moral good.

Eleanor Lyon presents the results of a systematic content analysis focusing on the presentation of violence in prime-time, fictional television programs. She begins with an overview of the research into TV violence and the controversy surrounding its supposed social impact. Within this context Lyon discusses who is portrayed as perpetrating violence, who is victimized, the relationship between the "violent" and the victim, the types of violence employed, and the consequences of the violent interactions. Of most interest are the various ways in which media violence is a distortion of "real life" violence. For example, perpetrators and victims tend most commonly to be white, middle-class males—interestingly, the characteristics of the writers, producers, directors, and other key decision-makers involved with these programs. Further, as is emphasized in Crew's paper on cop shows, Lyon's research supports the observation that a high proportion of violence is engaged in by "good" characters for "good" (ie., socially approved) reasons. The paper concludes by focusing on the distorted perceptions of reality which TV viewers draw from their exposure to media violence and their consequent support for particular political ideologies and policies.

In the concluding piece in this collection, Jon Cruz focuses on the newly popular TV genre of "infotainment" or "tabloid journalism." As a major figure employing this format, Morton Downey, Jr. uses a pseudo-populist image to carry the conservative political message that deviance is an everpresent threat caused by the "liberal" establishment and its ideology. Through his theatrical manipulation of the members of a committed socio-political taste culture, Downey reinforces the preexisting definitions of reality which underlie their moral resentment. Deviance is a highly emotional issue and its portrayal in the popular media is a launching pad for egotistic opinion leaders and their ideas of appropriate political action. Cruz's discussion is of particular interest in our understanding of the connections between popular culture and deviance in that it deals with a presentational form that clearly violates established media conventions. Downey's show and those like it are examples of innovative deviance as they breach the more-or-less cooperative tradition of TV talk shows and informational programming. Emotion is substituted for reason, discussion gives way to confrontation, and overt advocacy replaces the apparent objective evenhandedness which has traditionally acted as the cover for the somewhat more subtle forms of reality shaping used by media gatekeepers to structure public understandings of deviance and reinforce established interests.

Warning—Passion Can Be Hazardous to Your Health: The Portrayal of AIDS on Broadcast Series Television

Rod Carveth

Perhaps no disease has caused as much nationwide hysteria as that of Acquired Immune Deficiency Syndrome, commonly referred to as AIDS. Such is the furor over AIDS that schools struggle over whether to admit students with AIDS, corporations ponder whether or not to let AIDS-afflicted employees go, and the federal government balances political and economic agendas regarding AIDS victims.

Complicating the picture is the curious portrayal of AIDS in the media, in terms of both news and entertainment. Media reports on, and depictions of, AIDS vary in degree of accuracy and sensationalism. Nowhere does a more muddled picture emerge than the one beamed forth on television.

There is no question that TV serves as the predominant form of popular culture in our society. Television is watched over seven hours per day in the average U.S. household. More Americans get their news from television than from any other news source. The average price of a unit of television advertising costs more than that of any other medium. Television also functions as one of the primary institutions of socialization in society.

Communication researcher George Gerbner (Gerbner and Gross, 1976) likens TV's socializing role to that of tribal myths, presenting the dominant norms and values of American culture. According to Gerbner, TV portrays what is in the acceptable cultural "mainstream." What lies outside this mainstream—deviant groups and behaviors—is either trivialized or ignored. This discussion, an extension of previous research (Carveth, 1986), illustrates how TV has both delegitimized a class of AIDS victims while romanticizing another class. The institution of television has done this by giving disproportionate coverage to "mainstream" AIDS victims while virtually ignoring the majority of AIDS patients—those of the gay community.

This presentation restricts its review to broadcast series television portrayals. While TV movies such as *An Early Frost, Just a Regular Kid: An AIDS Story* and *Go Toward the Light,* have dealt with the issue of AIDS, their broadcasts were "one-shot" deals. Viewers tend to follow network series from week to week, thereby becoming familiar with the characters

An earlier version of this paper was presented at the Annual Convention of the Popular Culture Association in Atlanta, GA, April 1986.

84

that inhabit the shows. The networks have more at stake with these continuing series as well. Should too many viewers object to a storyline of a particular series, viewership may decline, and with it, advertising revenues.

Before beginning the discussion of AIDS on network series TV, it is instructive to briefly note its portrayal in TV news.

TV News and AIDS

Todd Gitlin (1980) describes in his book, *The Whole World is Watching*, how the mass media worked to delegitimize the student movement. By focusing on the most deviant acts of the student protesters, such as bizarre dress or violent episodes, the TV networks presented a distorted picture of the protesters to the American public. In doing so, the networks—who are dependent upon advertising revenues for their economic survival—were able to uphold the political status quo during the mid-sixties, when the American public still supported the war in Vietnam. In much the same way, TV, in the early days of the AIDS epidemic, virtually ignored the disease.

For the first two years of the AIDS epidemic (when the disease was still referred to as Gay Related Immune Deficiency Syndrome), no network TV news coverage of the malady existed. This is not to say that TV was alone in discounting the disease. Few print articles existed in the mainstream printed press, such as the *New York Times* or the *Washington Post* (Shilts, 1987). Most coverage of the AIDS epidemic was relegated to the so-called "gay press," such as the *New York Native* and *Bay Area Chronicle*. Network TV news did not begin to cover the disease until reports of heterosexual AIDS victims began to appear. Even then, network TV news virtually ignored the crisis.

The event that propelled AIDS into the television spotlight was the 1985 death of Rock Hudson, a film and television star of the 1950s through the 1980s. His death signaled an alarm, because, even though Hudson had long been rumored to be gay, he portrayed the macho, heterosexual matinee idol, so esteemed by the societal "mainstream." Overwhelming media attention focused on AIDS in the aftermath of Hudson's death. Each network began examining the disease in detail on nightly newscasts and special reports, focusing on how the average audience member (white, middle class heterosexuals) might contract and/or prevent AIDS.[1] Other stories illustrated high profile events, such as Hollywood celebrity-studded AIDS benefits.

The results of the focused media coverage of AIDS have been mixed. Some critics (eg. Goldberg, 1987) have lauded TV for alerting the public to the dangers of AIDS. Others (Hooper, 1988; Tierney, 1988) have objected to the "hyping," or overdramatization, of the risks to the non-drug-using heterosexual population. These critics protest that TV and other media have presented a distorted picture of the AIDS epidemic.

AIDS and TV Entertainment

The topic of AIDS began to appear in network entertainment programming shortly after TV news began to focus on the disease. However, TV has approached the topic of AIDS in its entertainment programming with considerable trepidation. The TV-movie, *An Early Frost,* aired in November 1985 to respectable audience ratings. However, few regularly-scheduled series since that time have tackled the topic. The prime time program that has dealt most extensively with AIDS has been *St. Elsewhere,* a prime time medical show that aired on NBC from 1982 until 1988. The show first dealt with the topic of AIDS during the 1985-6 TV season. Mark Harmon portrayed Dr. Bobby Caldwell, a handsome plastic surgeon at the fictional hospital St. Eligius, ("St. Elsewhere") whose medical skills were exceeded only by his libido. On a vacation to Cape Cod, Caldwell entered into an affair with a neighbor. Unbeknownst to Caldwell, his conquest had a penchant for cocaine and razor blades, and performed surprise "surgery" to Caldwell's face. In a later episode, when Caldwell himself was being readied for plastic surgery, he insisted on storing his own blood for possible transfusion during the upcoming operation because of the AIDS scare. Ironically, screening of his blood revealed that Caldwell had AIDS.

Caldwell contracted AIDS from a prostitute. Rather than deal with homosexuality or bisexuality, the producers chose to have the character become exposed to the malady through his heterosexual exploits. The message communicated to the viewer is to scale back sexual activity—to control one's passion—for AIDS might be the consequence.

One should note the parallel with news coverage of AIDS. AIDS failed to get much in the way of mention in the press until groups other than gays got the disease, such as drug addicts and transfusion cases. Given that TV has rarely portrayed a gay character (despite estimates of up to 10% of the U.S. population being gay),[2] it is not surprising that the first regularly recurring TV series character to get AIDS would be heterosexual. With one exception, the residents of St. Eligius rallied around Dr. Caldwell with their support. The lone unenlightened voice was raised by Dr. Mark Craig (William Daniels), the chief of surgery. The character of Craig on *St. Elsewhere* was shown to be at varying times racist, sexist, and homophobic. This trait is best exemplified by his remarks during an argument with Caldwell over whether Caldwell would continue to practice medicine at St. Eligius:

CRAIG: What's this I hear about you staying?

CALDWELL: I'm going to work until I can't.

CRAIG: Are you out of your mind?! Have you had your teeth cleaned lately? Dentists are wearing masks and gloves. Nobody's fooling around with this thing.

CALDWELL: What am I supposed to do, fold a tent and walk away?

CRAIG: Everybody you touch will have to be told.

CALDWELL: My medical status is confidential.

CRAIG: In this place, are you kidding?! When the word gets out, we'll be able to fire a cannon down the hall without hitting a patient.

CRAIG: Bobby, I don't take any pleasure asking you to leave. I brought you up here from Duke myself. But for crying out loud...[CALDWELL turns to leave] What's it been, two years? I never knew you were a fag.

CALDWELL: I'm not.

CRAIG: It doesn't make any difference. You're still out.

After pondering his future, including suicide, Caldwell left for an AIDS hospice in California.

The topic of AIDS became a recurring sub-plot during the series' season (1987-8). This subplot involved Seth Griffin (Bruce Greenwood) who is exposed to the retrovirus via a needle prick while drawing blood from an AIDS patient.

Seth Griffin was introduced as a character during the 1986-7 season of *St. Elsewhere*. Among other misdeeds, Griffin allowed a fellow resident to take the blame for a patient's demise, and impregnated the daughter of Dr. Donald Westphal (Ed Flanders), the head of medicine.

The AIDS subplot was foreshadowed during the first episode of the series' 1987-8 season. During that episode, St. Eligius was reopened under the direction of Ecumena Corporation, a major health-care provider (the ever-tottering hospital had been closed and faced the wrecking ball during the last episode of the 1986-87 TV season).[3] Dr. Wayne Fiscus (Howie Mandel), the resident assigned to emergency room care, finds an abandoned baby. Tests reveal that the baby has an unusual form of pneumonia (most likely, carinii pneumocystis). Follow-up diagnostics show that the baby has AIDS, prompting Dr. John Gideon (Ronny Cox), the new business-oriented chief of staff, to order the transfer of the baby to another hospital.

When the baby is about to be shipped to the other hospital, Fiscus notices the attendant donning rubber surgical gloves. Fiscus has grown attached to the baby, who he presumes has been abandoned by an addict mother.

FISCUS: This is an infant. He needs the warmth of a human touch.

ATTENDANT: They say you can't get infected through incidental contact, but let someone else take the risk.

FISCUS: We'll take the risk. You can go. This baby's not leaving.

Fiscus then lies to Gideon, stating that Dr. Westphal has ordered further tests. Gideon later confronts Westphal about the deception. Gideon claims that he wasn't fooled by Fiscus' lie, but allowed the ruse to continue so as to not dampen Fiscus' spirits. Gideon, ever aware of dollars and cents, notes that each state will spend up to a billion dollars per year by 1991 treating AIDS patients.

Westphal, who is seen feeding the baby, admonishes Gideon:

WESTPHAL: Dr. Gideon, everyone says that Ecumena is gonna make this place into a promised land. But if we're spending all our time or the money it takes to put paintings on the wall, then we've done this community a great disservice by stopping the wrecking ball.

The episode is instructive. The most heart-rending victims of AIDS are babies. Unlike gays, drug addicts or prostitutes, they are not considered to be responsible for acquiring the syndrome. Hence, in the episode described above, the most sympathetic type of character is seen as having AIDS. In addition, the baby becomes a symbol for the purpose of medicine—not the concern over paying for medical care, but the providing of it.

Three episodes later, Seth Griffin meets a cruel twist of fate. Griffin grudgingly tends to AIDS patient Brett Johnston (Kyle Secor). Griffin finds the assignment particularly distasteful, and wants to discharge the patient as soon as he can. Griffin impatiently awaits a blood test that might reveal that Brett is well enough to go home. When the lab work begins to back up, Griffin decides to take the blood from Brett himself. In rushing to complete the test, Griffin pricks himself with the needle. Despite assurances from the St. Eligius medical staff that it is unlikely he has AIDS, Griffin is convinced that he will come down with the disease. He announces that if he has AIDS, "he will put a bullet in his head." The manner by which Griffin is exposed to AIDS is highly unlikely in real life. However, the accidental exposure parallels the concerns of many hospital workers, many of whom have quit their jobs rather than risk infection by treating AIDS patients.

Griffin's outlook does not improve when, in a later episode, the storyline of Bobby Caldwell and Seth Griffin finally converge. In the residents' lounge, Dr. Victor Ehrlich (Ed Begley, Jr.) announces to Dr. Jack Morrison (David Morse) that Caldwell finally died in the AIDS hospice. Ehrlich tells Morrison that Caldwell "was down to 95 pounds" and that AIDS "affected his brain." Morrison laments that "Bobby Caldwell is the first friend I know to die of AIDS." In the bottom bunk, under a newspaper covering his face, we see the expression of Seth Griffin, an expression of a person who fully realizes the tragic consequences of the disease.

The relationship between Seth Griffin and Brett Johnston grows in an unlikely fashion during the course of the season. At first, Seth wants nothing to do with Brett, as demonstrated by this scene following Griffin's accidental exposure to the AIDS virus:

JOHNSTON: Nurse Papandrao said that you might still be here.

GRIFFIN: What the hell do you want?

JOHNSTON: Well, I came by to tell you that I'm sorry about what happened.

GRIFFIN: I don't need your apology.

JOHNSTON: I'm not apologizing. Just sorry.

GRIFFIN: If it weren't for you, I wouldn't be lying here worrying about what's left of my life.

JOHNSTON: Gay men are not responsible for this disease.

GRIFFIN: I know. But I used to think if a guy wants to do it with a guy, that's OK, 'cause it doesn't affect me. Now that's changed.

JOHNSTON: I've had sex exactly with two people. I was in love with both of them.

GRIFFIN: Look, I've got my own problems. So get the message—I don't really care about you.

JOHNSTON: I don't expect you to. I'm used to that. That's the way of the world. People reacting to their fears. Because of AIDS, we're all in danger of losing the comfort of human contact. Whether it's with gloves, or condoms, or sterile masks covering someone's smiles. We're pulling apart. Lines are being formed.

GRIFFIN: Just leave me alone.

However, as the season progresses, Griffin develops a much fuller understanding of both the disease and of being gay. He watches Brett's parents dismiss Brett's lover, while refusing to accept Brett's sexual orientation. Griffin witnesses gay-bashing while in the streets of Boston. He watches Brett waste away from the disease, eventually falling victim to AIDS-related dementia. He also sees the anguish on the face of Brett's lover, who now carries the virus, and will never be able to have further sexual relations.

Griffin acquires these insights while he undergoes a major transformation of his character. At the memorial service for Bobby Caldwell, Griffin is touched by the chaplain's sermon, and decides to "accept Christ in his life." By doing so, Griffin slowly achieves some peace of mind concerning his affliction. In addition, he becomes a much more sympathetic character. Toward the end of the season, Griffin faces a major crisis when his blood tests positive for HIV. In the series finale, however, further test results show the previous diagnosis was based on a "false positive" reading. He attributes this reversal in fortunes to "God's work." Has Divine intervention spared Griffin? The message the producers provide the audience here is that getting AIDS is a direct result of having a bad character. Adhering to a higher moral code will help one cope with AIDS. However, in the last scene Griffin is in, he hostilely berates a first-year resident for a mistake. It is apparent that the character transformation that Dr. Griffin has undergone is about to be undone.

Another medical show to deal with AIDS has been *Heartbeat*, a medical drama that debuted on ABC in March 1988. *Heartbeat* revolved around the personal and professional crises of Drs. Joanne Springsteen, Eve Autry and Marilyn McGrath (Kate Mulgrew, Laura Johnson and Gail Strickland) who head the Women's Medical Arts practice. In the series' second episode, Dr. Eve Autry faces an ethical dilemma. She is about to operate on a female patient named Cindy when she discovers that the blood her lover, Herb, donated for her surgery tested HIV positive. Eve wants Herb to tell Cindy he has the AIDS virus, but he refuses. Eve finds that the law is ambiguous— she could very well be sued and lose her medical license and practice if she tells Cindy that Herb has the AIDS virus. She is warned by the practice's top administrator not to reveal anything.

Eve decides to resolve her dilemma by confronting Herb, described below:

HERB: I've talked to my lawyer. You better talk to yours before you say any more to me, doctor.

EVE: I have.

HERB: So you know you could lose your license. That's the bottom line.

EVE: My license is no good to me if I don't use it to save lives.

HERB: Look. I don't want to hurt Cindy. I love her. She's my whole life. But I know her. Now you're going to have to let me handle this.

EVE: Look, I'd much rather you tell Cindy yourself. But I don't want to leave it up in the air. The stakes are too high. I can't do surgery on her until she's told. I want you to tell her. Now!

HERB: Or what?

EVE: Or I will. *That's* the bottom line.

Herb eventually reveals to Cindy that he has the AIDS virus. The final shot of them depicts them in an embrace—love conquers all. And, Dr. Autry displays her heroism by not giving up her ideals despite serious legal and financial consequences.

AIDS has twice been a topic for the popular NBC lawyer series, *L.A. Law*. During the second episode of the inaugural season (1986-87), assistant district attorney Grace Van Owen (Susan Dey) prosecutes a gay AIDS victim for a mercy-killing of his dying lover. Though the fatal consequences of AIDS are described during the trial, the use of AIDS here is used as a plot device to discuss the legal and moral implications of euthanasia. AIDS also appeared briefly as a topic during the 1987-88 TV season when the character Douglas Brackman (Alan Rachins) thinks he may have contracted AIDS from a female lover, and submits to an AIDS test (he passed). Here AIDS is again used as "punishment" for uncontrolled passion.

Midnight Caller debuted on NBC during the 1988-89 network TV season. The series stars Gary Cole as Jack Killian, an ex-cop turned late night radio talk show host. During the second episode of the series, Jack discovers that his ex-girlfriend Tina has contracted the AIDS virus from a bisexual man named "Mike Barnes." Unfortunately, she cannot locate this man to tell him that she has the disease. Killian later finds out that "Barnes" not only knows that he has the disease, but is purposely spreading the virus. Killian tries to convince Barnes to stop, but, in the end, the audience is left unsure whether or not the AIDS carrier will cease preying on innocent victims.

The theme of "restraint" is echoed again in Killian's episode-ending talk show sign-off:

Killian: Remember, if you can't stand sleeping in an empty bed, it's not empty if you're sleeping in it. There are worse things than being alone. Harder burdens to bear than tears.

This December 13, 1988 episode of *Midnight Caller* spawned a great deal of protest from gay activist groups, who objected to the portrayal of the bisexual AIDS carrier as inaccurate. Though these groups did succeed in getting the script changed ten times, they were unable to prevent the show's broadcast.

Certainly, the topic of AIDS seems an unlikely one for TV comedy. However, one situation comedy did tackle the issue. *Designing Women* is a CBS situation comedy about four women who run an interior decorating business. Two of the women are sisters, Julia (Dixie Carter) and Suzanne (Delta Burke) Sugarbaker. The other two women, Mary Jo (Annie Potts) and Charlene (Jean Smart) are close friends and business associates.

The Sugarbaker design firm had a brief encounter with AIDS during the October 5, 1987 episode. During this show, Mary Jo's young friend Kendall Dobbs shows up at Sugarbaker's with an unusual offer—he wants them to design his funeral. He then reveals he has AIDS. This plot is superimposed upon a subplot whereby Mary Jo must debate a conservative fellow PTA participant over the issue of disseminating condom information in her daughter's high school. Later in the show, Kendall returns to Sugarbaker's while Imogene, a long-time friend of Julia's, is present. Imogene overhears that Kendall has AIDS, and verbally attacks him. Julia rushes to present a spirited defense of Kendall:

IMOGENE: You reap what you sow. And you boys brought this on yourselves. As far as I'm concerned, this disease has one thing going for it. It's killing all the right people.

JULIA: Imogene, I'm terribly sorry. I'm going to have to ask you to move your car.

IMOGENE: Why?

JULIA: Because you're leaving.

IMOGENE: What are you talking about?

JULIA: I'm talking about the only thing worse than these people who never had morals before AIDS is all you holier than thou types who think you're exempt from getting it.

IMOGENE: For your information, I am exempt. I haven't lived like those people. And I don't care what you say, Julia Sugarbaker, I believe this is God's punishment for what they've done.

SUZANNE: Oh yeah? Then why do lesbians get it less?

IMOGENE: That's not for me to say. I just know that these people are getting what they deserve.

JULIA: Imogene, who do you think you're talking to? I've known you for twenty-seven years. If God was giving out sexually transmitted diseases as a punishment for sinning, *you* would be at the Free Clinic *all the time.*

Julia's diatribe against Imogene inspires Mary Jo to win her debate over her PTA opponent. The episode ends with the funeral of Kendall, set in the funeral home decorated according to his wishes.

AIDS and Daytime Drama

AIDS made its way to daytime drama, where, in 1988, three soap operas introduced characters afflicted by AIDS. Daytime television has had a tougher time tackling the subject of AIDS, due in part to its own taboos. Most AIDS victims have been gay men, who don't currently exist on daytime TV. However, given the publicity given over to the increasing number of heterosexual AIDS victims—intravenous drug users and women—soap operas have found a way to dramatize the epidemic. Interestingly, all three victims have been white adult females.

The character of Dawn Rollo briefly inhabited Bay City on *Another World*. Dawn was a truly unfortunate soul. Though a virgin, Dawn managed to contract AIDS through a blood transfusion. The donor turned out to be her mother, a prostitute. Despite the affliction, Dawn fought to save her job as an instructor in the local music school. While Dawn won a court fight to keep her job at the school, she quickly succumbed to AIDS. She passed quietly, without evidencing the variety of horrific infections that real world AIDS patients are subject to.

Jessica Blair of *The Young and the Restless* journeyed to Genoa City to try to make peace with her estranged teenaged daughter Cricket. Jessica acquired AIDS during her career as a prostitute. While in Genoa City, she met and fell in love with powerful perfume magnate John Abbott. Her disease began to progress, however, so she tried to depart. Cricket stopped her, but not before Jessica confessed that she had AIDS. Both Cricket and John professed that they would stand by Jessica. In fact, though he appreciated the seriousness of the disease (and would have to abstain from having sex), John Abbott still married Jessica Blair. Jessica's condition progressively worsened. Finally, after a brief hospitalization, and with her family at her side, she died. The theme here is that love can conquer all.

Cindy Parker on *All My Children* was given AIDS by her husband, a drug user who died of AIDS. She was left to raise a young boy, and went to work at the local beauty parlor. Shortly after her arrival in fictional Pine Valley, she discovered she had the AIDS virus.

The plot of Cindy on *All My Children* is particularly interesting as she married Stuart Chandler (David Canary). The character of Stuart spent most of his life in a mental institution, where his emotional development was retarded. A talented artist, Stuart met Cindy while he was teaching her son art. While Stuart understood that Cindy is very ill, he lacked a full understanding of the disease. Consequently, he did not share the same fear of AIDS as others in Pine Valley. While the message here is similar to the John/Jessica plotline of *The Young and the Restless*, another interpretation could be that one must be "crazy" to marry an AIDS patient.

To be fair, the producers of *All My Children* took great pains to portray AIDS authentically. The show employed three AIDS consultants, including Max Navarre, president of The People with AIDS Coalition, who himself has the disease (Rourke, 1988), and the soap has dealt with the discrimination AIDS patients have faced. For instance, customers at the beauty parlor where Cindy works began to avoid the shop. The show also examined the issue of quack doctors who prey an AIDS victims desperate for hope. Eventually, Cindy also succumbed to the disease. Because of the close relationship of "soap opera time" to real time, daytime serials have done a more realistic job of dealing with the irrational fear of people with AIDS than have prime time programs.

The Conflicting Messages About AIDS on TV

TV entertainment programming has presented the audience with mixed messages concerning AIDS and its victims. For instance, there is the message that one shouldn't fear the AIDS patient. No one shunned Bobby Caldwell or Seth Griffin at St. Eligius even though they knew the two doctors had (or may have had) the AIDS virus. The women at Sugarbakers took an immediate enlightened attitude toward their AIDS-afflicted friend. Televised entertainment portrayals of AIDS have also raised some of the emotional and ethical issues surrounding the disease, such as patient medical condition confidentiality, and job harassment.

On the other hand, much is missing from the portrayal of AIDS on broadcast television. Only two central characters—Kendall in *Designing Women* and Brett in *St. Elsewhere*—were gay. One other character—Mike Barnes in *Midnight Caller*—were bisexual. Even then, the characters Mike Barnes, and Kendall appeared in only one episode each of a series, and the character of Brett was a supporting player. For regularly recurring characters, two (Bobby Caldwell and Seth Griffin) have been white male heterosexual professionals, and three have been white female heterosexuals (Dawn Rollo, Cindy Parker and Jessica Blair). There have been no minority victims, and no drug addicts. In other words, AIDS has been shown to be a disease that will affect the audience member via heterosexual intercourse. The theme becomes that one should control one's passion, because not to do so invites possible death.

Perhaps the best (and most ironic) exposition of that theme came from the aforementioned Julia Sugarbaker of *Designing Women:*

JULIA: I was reading in yesterday's papers about that all these Hollywood producers who are now going to depict people not sleeping around because of AIDS.

What I want to know is, what was wrong with not sleeping around before AIDS?

I mean, God forbid that anybody would be sexually discriminating because it's virtuous, or loyal, or classy. No. Now it's as if they found a whole new reason for people to have morals again.

Conclusion: Setting the AIDS Agenda

George Gerbner (1972) and Gaye Tuchman (1977) distinguish between "symbolic representation" and "symbolic annihilation." Representation in the world of television announces to the audience member that a social characteristic is valued and approved. For example, the portrayal of punishment following criminal acts signifies to the audience that "crime does not pay," a message that is valued by a society that values social control.

The process of establishing symbolic representation is also known as agenda-setting. McCombs and Shaw (1972) first proposed agenda-setting to describe the news media's impact on the public's voting behavior. According to their proposition, the more coverage the news media devotes to an issue, the more salience the audience member attributes to that issue. Lang and Lang (1981) extend this notion in their discussion of agenda-building, the process whereby an issue becomes placed on the news media, and public, agendas.

This notion of agenda-setting has been applied to entertainment programming. Gerbner (1976) reconceptualizes agenda-setting in his cultivation hypothesis. Simply put, the cultivation hypothesis proposes that the more a viewer watches television—the more a viewer is exposed to television's symbolic representations—the more that viewer will perceive the real world as the world of television.

Thus, a symbolic representation that emerges from TV's portrayal of AIDS and its victims is that unrestrained passion can be deadly. Characters who have been promiscuous, such as Bobby Caldwell on *St. Elsewhere* or Jessica Blair on *The Young and the Restless,* eventually pay for their past indiscretions with their lives. Even one failure to maintain control can be fatal, as Killian's girl friend Tina discovered in *Midnight Caller.* Therefore, the audience is warned: to be safe, be chaste.

On the other hand, representations that are trivialized, condemned or completely absent constitute "symbolic annihilation." Feminist critics such as Tuchman have argued that because women are depicted on television either as unemployed, or employed in too few occupations, they are subject to symbolic annihilation. Similarly, a class of AIDS victims are "symbolically annihilated." The majority of AIDS victims in the U.S. are gay males. Their representation as AIDS patients on television is vastly underrepresented. This underrepresentation stems from two factors.

First, network television has historically been uncomfortable about homosexuality. When NBC aired the pilot for the situation comedy *Sydney Shorr,* the title character was described as a homosexual. When the series finally aired, Sydney became asexual—no further references were made to his homosexuality. Two other homosexual characters, Jodie of the ABC situation comedy *Soap,* and Steven Carrington of the ABC prime time soap opera *Dynasty,* switched between gay and straight lifestyles. Ellen Wheeler, who plays Cindy Parker on *All My Children,* stated on the ABC show *Good Morning America,* that the producers decided to have a woman have AIDS rather than a gay male so that people would "tune in" to the plotline *(Good Morning America,* December 28, 1988). Ms. Wheeler's statement implies that the audience would vehemently reject a regular gay male character with AIDS. Given the networks' discomfort with homosexuality, it is not surprising that they have a difficult time with AIDS portrayals. To portray AIDS victims in their proportion to the population would require presenting many more homosexual characters.

Ironically, even though the issues have become inextricably entwined, the networks prefer to deal with the issue of AIDS in a somewhat different way than they deal with the issue of condoms. Once U.S. Surgeon General C. Everett Koop announced that condoms were the best protection against AIDS other than abstinence, many called for the networks to air condom ads and public service announcements (PSAs). The networks, however, refused to air condom ads, and reluctantly aired AIDS PSAs. The networks argued that it was better to deal with the issue in entertainment fare (Carveth, 1987). Apparently, airing commercial-type messages dealing with sexual responsibility and disease prevention is more controversial than mentions of such messages in sitcoms or dramatic shows. As a result, both prime time and daytime shows began to openly discuss the use of condoms.[4]

Second, there is Gitlin's notion, derived from Gramsci (1971), of cultural hegemony—"a ruling class's (or alliance's) domination of subordinate classes and groups through the elaboration and penetration of ideology (ideas and assumptions) into their common sense and everyday practice" (Gitlin, 1979). The media provide an ideological frame by which the audience should perceive the world. As Tuchman (1978) notes:

The view through a window depends upon whether the window is large or small, has many panes or few, whether the glass is opaque or clear, whether the window faces a street or a backyard.

The television networks are major corporate institutions in society. They depend upon significant audience viewership of their programs for their economic survival. The size of the viewership determines the rates charged for advertising. Hence, the networks need to take care not to offend. Their economic drive forces them to be responsive to contemporaneous popular movements.

Over the past decade, opinion polls reveal that the majority of the American public supports the pro-family sociopolitical agenda of the Reagan-Bush administrations. Hence, by continually portraying an America that is pro-family—and, consequently anti-gay—the networks can establish and reinforce the dominant sociopolitical ideology of U.S. society. Thus, the hegemonic process of network television—the dominant form of popular culture in our society—works to 1) condemn the giving in to sexual passion for unmarried heterosexual partners and to 2) trivialize and symbolically annihilate societal "deviants" such as gays.

There are competing images of AIDS victims that do come into many U.S. homes. Pay cable services, which are not subject to the same commercial advertising pressures as network broadcast television, have begun to deal with the topic of AIDS in greater detail. For example, since 1986, the topic of AIDS has been dealt with in the sitcom *Brothers* as well as made-for-cable movies such as *As Is* (Showtime) and *Tidy Endings* (HBO). Unfortunately, less than 40% of all U.S. households subscribe to pay cable services, and of those that do, only about 1% ever see these shows.[5]

Will AIDS continue to be portrayed in such a limited and distorted fashion? Probably not. According to Gitlin (1979), the hegemonic process "has continually to be reproduced, continually superimposed, continually to be negotiated and managed, in order to override the alternative and, occasionally, the oppositional forms." The hegemonic frame through which the media present images continually shifts. Just as the hegemonic frame of the news media shifted in the 1960s from supporting the Vietnam War to questioning the U.S. role in the war, so does the hegemonic frame of the entertainment media shift.

For example, where once conservative sexual attitudes kept married characters Rob and Laura Petrie sleeping in separate beds on the *Dick Van Dyke Show*, the frame has now shifted so that Elliot and Nancy can openly talk about sex in the same bed on *thirtysomething* also featured two gay males sharing the same bed together in an episode that aired in November 1989. Even daytime drama experimented with a regularly appearing gay male character, Hank Elliott of *As the World Turns*, though the character lasted only a few months (Elliott left to go back to his off-screen lover, who was dying of AIDS).

Thus, the hegemonic frame of television will shift, not radically, but in a way that comfortably confines the audience in the security of the status quo.

Notes

[1] It is not always easy to distinguish informational from entertainment programming. Those viewers expecting to see *St. Elsewhere* on Wednesday, December 30, 1987 were treated instead to an NBC news special entitled *Scared Sexless*, dealing with the "new sexual morality" in the era of AIDS. Hosted by Connie Chung, this documentary has been decried for its sensationalism.

[2] The still most reliable source of information on the population of gays in the U.S. is the Kinsey Report on male sexual behavior.

[3] Interestingly enough, Humana Corporation objected to the parallel in the name Ecumena, and won from MTM Enterprises, the producers of *St. Elsewhere*, a concession of a disclaimer at the end of the show disassociating the name from the corporation.

[4] However, when NBC aired an episode of the situation comedy *Valerie* dealing with condoms, several stations either delayed its broadcast until late night or refused to air the show altogether.

[5] In addition, Lifetime, an advertiser-supported cable service, aired an episode of the failed CBS detective series *Leg Work* whose plot centered on finding an AIDS carrier (interestingly, a bisexual). Ironically, that particular episode, though produced and paid for by CBS, never aired on that network during its brief run.

Bibliography

Carveth, R. (1987) "The not-ready-for-prime time ads: Broadcasting contraceptive commercials." Presented at the annual meeting of the Speech Communication Association.

_____ (1986) "Agenda-building and the AIDS issue." Presented at the Popular Culture Association Convention.

Gerbner, G. (1972) "Violence in television drama: Trends and symbolic functions," in Television and Social Behavior. Washington DC: U.S. Government Printing Office.

Gerbner, G. and L. Gross (1976) "Living with television: The violence profile." Journal of Communication, 26.

Gitlin, T. (1980) The Whole World is Watching. Berkeley: University of California Press.

_____ (1979, February) "Prime time ideology: the hegemonic process in television entertainment." Social Problems, Vol. 26, No. 3.

Goldberg, M. (1987, November 28—December 4) "TV has done more to contain AIDS than any other single factor." TV Guide, pp. 4-6.

Gramsci, A. (1971) Selections From the Prison Notebooks. Quinton Hoare and Geoffrey Nowell Smith (eds.), New York: International Publishers.

Hooper, J. (1988, September/October) "Sex and circulation: Why media hypes hetero risk." Utne Reader, pp. 69-70.

Lang, G. and K. Lang (1981) "Watergate: An exploration of the agenda-building process," in G.C. Wilhoit and H. deBock (eds.) Mass Communication Review Yearbook 2. Newbury Park: Sage.

McCombs, M. and D. Shaw (1972) "The agenda-setting function of the mass media." Public Opinion Quarterly, 36.

Rourke, R. (1988, March 22) "Love and death on *All My Children*." *Soap Opera Digest*.

Shilts, R. (1987) And the Band Played On. New York: St. Martin's Press.

Tierney, J. (1988, November 17) "Straight talk." Rolling Stone, pp. 122-137.

Tuchman, G. (1978) Making News. New York: The Free Press.

_____ (1977) "The symbolic annihilation of women by the mass media," in Gaye Tuchman, Arlene Kaplan Daniels and James Benet (eds.) Hearth and Home. New York: Oxford University Press.

Decoding the Mass Media and Terrorism Connection: Militant Extremism As Systemic and Symbiotic Processes

Russell F. Farnen
Assisted by
Marek Payerhin

Introduction

The public role of the mass media in most western industrialized societies (in addition to making a profit) is to inform and educate citizens in the ways of democracy. By contrast, the goal of organized terrorist groups is to upset these orderly processes, and to achieve private, usually unpopular, political informational goals. Along the way, these violent groups use and abuse the media and the state; they, in turn, are reciprocally used and abused in the process. Media became witting and unwitting winners and losers in this process, which shares elements of both a game and a drama. In order to perform their controlling and socially-reinforcing role in the communications processes, media must regularly capture the public's attention, i.e., they must force the public to digest important news and consumer information. Therefore, media seduce consumers with sports, comics, human interest stories, crime, scare headlines, and enticing leads.

The "gatekeeping" function of the media is most relevant to the subject of terrorist news. Knowledge and information, the media's tools, are used to ensure system maintenance through feedback and distribution control. In complex pluralistic and interdependent societies, the print and broadcast journalists serve as arbiters of conflict management by playing watchdog or surveillance roles. This allows social stresses or subsystem dysfunctions to be resolved or handled, without resort to civil strife and resultant social chaos. News broadcasts and stories serve to keep the flow of information moving so that tension and ultimate release (resolution) follow the very crisis which the media helped to create. The media provide discrete knowledge of an issue or event rather than in-depth knowledge about a controversy or public policy. Media often avoid the latter, since those dangerous topics may require delving into causes and proposed solutions, both of which may be extremely divisive. Instead, the media selectively combine sights, sounds, images, and symbols into a meta-reality. These not only depict, but actually recreate, replace, or displace reality, as is well documented in post-modern semiotic, humanistic, and cultural studies of the news genre (Graber, 1980: 117-154; Agee, et al., 1982: 17-33; Robinson, 1984: 199-221).

Of course, violent bombings, kidnappings, or robberies actually involve very few perpetrators and relatively few victims. Any small war or state military action, such as the Grenada invasion or recurrent "police actions" in Libya (which some label "state terrorism"), are far more elaborate in both the number of killers and killed, just as are the weekly totals of mayhem on American highways. So the scale of militant violence or the extent of public risk of physical injury is relatively small. In fact, the number of actual terrorist incidents was only 127 out of 258 reports in the *Los Angeles Times*, *Washington Post*, and *New York Times* in the 1980-1985 period; i.e., an average of about 25 per year (Picard and Adams, 1988: 1).

Examining the statistics from another perspective, the number of international terrorist incidents reported in 1985 was 812 (a 36% increase over 1984), with 177 involving U.S. targets. Domestically, that same year, there were only seven actual incidents (with twenty-three thwarted attempts, according to FBI reports). Of course, certain highly visible incidents caught the media's and the public's attention. Among these were the TWA 847, Achille Lauro, and Rome and Vienna airport assaults in which American nationals were also victimized (Picard and Adams, 1988: 1). Despite these decreases in numbers, what we remember is the residue of psychological threats, diminution of national pride, and challenges to sacred morals, precious symbols, and hallowed myths. These have longer lasting and more qualitative significance to the citizenry and its leaders. This is why the most proficient terrorists seek to strike at the heart of the state and the core of the establishment, aiming to destroy that which carries the highest symbolic and media value—American tourists, flagship carriers, or military personnel.

The interactions between mass media and violent terrorism are akin to host (media) and parasite (violent terrorism). This symbiotic relationship requires the media to use violence to sell magazines/newspapers and gain viewers/listeners. They seek to increase readership/audience share in order to sell billions of dollars of advertising, which increases everyone's, except the terrorists, profitability. In Western state-controlled mass media societies, whose numbers decrease daily, publicly-owned media usually cover highly visible terrorist violence. Why? Because the news canon requires their reportage of all major events to ensure their continued legitimacy and credibility as a truthful or free press. Even the Eastern Socialist press covers terrorist events to maintain credibility and to benefit from invidious comparisons between the "wild West" and the "orderly East," where peace and quiet reign supreme.

This situation leads to the need to examine a series of interrelationships among the media and terrorism. Among others, two of the most interesting questions are: (1) do the media actually help or hinder terrorism despite their societal role as a cheerleader in support of basic anti-violent norms? (i.e., this is the "contagion" or "epidemic" theory regarding the spread of the terrorist "virus" or "infection.") And, (2) do media/publicity starved terrorist groups not only recognize this media dependence on violence, but do they also structure their campaigns to insure maximum media coverage and involvement for their own purposes? In addition to partial answers to these two questions, some suggestions for changing the cycle of violence system are also offered for consideration. These are presented in the context of public/media policy making in the future.

International Terrorism Defined and Described

The terrorist is the "ultimate criminal." Whole nations, it is claimed, can be held hostage by a small band of unified and dedicated, seemingly irrational, instantly important, and ultimately threatening and dangerous men and women (usually young) who, supposedly, may do violence to us all. Terrorists, though relatively impotent, also try to plan and control the calculated use of violence, mayhem, and death. Their aim is to provoke and inspire extreme fear and dread among individuals, groups, nations, and international agencies and institutions.

During the 1980s we have the dubious advantage of more than one hundred operative definitions of terrorism. One expert on the subject, Martha Crenshaw, defines terrorism as "a strategy any political actor can use." She also says that it requires few resources (i.e., it is "cheap"); it involves "violent coercion" in order "to intimidate an opponent;" and "it is intended to compel a change in an enemy's behavior by affecting his will, not to destroy the enemy physically." Terrorism also relies on "suspense," and "psychological reactions of shock, outrage, and sometimes, enthusiasm." Moreover, terrorism usually occurs in times of peace rather than war. Non-combatants are the usual objects, and the targets or victims have symbolic value, being representatives of a class, nation, or a cause. Crenshaw concludes: "Terrorism is fundamentally a strategy of demoralization, directed against the entire population of a nation rather than its armed forces, as would be the case in traditional warfare" (Crenshaw, 1987: 4-8).

In her writings, Crenshaw tries, as she says, to avoid a "normative judgement" about terrorism. However, Walter Laqueur, not known for the neutrality of his views on the subject, says that "there is no such thing as pure, unalloyed, unchanging terrorism, but there are many forms of terrorism. In the circumstances a case may be made for broader and, of necessity, vaguer definitions" (Laqueur, 1987: 145). More typical of such definitions was that of the U.S. Task Force on Disorders and Terrorism (1976) which defined terrorism as "violent criminal behavior designed primarily to generate fear in the community...for political purposes." Other definitions of terrorism include within them individual hijackings of commercial transport vehicles or state terrorism, which involves training and deployment of assassins and para-military guerrilla bands to invade another land. In terms of objectives, some groups seek financial reward ("criminals"), personal glory and fame ("crazies"), and others use violence for political goals ("crusaders") (Hacker, 1976).

Terrorists themselves advertise their political goals preferring to be called "freedom fighters," "revolutionaries," "liberators," "soldiers," or "nationalists." These defensive terms are meant to combat the pejorative abuse uniformly heaped upon them in most mass media. Occasionally, however, extremist or marginal newspapers, like certain government controlled media, have used similar favorable terms to describe those militant bands with whose violent motives or politics they agree. Simply put, terrorists may be red, brown, or black, uniformed or dressed in ethnic regalia, or otherwise decked out to communicate and symbolize their "just" cause against a powerful and evil enemy, the state.

In more technologically primitive days, terrorists frequently demanded media interviews, press releases, printing of demands, statements, or photographs, and the like. More recently, however, terrorist (or "quasi-terrorist") groups have produced videotaped reports on the condition of hostages, used hostages as spokespersons, spoken directly to television audiences, or even compiled a documentary record for publication of their exploits (as the Animal Liberation Front did in 1985 after a California laboratory break-in). Their increasing use of new video technology is evidence of the parallel development between terrorism and the media. As Laqueur says, "the media are the terrorists best friends." He also maintains that "the terrorist's act by itself is nothing; publicity is all" (Laqueur, 1976: 104). So close is this connection that one Associated Press correspondent recently claimed that terrorists are so media-wise that they now play journalists "like a violin" (Livingstone in Livingstone and Arnold, 1984: 220). The most severe critics of media's role in publicizing terrorist exploits would, of course, like to enroll media as a front line soldier in "fighting back" or "winning the war" against terrorism, labelled a "hydra of carnage," in "low-intensity operations," military jargon for a small war (See Livingstone and Arnold, 1984 and Ra'anan, et al., 1986).

Picard and Adams (1988: 9) point out that media, victims, and witnesses to acts of political violence actually use more neutral nominal characteristics (such as "shooting" and "attacker") to delineate events. By contrast, government officials use highly charged descriptive words (such as "criminals," "terrorists," "murderers"). The latter are more "judgmental, inflammatory, and sensationalistic." However, in these stories the primary media characterizations were of their own making. Media seldom quoted primary sources. This occurred only six percent of the time in relevant *Los Angeles Times*, *New York Times*, and *Washington Post* stories from 1980-85.

Complaining that journalists also have no real understanding of terrorism, T.W. Cooper (1988: 5) defines the problem in this way:

The sum total of people categorized as terrorists do not fit a pat, unchanging stereotype. In-depth interviews with those depicted as terrorists in many countries do not reveal a uniform pattern of deranged, hostile, illiterate, macho psychotic madmen. Although such people exist, much, if not all, of our monolithic image of terrorists is presented to us, not by people who call themselves terrorists, but by mass media.

Since few, if any, of us has seen (or is likely to), spoken to, or met a terrorist, we are at some disadvantage, just as when we appraise the worth of foreign news personalities such as Yasser Arafat and Muammar Qaddafi. Much the same ignorance prevails among those strangers who label Americans as "state terrorists." Actually, we may each share the undesirable attributes we assign to others: a low estimation of human life; lack of mutual respect; projection of power orientations; demonstrated rigidity; and espousal of self-serving ideologies. America's violent films, political assassinations, racial conflict, violent strikes, use and threat of military force and massive retaliation, drug wars among urban guerrillas, and thousands of annual industrial injuries and deaths seem to validate America as a violent society. By comparison, the George Washington/Charles DeGaulle of the P.L.O. (Arafat) claims to be a freedom fighter resisting the "state terrorism" of the Israelis and their American allies.

Claims of P.L.O. "terrorism," American "Ramboism," Qaddafi "irrationality" and like creations are products of the mass media, bearing only some, if little, resemblance to reality. Terrorist groups are frequently foreign or exotic, unknown or inexplicable, or religious based. They also produce disinformation and thrive on military secrecy, bonds, or a blood pact. When mass media approach such groups, they are bound to fail in their comprehension, story telling, or reporting since their perceptions are seldom realistic, often adversarial, and always distorted. They are also at times self-serving, biased, or ethnocentric, and are frequently rigid, ideological, purposeful, and negative. While terrorism is at best unpleasant, it deserves the benefit of a realistic treatment. We not only are dishonest to ourselves when we deny such treatment, but we infuriate and heighten the animosity of these supposed adversaries, both today and tomorrow (Cooper, 1988: 5).

ABC's Sander Vanocur discounts the "enlightenment or education business" functions of mass media as well as "the people's right-to-know" argument for a free press. He says that media "are in a business, the business of information. Whatever anyone else may claim for us, that is what we are supposed to do—pass on information, as best we can, as quickly as we can" (Vanocur in Ra'anan, 1986: 259).

Even if the mass media are not primarily educational or enlightenment agencies, it may be useful and more accurate to accept some of Vanocur's argument. That is, the media (particularly radio and television) are mainly in the profitable entertainment business, and sexual and violent entertainment at that. Mass media operate on providing minimum context, broad and quick coverage, and giving readers/viewers what they want. The context for news is, at best, the standard journalistic litany of answering the who, what, when, where, how and, occasionally, why questions learned in Journalism 101. Seldom do the media provide the readers with background, context, or parallel information needed to follow a story over time or to understand a topic in-depth. It is a small wonder that readers/viewers cannot internalize, assimilate, and conceptualize a story into their highly valuative, cognitive maps and perceptual frames of reference. The texts themselves of news stories and television scripts are often more "writerly" than "readerly." In the absence of regular coverage, with context, for an important continuing story or recurrent social theme (such as on work hazards, defense, or violence toward others), the reader cannot realistically understand the news. When Bhophal, defense corruption, or the latest terrorist story catapult on the screen or front page week after week, they remain unique, vague, strange, and forever inexplicable and meaningless.

The predominant journalistic values require news to be about *unexpected, sensational,* and *conflictive* events. Violent groups are more than willing to supply an ample measure of each ingredient required for a newsworthy story.

Media and Terrorism: Symbiotic Relationships

Terrorism is different, dramatic, and potentially violent. It frequently develops over a period of time, occurs in exotic locations, offers a clear confrontation, involves bizarre characters, and is politically noteworthy. Finally, it is of concern to the public (Hoge, 1982: 91).

Since terrorism so clearly fills the bill as a major news event, media fiercely compete for coverage, "scoops," and live footage or photographs which can be labelled "exclusives." This drive to win, as Jody Powell says, is a direct product of the competition "for ratings and circulation between newspapers and networks and for personal advancement within a given news organization" (Powell, quoted in Livingstone, W., 1985: 219).

The history of media coverage of terrorism has also proved the validity of Daniel Schorr's observation that "many people have found that the royal road to identity is to do something violent" (Schorr quoted in Anzovin, ed., 1986: 101). For example, the Palestine terrorists who, in 1972 attacked the Israeli Olympic team in Munich, instantly found themselves in the living rooms of over 800 million people. Through creating a climate of fear in an attack on (or even killing) unknown victims, the relatively powerless terrorist hopes to compel far more powerful state or media officials to comply with his wishes. Since the terrorist is so much weaker than the establishment he is challenging, he must use guerrilla hit and run tactics in order to create the psychological state of mind needed to ensure public and official compliance with, or acceptance of, certain aggressive goals.

The motto of the Italian Red Brigades (*Brigate Rosse* or *B.R.*) "Strike One to Educate One Hundred" is also worth noting here. The *B.R.* struck violently in 1978 by kidnapping Christian Democrat party president Aldo Moro. (Moro was previously prime minister of Italy for six years.) Yet the education of the public was left to the media, with the *B.R.* serving as principal accomplice in the journalistic orgy which followed. Earlier, the *B.R.* had targeted the media and prominent journalists themselves as potential victims in its war against the multinationals and the "imperialist state." By 1977 journalists, editors, and members of the Italian press had been branded "servants of the imperialist apparatus of repression." After several journalists were "kneecapped" or shot dead in quick succession, the popular and press reaction to these violent incidents was equivalent to that following an invasion from outer space. Later, however, the *B.R.* deliberately confined its attacks to "the heart of the state" by enlisting the media to publicize its cause through the Moro kidnapping.

The Moro case signalled the *B.R.'s* change of tactics to "armed propaganda, seeking political recognition, and through attacks at the heart of the state." Its goal was to prove that revolution was "within...reach." Media were transformed from objects of attack to a useful instrument of war. For example, after the assassination of Moro (in which the government, the terrorists, and everyone but Moro himself exploited the media), the *B.R.* kidnapping of a prominent judge (Giovanni D'Urso) in 1980 also allowed them to use media for their own purposes before releasing their prisoner. A year later, after rejection of their demand for media time, the *B.R.* shot a hostage. The kneecappings of journalists and media brutality of the 1970s were not reinstituted in the 1980s. Instead, the *B.R.* created its own media research and coordination group for public relations, fighting a new war on the "psychological front."

As Daniel Schorr observes, television has a "love affair with drama and a love affair with violence" (Schorr quoted in Anzovin, 1986: 101). Ted Koppel, ABC's "Nightline" host is of a like mind saying:

Without television, terrorism becomes rather like the philosopher's hypothetical tree falling in the forest: no one hears it fall and therefore it has no reason for being. And television, without terrorism, while not deprived of all interesting things in the world, is none the less deprived of one of the most interesting" (Koppel, quoted in Anzovin, 1986: 97).

Mass media's coverage of the news is mainly focused on politicians, corporate leaders, criminals, athletes, and other public and entertainment figures who have "star quality." Terrorist leaders also recognize the importance of mass media just as New Left advocate Jerry Rubin did. He exhorted his revolutionary brothers for being "too puritanical" in mass media use, perhaps because "Karl Marx never watched television." "You can't be a revolutionary today without a television set," he wrote. "It's as important as a gun" (Rubin, 1970: 108).

Even a spokesman for the P.L.O. recognized the importance of media in its quest for United Nations observer status and legitimacy saying: "The first hijackings aroused the consciousness of the world and awakened the media and world opinion much more—and more efficiently—than 20 years of pleading at the United Nations" (Hickey, 1976: 10). The media also provide a "status-conferral" function for terrorists as Paul Lazarsfeld and Robert K. Merton recognized in 1948, i.e., by singling out terrorism for the mass audience, these behaviors and opinions are seen as significant enough to deserve public notice (Lazarsfeld and Merton, 1971). Moreover, media coverage of terrorism not only provides free publicity, but also, it is claimed, may establish role models for the imitative behavior of others (Schmid and de Graaf, 1982: 53-54).

There also may be a spiraling cycle of violence, i.e., an interactive effect between the quantity of media coverage and the subsequent intensity of terrorist activity. However, which factor (media or violent incident) causes this or what else causes both is often unclear. Media coverage affects the public and combative groups alike. Regardless of their motives, as terrorists upscale their violence, they are reinforced and rewarded with more media coverage. In turn, as media coverage increases, terrorists are encouraged to top their last execution, threat, or demand (Weimann, 1983: 43-44; Tan, 1987: 151).

However, this view of terrorism as an epidemic which the news media spread, (though widely believed by public, press, and some experts) is not supported in the social science literature as other than a contributing cause. Beliefs that new groups form, new actions are incited, public support is generated, the level of violence is escalated, and media control is lost by default to the terrorists are just some of the associated allegations which also remain unsubstantiated.

There is little proof that the press is so powerful as either potential censors or terrorist groups may imagine. Nevertheless, Prime Minister Margaret Thatcher called in 1985 for press controls which would deny terrorists and hijackers the "oxygen of publicity" which feeds their violence. Edwin Diamond of New York University's News Study Group claimed in a *TV Guide* article that once the television put a human face on the TWA Flight 847 passengers and crew and charged the incident with "everyday emotions" then "all military options were dead." CBS's Lesley Stahl says of the press: "We are an instrument for the hostages. We force the administration to put their lives above policy." Consequently, these events become "institutionalized crises" which crowd out all other news (Picard, 1988: 1). Michael J. Davies, publisher of the *Hartford Courant* and former president of the Associated Press Managing Editors, typifies editorial attitudes when he says:

Publicity is the lifeblood of terrorism. Without it, these abominable acts against the innocent would wither quickly away. Yet few responsible critics would suggest that the media enter into a conspiracy of silence that would ignore all acts of international terrorism (Davies, 1985: 4-5).

By and large the media-as-contagion theory depends on transference of the findings on televised violence and aggression over to the terrorism arena. Moreover, widespread public perceptions also support this relationship. The popularity of this view among law enforcement officials has helped gain support from some experts (such as M.C. Bassiouni) who say that, except for the "ideologically motivated," there is a certain "intuitive reasonableness" to the contagion theory. A. Schmid and J. de Graaf, two Dutch experts, also claim media reports help to "reduce inhibitions" and offer "models," "know-how," and motivation to potential terrorists (Bassiouni and Schmid and de Graaf are quoted in Picard, 1988: 2-3).

In response, others such as Brian Jenkins of the Rand Corporation reply that "the news media are responsible for terrorism to about the same extent that the commercial aviation is responsible for the airline hijackings," i.e., the media are just "another vulnerability" in highly vulnerable technological and free societies. Other related studies have shed some light on this phenomenon. For example, hierarchy was used in one study (by M.I. Midlarsky, M. Crenshaw, and F. Yoshida) in 1980 as a theory to explain the spread of terrorism "from the least powerful" and "from the weak states to the strong," e.g., from Latin America to Western Europe. (For a description of these studies using diffusion and hierarchy as conceptual frameworks of analysis, see Picard, 1988: 1-7). European terrorist groups borrow ideology, rhetoric, and methods from the third world as well as techniques of bombing. Each transfers quite easily across boundaries through intergroup cooperation to new locations, providing suitable sites for new violence. The careful planning and specialized technical knowledge which some groups display were not learned on television or in newspapers. Diffusion of these ideas is more likely based on interpersonal channels of communications. While the media can reinforce public awareness of terrorism, this may not apply to the evaluation, acceptance, and adaptation parts of the same process. At any rate, diffusion theory probably offers a better line of research than does the imitative effect of copying violent acts, scenes, and situations.

Since media engage in sensationalism, can interfere with law enforcement, may endanger lives, and spread the contagion of fear, they have become closely associated with, though still not being the primary cause of, terrorism. Moreover, if terrorism really seeks the media publicity it gets through violence, why should potential terrorists not receive media coverage for their grievances before they resort to violence? Not only can the media adopt a responsible, reasoned, and measured approach to terrorism, once begun, but they can regularly provide ample outlets for expressions of public and group concerns, thereby reducing grievances while evaluating current public policy. This response to terrorism would actually require more, not less (although very different) coverage of terrorist and other violence. This could be done without glamorizing the perpetrators. Media can provide useful and valid information, consider consequences of past or hypothetical acts, improve public capacity to deal with large crises, aim to reduce public fear, and increase public understanding to help reduce the general level of violence in the society (U.S. Department of Justice, 1976: 65; Picard, 1988: 3-5).

As a terrorist sideshow unfolds, the black and white spectacle of heroes and villains fighting it out usually mesmerizes the public. This is not the set of "Miami Vice," but a real scene with real guns, bullets, bombs, hostages, and murders. The viewers are eyewitnesses to a human morality play, with its real winners and losers. In a way, this portrayal even becomes the "theatre of the obscene" in that the television screen (reinforced by radio, newspapers, and magazines) displays a huge international "snuff film" rivaling the execution scenes in World War II and Vietnam documentary footage. These real life scenarios are left to the viewer to interpret alone, since the media seldom report what the social, economic, or political objectives or rationales are for the unpaid terrorist actors who are not even members of Actors Equity (Paletz, Ayanian, and Fozzard, 1982: 166-167).

Indeed, the media's message, though anti-violent, may have other appeals to different audiences. As Schmid and de Graaf (1982: 98) concluded:

Through the way the media present terroristic news, through selection of some facts out of the multitude of potentially relevant facts, through the associations they lay between the terroristic act and the social context, the media can have a profound influence that can create public hysteria, witchhunts, fatalism, and all sorts of other reactions that serve certain political interests—and not only those of the terrorists.

The Systemic Relationship between Terrorism and the Media

We cannot simply define or describe all forms of terrorism or generalize about their relationships to different news media and governments. Nevertheless, it is possible to capture some of these essential relationships using a schematic. Figure 1 lays out some of the key elements in this dynamic, *interactive* relationship among terrorist groups, the media, terrorism, public opinion, and public policy decisions. A hypothetical democratic political system is assumed in which a relatively free and unfettered press normally functions.

"Deviance amplification" is a useful construct for an analysis of the relationship between terrorism and mass media. The work of Leslie Wilkins (1965) and Jock Young (1973) describes this process as it applies to drug use. Their work depicts a "deviancy amplification spiral," whereby society defines a group as deviant, then isolates its members. The ensuing group alienation results in increased deviancy and increased social reaction. This supports more deviancy, more isolation, and further escalation of the initial "abnormality." Information provided through the mass media influences the dynamics of the interactions between the agencies of social control and the deviant group. This involves drug users, the police, the extent of public indignation, possible societal responses, and statistics on drug abuse. The whole "fantasy stereotype" of the drug taker is a media fabrication. While untrue early in the process, it assumes greater validity as self-fulfilliing prophesies about the drug culture increase. Increases in isolation, secrecy, ossification of values, group cohesion, professional distribution of drugs, and public demands for solutions and social control are observed. Much the same process occurs with respect to the interaction between media and terrorist groups in that the nature of terrorism has been greatly changed with the help of the mass media (Young, 1973: 350-359).

Going through the diagram, from a given terrorist group with its peculiar or unique aims and style of violence (1), reports are picked up as news by the ever-watchful media (after coverage of a violent incident or release of a group's claim of responsibility for an act). The media lens or filter (2) starts the magnification process (using terms and negative imagery such as "disorder," "violence," "threat," "irrationality," "secret society," "ruthless criminals," "fanatics," etc. as the usual magnifiers) which produces a new and larger social phenomenon labelled TERRORISM (3).

"Terrorism" has certain encoded meanings (e.g., "civil war," "guerrilla actions," "widespread violence," "crisis," "proletarian uprising," "Marxist revolutionaries," "irrationality," "siege," "rebellion," and "extremism") with highly negative valence. "Terrorism" then impacts upon (4) public opinion (regarding the terrorist group, its motives, its cause or objectives, government's alternatives, media reports, treatment of terrorists, victims, handling of new threats and demands, negotiations process, and surrender).

But the public does not take the raw news as gospel. People, instead, filter, compress, and interpret the news through the two-step flow of communications/"opinion influencers," and conceptual frames of reference (filters). This is the sum total of previous information/attitudes about such political events as terrorist attacks, governmental corruption, trust and cynicism, and good and bad politicians. Some of the resulting impressions are either neutralized/inhibited or blocked, while others are scattered or dispersed (like light through a prism). Still others become more closely focused on political decision makers in terms of supports or demands (much as light passes through a convex lens).

Finally, the process results in (5), official short and long-term actions or public policies. These include meeting demands, mounting rescue operations, anti-terrorist/media controls or guidelines for coverage, negotiation, stonewalling, news releases, etc.. These are the result of information, media reports, public opinion, input from other governments, and previous public policy positions on terrorism.

These events occur over long (Moro and Iran hostage cases) or short (Achille Lauro hijacking, Munich Olympics, and TWA Flight 847 hostage cases) periods of time. They also occur within a political environment which has its own levels of order, violence, or limits on legally permissible behavior. For example, the level of normal or acceptable violence may vary from that seen in relatively more violent societies (such as the USA, Lebanon, and Italy), to that in less violent societies (e.g. the Netherlands, Sweden, or West Germany) or on the high seas (where international law carries the threat of certain moral sanctions). In other settings, where nationals of one country may be victimized by an international band of terrorists on the soil of a third (neutral, biased, or friendly) country, the legal restrictions, governing laws, or permissible level of violence also condition the environmental context in which the event occurs or is played out.

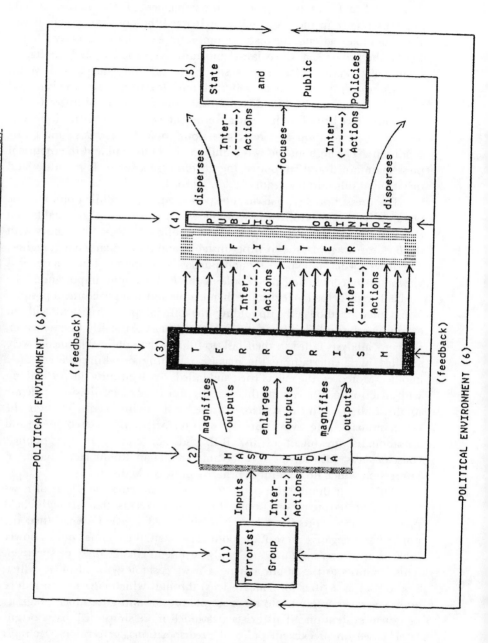

TERRORISM AND THE MASS MEDIA: AN INTERACTIVE SYSTEM

The political climate or culture of a country may help explain public policies taken to resolve a given terrorist incident. For example, in Italy in 1978 violence in the streets daily challenged the political system. It was also about to experience the historic compromise of a parliamentary alliance among the progressive Christian Democrats, the Socialists, and the Italian Communist Party. Worker protests, high unemployment, and youth demonstrations promoted or reflected anti-governmental cynicism and popular alienation. Within this political culture, Prime Minister Giulio Andreotti voiced the intransigent government position. This position was one of no negotiation and no concessions to *B.R.* terrorists, under any conditions. Throughout the two-month crisis the Italian and international press maintained and supported the government's stand. It naturally and inevitably resulted in the death of Aldo Moro.

The press, however, had an unexpected effect on public opinion. The news audience soon realized how feeble was the threat to the unstable and fragile system which the *B.R.* posed. The public also began to identify with the *B.R.* cause against the corrupt, unstable, and unpopular Roman regime. The news media, unexpectedly and purposely, helped to bring about this viewpoint by convincing the people of the *B.R.'s* public importance. The media thereby helped to legitimize their claims and anti-government posture, if not their methods. By upholding the official party line and without examining the underlying societal links and causes of the *B.R.* phenomenon, the news analysts failed in their task to inform the public. The media were satisfied with entertaining the masses, reporting one bizarre event after another. Moreover, the media tried and failed to delegitimize the *B.R.* (along with all terrorists). Preventing this were deeply rooted social divisions endemic to the Italian political system, culture, and environment. Though the establishment line was harshly anti-terrorist, the stereotyped and sensationalist treatment of the *B.R.* did not endure in the public's consciousness. Instead, the *B.R.* became an Italian Robin Hood band, an impression which no amount of negative press could dispel.

This result should give pause to those considering the effects of news coverage of terrorism on public opinion. It seems that strongly held preexistent views provide a barrier against media penetration. When the public has a negative view of the political system, the regime, and its power brokers, any news story may not easily be able to change these perspectives. This amounts to the public having a news cosmology or ideology which it also uses as a filter (or concave lens) through which citizens can reduce an exaggerated account into more simple pro- or anti-government, regime, or system evaluations. This exists at a much more simplified, basic or gut level, based on preexistent political predispositions, perceptions, feelings, attitudes, and cognitions. Therefore, the desire of the government or media for public support of a predetermined public policy stance may not be forthcoming in the face of a solidified, unified, and clear expression of popular opinions. This situation, which sometimes may allow the government to carry out an unpopular policy without public hindrance or objection, may not always be transferable to another, later, or similar incident. It may not result in renewed public support for the regime, system, or office holders.

What a different tack on the part of government or mass media would yield remains to be seen since there is seldom, in any country (with the possible exception of Great Britain), a concern for an in-depth media analysis of causes, motives, social conditions, or alternative contexts (or lenses in this illustration) for interpreting news about terrorist acts. Meanwhile, the public remains mystified about the roots, manifestations, and solutions to terrorism (e.g., is more or less democracy necessary?) and puts such incidents in the category of the "wrath of nature," much like an earthquake, volcanic eruption, or hurricane—here today, gone tomorrow—lacking any rhyme or reason.

Conclusions and Implications for Media and Public Policy

Statistics on both international and U.S. domestic terrorism indicate a decided decline during the 1980s as compared with the number of incidents in the '70s. In 1978, for example, there were 2,725 international incidents reported, some sixty of them attributed to the *B.R.*, with sixteen deaths in Italy. During the 1980s decade the total number of such incidents varied from 600 to 800 per year with about 150 aimed at U.S. nationals or American targets. Domestically, in 1985, for example, there were only ten actual incidents (as contrasted with 112 in 1977) due to a changed political climate, better airport security, counter terrorist activities, and more frequently thwarted attempts (e.g., 23 preventions in 1985). Though fewer in number, there was also a commensurate increase in the symbolic significance afforded attacks such as the Terry Anderson kidnapping, the Achille Lauro/ Klinghoffer incident, the TWA 847 hijacking, and the Berlin Disco bombing. Each such incident has been associated with real or alleged American links to Israel, the West Bank and the Gaza Strip, Lebanon, or other Middle Eastern conflicts (Genovese, 1986: 143ff.).

In Gerbner's discussion of symbolism, violence, and terror (1988a and 1988b: 1-4) he maintains that such "symbolic uses benefit those who control them: they are usually states and media establishments, not small-scale or isolated actors or insurgents." Gerbner also observes:

"though perpetrators of small-scale acts of violence and terror may occasionally force media attention and...seem to advance their cause,...such a challenge seems to enhance media credibility...and is used to mobilize support for repression often in the form of wholesale state violence and terror or military action, presented as justified by provocation" (1988b: 1).

Cross-national survey results at the end of the 1970s indicated that most West Germans, British, and Americans believed terrorism was a "very serious" problem. Despite these popular fears, Gerbner maintains the greater threat is "collective, official, organized, and legitimized violence." Television violence and small-scale terrorist attacks are not as dangerous to social stability as are "illicit commerce, wars, unemployment, and other social trends" which allow the wielders of power "to depersonalize enemies, to cultivate vulnerability and dependence in subordinates, to achieve instant support for swift and tough measures at home and abroad in what is presented as an exceedingly mean and scary world" (Gerbner, 1988b: 3).

Just why the U.S. government should be seeking self-restraint or prior restraint on media's (especially television's) coverage of terrorism or enlisting the media as an ally in the "war" against terrorism is not easily explained. With such limitations in place, the media establishment's quasi-adversarial role *vis à vis* the government would be further compromised through a form of governmental co-optation. When the concept of a "war on terrorism" comes into being, the media partners risk becoming tools or voices for the state, much as they did with managed news events such as the Grenada invasion, the Libyan air strike, and other military operations against Libyan aircraft and the Achille Lauro hijackers.

Press treatment of incidents such as the TWA 847 case are usually rather bland, pro-governmentally biased, and hostage oriented. Atwater's (1988: 1-8) study of network news coverage of the TWA Flight 847 hijacking indicated that there was massive television coverage of this event, with twelve hours of coverage devoted to it over the June 14-30, 1985 period. Whereas Laqueur (1977) and Alexander (1978) maintained that publicity was the key to terrorism's success and that "establishment" media wittingly or unwittingly were tools of terrorist strategy, this was not true in the TWA case study.

Atwater found that most reports came from Washington or New York, with few from the actual site. Over half the stories were on hostage conditions and U.S. government reactions, and far fewer focused on terrorist demands, acts, Islam, or Lebanon's internal or external difficulties. While the coverage was "dramatic, reactive, and extensive," the Iranian crisis mode of reporting was used. It had great detail, but no interpretation or education of the viewers. This finding was similar to that noted in the Paletz, et al. (1982: 145-165) study of the I.R.A., F.A.L.N. and Red Brigades coverage in network news. The networks treated these groups evenly, covering the same events with a similar portrayal; there was no legitimacy afforded the groups; their causes were not defined as just; no explanation was given of the causes or objectives behind the acts of violence; and most stories did not even mention the organization or its supporters.

Since governments have (or ought to have) control of the scene of the crisis or crime, they can limit media access as they would in any war, crisis, or emergency zone. Publishing or reporting terrorist events, however, are the responsibility of the press, not the government. As Ralph Langer, *The Dallas Morning News* executive editor says, "the basic cause of terrorism is not news coverage....Terrorism comes from real or perceived disputes and problems that aren't resolved" (quoted in Genovese, 1988: 151). Similarly, *Chicago Tribune* Editor James Squires maintains:

No policy other than a policy balancing hostages with national security and readers' interests is all that can be hoped for in a free and responsible press environment....We don't want to be used and manipulated by anyone. So we try to be as skeptical and as cautious about being compromised in the interest of some special cause or group of people as we are on a day-to-day basis when we deal with government (quoted in Genovese, 1986: 151-152).

When the government seeks involuntary guidelines and prior restraint, the classic case of the sovereign's blaming the messenger for bringing the bad news comes to mind. Should the press be forced to surrender its historical role as the fourth estate's check on governmental power as a specious palliative to quiet minimalist terrorism? The government and the terrorists may each share an interest in controlling the press, but the public's interest is certainly not served thereby.

In this regard, R.J. Rummel's (1988) study of the relationships among political systems, violence, and war is worth noting. He concluded that: "In a nutshell, democratic freedom promotes non-violence." To "minimize collective violence" and elements of war, "...one must embrace and foster democratic institutions, civil liberties, and political rights here and abroad." This proactive democratic stance toward preventing internal and external violence may also be applicable as a tool in future campaigns against terrorism at home and abroad.

Other advocates of proactive media roles for conflict resolution hope to reduce group grievances, frustration, and despair through use of forums and the encouragement of free expression. These vehicles would afford a hearing, provide legitimacy, and lend credibility to the unnecessary use of violence in media rich societies. Present media modes reward terrorists for using violence; new modes could reward the sensible discussion of non-violent alternatives to past aggression, fearsome reports, coerced coverage, and lengthy media-prolonged violence. Though these alternatives, like the diffusion theory (as an alternative to the contagion theory), are worthy of consideration, they (like alleged media—exacerbating behavior) are also based on informed judgments or suppositions. That is, they are equally sound ideas worthy of testing.

The provision of a U.N.O. office to the P.L.O., extensive western media coverage of Yasser Arafat, Gaza and West Bank Palestinian uprisings, and P.L.O. acceptance of Israel and rejection of terrorism are all recent and relevant developments. They indicate that what Secretary of State George Shultz called a terrorist group in 1988 (thus refusing Arafat a U.S. visa to speak at the United Nations) may very likely enjoy U.N. observer status in the 1990s.

Of course, post hoc interviews with those responsible for prior violent acts (such as the I.R.A., P.L.F., Red Army, or Animal Liberationists) make some sense. The group's motives, grievances, plans, and demands can be safely revealed in these "media therapy" sessions which provide a safety valve and a legitimate platform for dissenting views. Causes, policies, alternatives, shared selection of and control over topics, counter-propaganda, and deep and informed questioning would be necessary parts of what critics are sure to label the "meet your friendly neighborhood terrorist" shows. Unless the national government both supports and participates in such programs, they are likely to fail. The recent Columbia School of Journalism Media Studies Center series (which focused on the media and terrorism) also failed to have any "guests of dishonor" at the event. No P.L.O., I.R.A., P.Q., Basque, or Puerto Rican nationalist advocates or spokespersons were present. Trying terrorism in absentia in such forums, which specialize in exchanging the conventional wisdom about media guidelines (voluntary or imposed) versus press freedom, will do little to prevent forthcoming violence in which media are sure to be major actors.

The British government (since 1982) has actually used the threat of I.R.A. terrorism to restrict English press freedom, and, more recently to circumscribe the right of witnesses against self-incrimination—a procedural due process rule change which applies to all citizens, terrorists and non-terrorists alike. Similarly, the U.S. State Department strenuously opposed an NBC news interview (of three and one-half minutes duration) in May, 1986 with a P.L.F. leader involved in the Achille Lauro hijack. A spokesperson claimed that "terrorism thrives on this kind of publicity" and it "encourages that which we are seeking to deter" (quoted in Picard, 1988: 6).

Healthy debates about the broader causes of violence (e.g., publicity seeking, easy transport, cheap weapons and explosives, private and governmental funding, and media and governmental intransigence) may be more useful contexts for media based discussions of the terrorism dilemma (Picard, 1988: 5-6). Rather than seeking a single cause for this seemingly irrational and anti-statist form of protest (which has existed for thousands of years), terrorism must be placed in the context of typical violent reactions in typically violent societies. Moreover, the realities of modern technology have promoted the state's monopoly on the use of force. World arms sales annually total in the hundreds of billions of dollars. A puny group of terrorist is nothing compared with thousands of preventable highway and job-related deaths every year or a 3,000,000 person U.S. military establishment, with an annual budget of $300 billion per year. This is just one necessary part of the context needed for understanding terrorism in the late twentieth century.

The political environment or symbolic context for terrorism also relates to the centrality of the pledge of allegiance debate in the 1988 presidential elections. National pride and personal loyalty were introduced as campaign issues, just as they previously had been in the Klinghoffer case and the Achille Lauro hijacking and the TWA 847 incident, in which a living symbol of America's military was denigrated, brutalized, and murdered. When national emotions are allowed to exaggerate what is essentially a police matter into an international incident which provokes (as did the bombing of the Berlin disco) a military assault on Libya and the U.S. counter-hijacking of an Egyptian ally's plane as responses to terrorism, more sensible options must surely be available. This is merely "knee jerk" patriotism which invites even further provocation and combative retaliation.

As a case in point, on January 8, 1988, Ted Koppel, host of ABC's *Nightline* had Yasser Arafat as his guest. Arafat maintained that the U.S. and Israel were united in "state terrorism" against Palestinian, Libyan, and other peoples. Though Koppel pressed him, Arafat held his ground. On January 27, 1989, Colonel Qaddafi appeared on ABC's "20-20" news show. He attacked the Reagan administration, labelled the Fatah terrorists "revolutionaries," and sought dialogue with the Bush administration. Despite his increased sponsorship of state-supported violence, such public appearances, when combined with new U.S. diplomatic initiatives to quarantine his aggression, will allow world opinion to judge Qaddafi on his own merits or demerits. Moreover, the abundant international media coverage which Arafat received in 1988 during U.N.O. Geneva meetings, as a result of the U.S.A.-P.L.O. diplomatic rapprochement, neither inspired a rash of terrorist incidents nor pro-terrorist sentiment in the U.S. or elsewhere. Though Arafat received widespread media coverage, the state-directed anti-terrorist system has not collapsed. Censoring Arafat, Qaddafi, or other advocates of unpopular, anti-establishment positions in the U.S. makes no sense in a democratic society.

Before the business of government becomes regulation of the news business in the name of national security and symbolism, the press needs to inform the public about policy alternatives and just what is at stake. This may mean antagonizing the old or new power brokers who would have the media promote even more of their private financial and corporate interests, which deregulation has only encouraged. Mass media news coverage is tame, bland, and establishment-oriented as it is; to promote further restrictions would not only be redundant, it would also serve to erode our shrinking press freedoms even further.

Bibliography

Agee, W. et al. (1982) Perspectives on Mass Communications. New York: Harper & Row.

Alexander, Y. (1978) "Terrorism, the media, and the police." Journal of International Affairs 32: 101-113.

Anzovin, S. (ed.) (1986) Terrorism. New York: H.W. Wilson Co.

Cohen, S. and J. Young (1973) The Manufacture of News. Beverly Hills, CA: Sage.

Cooper, T. (1988) Terrorism and Perspectivist Philosophy. Boston, MA: Terrorism and the News Media Research Project, Emerson College, 1-6.

Crenshaw, M. (1987) "The international consequences of terrorism." Dudley, MA: Nichols College Institute for American Values, The Sovereign Citizen 2, 1: 4-8.

Genovese, M. (1988) "Terrorism." pp. 143-153 in R. Heibert and C. Reuss (eds.) Impact of Mass Media, New York: Longmans.

Gerbner, G. (1988a) "Violence and terror in the mass media." Reports and Papers in Mass Communications 102, Paris: UNESCO.

—— (1988b) Symbolic Functions of Violence and Terror. Boston, MA: Terrorism and the News Media Research Project, Emerson College, 1-4.

Graber, D. (1980) Mass Media and American Politics. Washington, D.C. Congressional Quarterly Press.

Hacker, F. (1976) Crusaders, Criminals, Crazies. New York: W.W. Norton.

Hoge, J.W. (1982) "The media and terrorism." in Miller A. (ed.) Terrorism and the Law. Dobbs Ferry, NY: Transnational Publishers.

Laqueur, W. (1976) "The futility of terrorism." in Harpers 104: 252.

—— (1977) Terrorism. Boston, MA: Little, Brown.

Lazarsfeld, P. and R. Merton (1948) "Mass communication, popular taste and organized social action." pp. 554-578 in Schramm, W. and Roberts, D.F. (eds.) The Process and Effects of Mass Communications. Urbana, IL: University of Illinois Press.

Livingstone, W.D. (1986) "Terrorism and the media revolution." pp. 213-227 in N. Livingstone and T. Arnold (eds.) Fighting Back. Lexington, MA: D.C. Heath.

Paletz, D., J. Ayanian, and P. Fozzard (1982) "Terrorism on tv news." pp. 143-165 in W. Adams (ed.) Television Coverage of International Affairs, Norwood: Ablex Publishing.

—— (1982) "The IRA, the Red Brigades, and the FALN in the New York Times." Journal of Communication 2: 166-168.

Payerhin, M. (1988) "Terrorism and The News Media: The Case of Moro" Storrs, CT.: Unpublished Master of Arts Thesis, Political Science Department, University of Connecticut.

Picard R. and P. Adams (1988) Characterizations of Acts and Perpetrators of Political Violence in Three Elite U.S. Daily Newspapers. Boston, MA: Terrorism and the News Media Research Project, Emerson College, 1-11.

Picard R. (1988) News Coverage as the Contagion of Terrorism. Boston, MA: Terrorism and the News Media Research Project, Emerson College, 1-7.

Ra'anan, U., et al. (1986) Hydra of Carnage. Lexington, MA: D.C. Heath.

Robinson, G. (1984) "Television news and the claim to facticity" in W. Rowland and B. Watkins (eds.) Interpreting Television, Beverly Hills, CA: Sage 12: 199-211.

Rummel, R.J. (1988) "Political systems, violence, and war" in Journal, Washington, D.C.: United States Institute of Peace 1, 4: 6.

Schmid, A. and J. De Graaf (1982) Violence as Communication. Beverly Hills, CA: Sage.

Schramm, W. and Roberts, D.F. (eds.) (1971), The Process and Effects of Mass Communications. Urbana, IL: University of Illinois Press.

Tan, Ch.-W.Z. (1987) "Mass media and insurgent terrorism." Ph.D. dissertation, Ann Arbor, MI: University of Michigan.

U.S. Department of Justice Task Force (1976), Disorders and Terrorism. Washington D.C.: U.S.G.P.O.

Weimann, G. (1983) "Theater of terror." Journal of Communication 33: 38-45.

Fantastic Outsiders:
Villains and Deviants in Animated Cartoons

Priscilla Kiehnle Warner

A flexible symbolic vehicle, animation gives character designers the potential to make a character fit a role to a greater extent than in any other medium. However, the structure of television programming, available resources, marketing considerations, and artistic and moral conventions constrain the content of televised cartoons visually and thematically. This analysis, informed by the sociological "production of culture" perspective (Becker, 1982; Peterson, 1976; Hirsch, 1972), discusses these constraints and how they affect cartoon creators' portrayals of villains and social deviants in animated cartoons.[1]

Character designers, animators, and story writers utilize stigmatizing visual and behavioral conventions to convey lessons about the causes and consequences of deviance in shows developed for the child audience. They provide explicit and implicit models of interpersonal morality and perpetuate the social typing of deviance. Creators present villainous characters who illustrate the appearances, motivations, and behaviors of figures who threaten the cohesiveness of integrated social groups.[2] Medium constraints and artistic and moral conventions combine to reinforce creators' tendencies to stereotype, limit their abilities to provide "personal history" for characters—which results in a focus on a "bad seed" theory of deviance—and warp the strength of pro-social creators' messages that deviance is negatively sanctioned.

Shared understandings deeply influence the things people do during the complex process of creating, distributing, and consuming cultural products (Lyon, 1974; Kealy, 1979; Faulkner, 1983). These understandings become *conventions* when they continue to meet people's needs successfully. Sanders (1982: 68) explains that *production* conventions facilitate the coordination of activities of artists and support personnel. "In effect, they are the norms which increase the predictability of and ease the problems inherent in the collective action." Character designers, for example, avoid technically troublesome ornamentation. Stan and Jan Berenstain (1981: 99-100) report that they altered their bear characters when they made the transition from printed pages to animation cells, "Papa's yellow plaid shirt presented a problem; animating a plaid apparently presents horrendous technical problems—and likewise the polka dots on Mama's dress..." Alternatively, *product* conventions are features of cultural products that when manipulated, altered, or avoided "influence the relationships between cultural producers and the consuming audience" (Sanders, 1982: 67). *They create the aesthetic experience.* Product conventions affect, for example, musical score cues, product dimensions, and visual displays (perspective, lighting styles, the use of color as opposed to black and white). Cartoon creators rely heavily on product conventions to communicate and add complexity to character identities and stories.

This analysis of recent cartoon images expands Needelman and Weiner's (1976) comments on the "physical appearance-moral status" convention (attractive heroes/unattractive or ugly villains) that, historically, artists have utilized in all types of art. Needelman and Weiner concluded that the use of unattractive heroes was the growing trend, especially in the performing arts. They anticipated that television's "blizzard of moral tales" would exhaust "once effective artistic devices" and that an increasingly educated public would be unresponsive to such unsophisticated contrivances.

Cartoon portrayals remain wedded to the unattractive appearance-low moral status convention. Three factors explain this: (1) a constant supply of new, unjaded children, with a perceived need for unambiguous morality plays, replenishes the cartoon audience. (2) Creators use moral stereotypes for immediate recognizability and visual impact. Television's time and budgetary constraints grossly aggravate the pressures against subtlety that exist to varying degrees in other media. (3) Finally, among all of television's audiences, children are the least able to communicate with the people making creative or programming decisions. If the child audience has been oversaturated by stale formulae, its members have few available channels through which they might voice dissatisfaction.

Medium Constraints and Effects

Stereotyping and type-casting are common in television short format programming because quick recognizability eases time and cost pressures. With a 20-25 minute format for all but a few cartoon shows (or 5 to 7 minutes for individual shorts), little opportunity exists for complex character development. The relatively greater development that existed in theater cartoons came from the imaginative ways that animators played with the movement possibilities of figures not bound by the laws of physical reality.[3] Before "limited" animation, motion was not only more fluid, character elasticity was also a major story component.[4] *Road Runner* episodes are classic examples. Wiley E. Coyote rebounded every time his eyes bugged out in triplicate, his body compressed into a pancake, or his fur flew off— all expressive of his resilient single-mindedness during each ravenous chase.

Episode time restrictions lead to characters who lack complex personal histories. Unless a viewer sees a series' pilot show, the heroic characters' fragmentary backgrounds appear most often as part of an opening credits montage, but this device is not used routinely. Star villains appear without historical grounding; they lack pasts or childhoods (although family relationships may provide links between characters, e.g. long lost siblings).

Time pressure limits creators' opportunities to impart information about factors affecting villainous character development.

Cartoons convey a sense of encapsulated timelessness and discrete episodes (unlinked story lines) facilitate re-scheduling flexibility.[5] Both characteristics allow stations to schedule episodes in various mixed or repeated combinations without confusion from one programming season to the next. Programs typically avoid direct references to current events although shows may draw their inspiration from current fashion styles or use popular slang. (Newer programs increasingly feature villains with spiked or mohawk haircuts.) Recent exceptions have been thinly veiled "just say no" messages. It is difficult to tell, however, if older shows appear more timeless than they really are because programmers shelved episodes with dated references.[6] Independent episodes and timelessness, however, contribute to discontinuities in characters' histories.

Creators use the plot device of allowing star villains to retreat to "home base" while essentially unscathed to enhance believability and continuity. How could Skeletor, the Supreme Oppressor, or Mumm-Ra reappear on a daily basis unless they escape consistently? More importantly from a commercial perspective, however, is the question whether toy marketing would be as effective for characters who appear only once. Shows are commonly only one aspect of massive marketing campaigns. *JEM*, *She-Ra*, and *Teddy Ruxpin*, for example, existed as toys before being turned into animated characters.[7] The commercial emphasis also explains the look-like community style groups (Care Bears, Smurfs, Little Ponies, Rainbow Brite sprites). Marginal differentiation through character names, decorations, or clothing accessories lends itself to efficient toy mass production.

In sum, medium constraints and the commercial orientation of televised cartoon production organizations reinforce stereotyping and type-casting tendencies, minimize creators' chances to provide information about villainous character development, and contribute to the sketchiness of characters' histories.

Presentation Conventions: Causes and Consequences of Deviance

The need for elements of conflict in a story (to stimulate viewer interest) does not dictate how creators explain the origins of or motivations for individual characters' behaviors. Pro-social program creators carefully construct and reinforce messages about what is acceptable or unacceptable behavior; however, while they are teaching these moral lessons, other, implicit, messages are available to young viewers. Creators unobtrusively reinforce individualistic explanations for the etiology of deviance and its consequences in cartoons.

Creators do not show villains becoming involved in deviant behavior through social processes or the influence of structural factors. The deviance "theories" implicit in cartoons are, at heart, biological or psychological rather than sociological. Creators visually reify deviant character.[8] They consistently link moral status to appearance, which repeatedly suggests to viewers that deviance originates genetically, not socially. Villains (and heroes or heroines) are not merely dressed in fantastic garb, their faces and bodies express their basic character. Villains are "bad seeds." Such characters typically possess constellations of negative traits attached to a deviant "master status" (Becker, 1972: 32). Unattractive evil sorcerers, aliens, etc. lack redeeming characteristics; they lie, cheat, steal, and covet; they abuse their associates, behave selfishly, and act mercilessly. Creators do not show these behaviors to be situationally specific or momentary aberrations; they derive from characters' enduring evil character.

"Criminal" characters lack a social context. They rise full-blown as career lawbreakers without reference to reasons why they might be in the position they now occupy—blocked opportunity structures, for example. This kind of explanation for anti-social behavior is too non-visual and complex to convey in cartoon form. To portray Skeletor and Mon*Star as, for example, victims of discrimination or as abused children would be problematic. But interpersonal violence, even child battering, has been offered as humor. A "Fractured Fairy Tales" segment that shows a little girl who, among other things, has a sister who sets her skirt afire, closes with the (satirical) moral, "Be it ever so painful, there's no place like home" (Jay Ward Productions, 1986). Cartoon creators identify deviants and deviant behavior without giving more than the simplest explanation for it.

Only basically good characters learn from mistakes. Repentance, or the lack of it, distinguishes good from deviant characters. Younger children's fantasy programs and some of the action-adventure series show good characters being rude, impatient, or greedy, but before the show ends they realize that they were wrong and apologize. For example, in "Something Old, Something New," an arrogant apprentice magician responds contritely to She-Ra/Adora's question as to whether he learned anything on his visit.

Eli: Yes, I have, Adora. I now know why my teacher sent me here. He knew I would learn something even better than magic. Through your kindness and patience I've learned not to brag and show off (Filmation, 1986).

In other action-adventure shows, heroic teammates reaffirm their solidarity after being unfriendly to each other through concilatory joking remarks. The villainous characters in the same shows do not admit to error or guilt and remain unchanged.[9] Unlike the heroic characters, villains leave the scene trying to pin the blame for failure on each other or their fool-type accomplices.

Deviants and villains never win in cartoons; the heroic characters thwart their evil goals. As ThunderCat leader Liono exclaims, "Evil always loses in the end." (Filmation advertisement, 1986) Two basic consequences exist for the perpetrators of villainous behavior: they lose a verbal or physical confrontation and experience immediate sanctions or they lose and flee the scene while vowing to return for revenge. Non-starring villains and criminals routinely go to jail or prison or are the subject of a beating or backfired plans.[10] Peripheral gunfighting characters may be killed. Star villains also sporadically receive physical punishment. The sanction is not always this severe, however. Characters are otherwise publicly degraded. They are laughed at, embarrassed, and made to look foolish. Master Blaster and the Copy Cats from *Kidd Video* routinely end up in a tangled heap as a result of their own ineptitude while the Kidd Video musical group characters look on.

Star villains escape long-term punishment repeatedly, an event that weakens the "deviance is negatively sanctioned" pro-social message.[11] Story creators struggle with the obvious moral dilemma. Heroic He-Man attempts to explain during the episode "Not So Blind":

Boy 1: I want to know something. How come He-man doesn't just go to Snake Mountain and smash Skeletor into little bones?

Old Storyteller:...Oh, children, what kind of talk is that? He-man never tries to hurt any living thing, evil or not.

Boy 1: But I don't understand. When I do something bad, I get punished. Why doesn't Skeletor?

Boy 2: Yeah, how come he gets away with everything?

He-Man: He will be punished for his evil deeds. Skeletor is not an ordinary criminal. You see when someone commits a crime, he's tried and if found guilty, well, he's punished.

Boy 1: Skeletor hasn't been punished.

Boy 2: I told ya. If you were powerful you could get away with anything.

He-man: Well, not really. The punishment is just delayed, that's all. You see, the more evil Skeletor does the worse his punishment will be. And each day we come closer to taking care of Skeletor once and for all.

Boy 1: I still think He-man should beat him up.

Storyteller: Well, that will be enough of that, young man.

(Filmation, 1986)

In short, creators perpetuate individualistic etiological theories. Deviants are portrayed as unreliable and incapable of reform. They never fully achieve their goals, but neither do star villains become subject to long-term sanctions.

Stigma Conventions

The product conventions animators use to convey villainy and deviance draw upon what Goffman (1963: 4) identified as three general categories of stigma: "abominations of the body", "tribal stigma", and "blemishes of individual character" (e.g. "weak will, domineering or unnatural passions,...dishonesty..."). Cartoon characters with the first type of stigma violate human appearance norms. These characters might be human sideshow style "freaks" (giants, "rubbermen", overweight women) or figures that combine animal, mechanical, and humanoid elements. Characters stigmatized by tribal differences transgress national, species, or ethnic boundaries. Morally suspect characters violate social norms, (including gender role expectations), legal codes, and political rules, Villains commonly exhibit more than one stigmatizing characteristic, but for descriptive purposes

I will discuss the conventions that animators and story creators use to communicate each stigma separately.

Cartoon artists repeatedly draw upon stock cultural symbols and stereotypes to distinguish villainous from virtuous characters. They borrow freely from literature, especially myths and fairy tales, or pirate their own medium.[12] For example, Katrina Stoneheart in Hanna-Barbera's *The Pound Puppies* is a milder version of Cruella DeVille in Disney's *101 Dalmations*. Katrina even sets up a factory to make fur coats from puppy hides, aided by a pair of inept goons. Nor is self-reflexivity a new device in cartoons, although it is taken to special extremes due to the flexibility of the medium.[13]

Appearance Conventions

Certain facial displays provide important clues to villainous identities. A head or face with a pronounced skull shape (prominent cheekbones, sunken eyes) signifies deviance. Males are apt to show heavy beard shadow (particularly in combination with an ethnic identity, e.g. Clyde, Woody Woodpecker's French Canadian nemesis or Blacque Jacque Shellacque in Warner Bros. episodes). Beards have lost the ability to signify deviant character reliably, but particular moustaches are closely associated with villains, for example, tiny Hitler brushes or long whiplash styles.

Dark ringed and deepset eyes appear on both men and women villains although on males eyeshadows are more distinctive when combined with bulging or bloodshot eyeballs. One of the most visually communicative shots in a *Mighty Mouse* episode titled "The Sky is Falling" is an opening sequence dominated by a fox's slanted bloodshot eyes glaring from behind a thicket of bushes. Villains are also likely to appear with one blind eye; they display either a pupil-less orb or wear an eyepatch. Villains who lack all other facial features (their faces are shadows enclosed by a hood) retain indications of eyes: glowing pinpoints or slanting pointed ovals. Rounded eyes in the darkened space, however, indicate innocence (e.g. Orko in *He-Man*). Eyes, of course, are a focal point for expression. Squints, lowered lids, and "crazed" stares signify evil character and intent. Male villains wear monocles rather than glasses, especially Nazi-styled characters. In non-deviant males, glasses carry connotations of seriousness and real or pseudo-intellectuality.

Tooth shape is one of the most consistent signs of bad character. Not all villainous characters have pointed teeth, but figures with fangs are nearly always bad; good characters have smooth rounded or squared teeth, even many of the feline characters (e.g. the *ThunderCats*). In fact, a character's teeth sometimes transform into fangs when he is about to do something bad.

The ugliest characters are male and female villains. Witches or "hag" queens are plagued by warts on large, crooked, or pointed noses. Lack of facial beauty means different things for each gender. Ugliness and advanced age carry special weight as motivating forces in female deviance. In a "Fractured Fairy Tales" segment that parodies the Cinderella story, narrator Edward Everett Horton reveals that two ugly older sisters beat and otherwise abuse the youngest sister, Sweet Little Beet, because she is "very pretty, very pretty indeed":

> Horton: How do you think that made her sister feel?
> Grenetta: Terrible!
> Horton: And what do you think they did?
> Prunelda: We treat her something awful of course! (Jay Ward Productions, 1986)

For ugly, even monstrous, males, however, physical appearance does not specifically motivate misbehavior.

Body type is an inconsistent indicator of human characters' deviance. Animators use endomorphic and mesomorphic characteristics, especially for slow-witted villainous accomplices, but a multitude of Hanna-Barbera characters (Yogi Bear, Huckleberry Hound, etc.) have large upper bodies and short legs whether good or bad. Stereotypes appear, e.g. hunchback assistants. However, many of the new characters in the action-adventure category, villainous and heroic, have exaggeratedly physically fit bodies with overstressed secondary sex characteristics.

Animal body types carry connotations. Certain animals communicate "badness" better than others: bats, snakes, lizards, alligators or crocodiles, spiders, scorpions, vultures, ravens, wolves, jackals, sharks, rats, gorillas, warthogs, dragons, and griffins. Frogs are usually cast as repulsive, monkeys are mischievous. Cats or cat-like humans appear in both villainous and innocent roles. Human or humanoid villains display characteristics of these animals, e.g. Cat-thra from *She-Ra* has a feline quality to her voice and makes biting remarks. Apart from villains having animal shapes and characteristics, wizard and witch characters (and others) have standard familiars (ravens, cats). Azrael, a cat, cohabits with the Smurfs' nemesis Gargamel, a bumbling wizard who considers Smurfs to be a desirable food source. "Azrael" is the name of the angel who, in Jewish and Moslem belief, parts the soul from the body at death (Webster's, 1970).

Monsters and "mutants" appear as villains. The *Inhumanoids* program has several star monster characters: Tendril, Decompose, and Metlar. Subtitled "the evil that lies within," it is the only show named after villains. The ThunderCats ceaselessly battle Mumm-Ra and his crew, plainly named "the Mutants," who include S-S-Slithe (fanged and frog featured), Vultureman, Jackelman, and Rataro. The *Wuzzles*, a show for younger children, includes characters with hybrid animal bodies (e.g. Bumblelion, a bee striped lion), but the narrator humorously describes the whole community setting as "mixed up" so that what viewers might consider a mutation is framed positively.

Language and voices provide clues. Mechanical or "Darth Vader" breathiness accompanies some villainous male appearances. Female deviants tend to have deeper (more masculine?) voices than do sweet heroines or victims. Adora transformed into She-Ra provides an exception, her voice deepens with the change; the fact that the transition is to a more powerful, action-oriented role may explain this. Tone of voice is a more reliable clue than is sound alone. Villains have relatively loud, hostile, haughty, whiney, or demanding voices. The distinction shows up clearly when a female villain tries to disguise herself as a good character but momentarily slips out of role when events do not go as she desires.

Jewelry is a gender sign so that earrings worn by males, usually by pirates, still conveys deviance. (An exception is Capt. Lou in *Hulk Hogan's Rock 'N' Wrestling*, a good character who has his cheek, not ear, pierced.) Male villains do wear other ornaments that are similar to jewelry.

Much like the skirt or pants sporting figures that adorn public restroom doors in an international gender code, villains wear skull symbols and heroines and non-deviant males wear hearts. In the Care Bears community (which includes heart-decorated Tenderheart, Nobleheart, Swiftheart Rabbit...), whose members' declared mission is to "help people share their feelings", the villain goes by the name of No-Heart. Skulls and skull insignias, more than any other symbols, are associated with villains. They also nearly monopolize spiked ornaments (spike-studded wristbands, shoulder decorations, and helmets (as opposed to crowns)). Tattoos almost never appear on starring non-deviant characters. Hefty Smurf, a secondary character, displays a *heart* tattoo on his arm (which dilutes its impact).[14]

Race and Nationality

Goffman (1963) developed his analysis from observations of human social interaction. Animators, of course, need not confine themselves to real characters. Traditional racial and ethnic portrayals as a form of deviance are not readily apparent in the most recent cartoons; this form of stigma has migrated into the fantasy realm. These stigmatized characters are identified by in/out group boundary clues, "us" vs. "them" distinctions.

A portion of the figures in the "deviance through racial aspect" category are created through contrast to "natural" humans. These are the space aliens, monsters, and supernatural characters (ghosts, dracula-types, living mummies). It is through the physical characteristics of the members of the group and the human characters' reaction to these differences that the concept "alien" (a "foreign" race) exists. Mutant characters also belong here. They are not only visually different, they form adversary groups (e.g. the space aliens vs. Josie and the (human) Pussycats, the Inhumanoids vs. the human Earthcore team).

Nationality (linked to country or planet-based ethnocentrism) is an issue in cartoons, particularly in the new mythical sagas or the patriotic programs. The G.I. Joe team consists of "Real American Heroes;" Mandrake the Magician and friends are "Defenders of the Earth." Political deviants are common: spies, Nazi-styled characters, demagogues, corrupt public officeholders, rebels against legitimate authority, and mercenaries. Several terrorist-style groups plague the heroes in current shows. Rambo outwits S.A.V.A.G.E. (the Secret Army of Vengence and Global Evil) and the M.A.S.K. team repels V.E.N.O.M. (Vicious Evil Network of Mayhem).

Ethnicity in connection with deviance appears in the oldest cartoons only. Some vestiges of it remain in the form of beard-shadowed mediterranean accomplices. Ethnic slurs have disappeared from new programs as a source of humor. The current pro-social cartoon creators are concerned with positive, if sparse, displays of racial or ethnic diversity. Blacks are members of the heroic action teams but very few Hispanics or Asians appear. Brasch writes that animation industry personnel believe that viewers and advertisers (the sources of income for cartoon production) are "more comfortable" with WASP names and character images (Brasch, 1983: 149-151). The absence of ethnic-based humor also comes from decreased emphasis on humor generally due to the rise of dramatic action-adventure plots. Following the Marvel Comics tradition, characters in these shows turn to sarcasm and satire as entertainment devices.

Character Flaws and Behavior Norms

Character flaws, of course, are not visible stigma; they must be inferred from behavioral indicators. Animated characters (anthropomorphized animals and humans) exhibit "blemishes of individual character" through actions, motivations, and expressed intentions. Evil thoughts and intentions are not visually obvious so animators use muted voice-overs to reveal a character's thoughts, "break the fourth wall" (the character speaks directly to the viewer), or have the character speak his thoughts without audience awareness. Mumm-Ra, for example, often peers into a magical pool while soliloquizing.

Norm violations range from gender role reversals to overtly criminal activities. In *The PawPaw Bears*, villain Darkpaw scorns persistently affectionate Prettypaw as a "love sick lump of bear grease." Extortionists, arsonists, kidnappers, "slavers," outlaw gunfighters, and trespassers trouble the defenders of law and order. Thieves, vandals, and saboteurs abound. Graft, bribery, and a new topic, consumer fraud occur. 1930s style gangsters seem to be fading from popular consciousness. They appear in older reruns, for example, Biggie Rat plots against King Leonardo, Noodles Romanov and his gang harass Roger Ramjet.

The dominant convention concerning behavior norms is to have villainous characters simultaneously violate a multitude of social rules. Villains are identifiable because they are so thoroughly bad. They engage in activities driven by interests or goals that provide no motivation to heroic characters. Good characters wage a constant reactionary battle to maintain or restore social order and cohesion. In fact, the major proportion of their energies is devoted to counteracting villains' and deviants' activities. Even the youthful anthropomorphic characters are kept busy resolving problems caused by less well-behaved animals: interpersonal friction or adventures gone awry. Heroic characters do not initiate conflict (even She-Ra who proclaims she leads "the rebellion" against evil Hordak). Typically, it is only in the more obvious pro-social cartoons that show good characters carrying on non-reactionary constructive activities.

The key characteristic of villains and deviants is disruptive competitiveness and desire for personal power. The pro-social message that cartoon creators convey repeatedly is the appropriateness and desirability of cooperative group effort (although not in an egalitarian group—leaders and followers definitely exist). Teamwork and friendship or other common bonds are highly valued. (In "The Tragic Flute," Ewok Latara observes, "I learned that my friends are the most valuable thing in the world"). "Winning" or success is keyed to cooperativeness. As one Potato Head Kid declares, "You know, when we work together we can do anything." Singing together in the "Trash Can Derby," the Kids emphasize the benefits of group effort and the work ethic:

> Everybody pitching in. That's what it takes to win. Everybody working for one goal.
> Keeping on through thick and thin. That's what it takes to win. Give it all you've got, both heart and soul.
> Nobody wins by wishing. It takes work to achieve a dream.
> And you really improve your chances when you're working as a team.
> [Jumping in[15]] and discipline. That's how you must begin.
> Add a little cooperation, lots of effort and concentration, lots of pluck and determination.
> That's what it takes to win. That's what it takes to win. That's what it takes to win. (Sunbow, 1986).

Deviants' desire for power leads them to form instrumental (rather than affective) relationships that are tossed aside when the possibility for individual gain or more advantageous relationships appears. As a *Galaxy Ranger* villain shouts in the face of danger, the code is "Every man for himself." Leader villains especially are highly untrustworthy and double-cross their associates. They may even temporarily team up with the heroic characters as in this *Galtar and the Golden Lance* "Antara the Terrible" episode:

> [Hero] Galtar's team helps [sorceress] Antara find a power bestowing stone:
> Antara: I have waited so long! The power!
> Princess Galeta: I only hope it can help us in our battle against [Lord] Torment.
> Antara: Torment shall finally be brought to his knees—And a new ruler shall rule above the land!
> Boy in Galtar's group: What's she talking about?
> Antara: Tonight will be the birth of a new reign. Antara, Antara the Terrible!
> Galtar: I don't think I like the sound of that, Antara.
> Antara: Ha ha! I didn't think you would. [She drops a magical loop over them.]
> Galtar: We've been tricked!
> Antara: SURPRISE! (Hanna-Barbera, 1986)

Villains fail to "take the role of the other;" they have little empathy. They operate their relationships on the principle of a zero-sum game so that they exult in others' misfortunes, jealously guard what they have, or covet what others possess. A conversation between villains from the same episode of *Galtar* illustrates this:

Lord Torment: Why do you despise her so?

Krim: Why? Why not? Antara was forever trying to outdo my magic. Mainly to impress our mother at my expense. But mother always did like me best.

Lord Torment: So where has your sister been all these years?

Krim: Long ago, on the eve of mother's birthday, Antara asked me to help her steal the perfect birthday gift. The magic of the Wizard Izzar.

Lord Torment: Izzar's magic? Hmm. Ambitious girl.

Krim: Too ambitious! I told her it was dangerous, that Izzar was too strong, but would she listen? Noooooo. Not Antara.

Lord Torment: What happened?

Krim: When we finally attacked Izzar he cast a spell which banished my wicked sister to another world...Believe me, Torment, mother did not call my sister "Antara the Terrible" for nothing. (Hanna-Barbera, 1986)

What Goffman (1963: 4) identified as "domineering or unnatural passions" for power, wealth, revenge, or recognition motivate villains and deviants into behaviors that demonstrate disrespect for the ideals of order and equality. Their disrespect for established authority figures or "crying wolf" endangers others' and their own security. Deviants cheat, lie, verbally and physically mistreat subordinates, are arrogant and immodest, and take credit for others' ideas.

Villains' cowardly selfishness and irresponsibility puts associates at risk, often to benefit themselves. (Antara the Terrible says about her brother, "Krim could have saved me but he chose to run away like a dog to protect his own miserable hide...") In sum, through their overweening self-interest, villains and deviants symbolize dangers to the cohesiveness of integrated social groups.

Summary and Conclusion

Sensitized by the production of culture perspective, this paper focused on constraints that affect the visual and thematic content of cartoon creators' works. In particular, medium and market pressures encourage the use of stereotypes and reduce character complexity. Programming needs for scheduling flexibility result in discrete, encapsulated episodes that limit creators' opportunities to develop character histories. Marketing plans, increasingly behind the appearance of new shows, and creators' needs for believability and continuity explain why star villains reappear consistently. Villains inconsistently experience vigilante retribution rather than being subject to the long term sanctions of law. Creators use of appearance, "tribal," and moral stigma conventions is an effective labelling device to delineate and maintain moral boundaries. In the process of passing on an accumulating symbolic culture to young viewers, cartoon creators perpetuate stereotypical understandings of deviance and function to reinforce consensual mythology about its sources.

Notes

I would like to thank Clinton R. Sanders for his comments and unfailing enthusiasm throughout the various stages of this analysis.

[1]The sample includes an episode of every cartoon show regularly scheduled on the non-cable channels in the Chicago market area. I took additional notes on non-videotaped episodes of each show. The September issues of *The Chicago Tribune TV Guide* listed 62 unique titles, but because various shows appeared multiple times during the day or as weekday series, the free channels were displaying 100.5 hours of animated cartoons per week.

[2]See Klapp (1956, 1962) for a general discussion of social typing. See Young (1973) for a discussion of images of deviants in news programs.

[3]Don Bluth's *The Secret of N.I.M.H.* or Richard Williams' *Who Framed Roger Rabbit* are recent feature length examples of sophisticated full animation.

[4]A response to the television market which created the need for more rapid means of production, "limited" animation requires as few as 4 frames per second to convey movement to up to 24 in full animation. In the 1940s, Bill Hanna and Joe Barbera Productions created fifty minutes of animated footage *per year;* from 1958 to 1963 their output increased to sixty minutes *per week;* by 1977, they had quadrupled that rate. (Slafer in Peary and Peary, 1980: 255-260).

[5]The creators of daily series shows are experimenting with thematically linked daily shows (*ThunderCat* Liono's leadership trials) and cliff-hanger endings (*My Little Ponies*). The cliff-hanger device, however, also reduces costs slightly because it allows re-use of footage to inform audiences about previous episodes.

[6]Racist or ethnic stereotypes became embarrassing to the networks.

[7]Diane Keener, character designer at Filmation, mentioned that the producer originally brought her a *She-Ra* doll from which she developed pose sheets for the animators. See also Diamond (1987) or "Talk of the Town: Marketing" (1987).

[8]The association between physical appearance and deviant identity parallels the Lombrosian (1911) perspective on deviance.

[9]A good character's temporary lapse is usually due to immaturity and situational temptation. Villains, however, are almost invariably adults.

[10]In "The Chase," the Silverhawks begin to read "Miranda rights" to a captured criminal before he escapes ("You have the right to remain silent...")

[11]Professional consultants who comment on the psychological or child development aspects of scripts are an additional constraint.

[12]Villainous and non-villainous characters have been inspired by live, literary, or televised images. Brasch (1983) identifies the origins of many characters. Of the characters that appear in my sample: Bert Lahr's cowardly lion was the model for Snagglepuss and Charles Boyer's movie role in *Algiers* inspired amorous skunk Pepe Le Pew; Top Cat is a caricature of Phil Silvers; Doggy Daddy parodies Jimmy Durante. The Flintstones are time distorted versions of *The Honeymooners*; Red Skelton's Sheriff Deadeye provided the seed image for both Yosemite Sam and Quick Draw McGraw (whose alter-ego, El Kabong, borrows his style from Zorro). Heckle and Jeckle's names are a variation of Dr. Jeckle and Mr. Hyde. Superman's success as a comic strip character and animated figure inspired I. Klein's Super Mouse, quickly renamed Mighty Mouse (Klein in Peary and Peary, 1980: 171-177). Cold war spy

character Boris Badenov (*The Bullwinkle Show*), "owed his name to Modest Mussorgsky's opera *Boris Godunov*. The cartoon name was a natural. It had political and phonological significance (it sounded foreign) and it had semantic significance ('bad enough'). It was also alliterative." (Brash, 1983: 100)

The *Bullwinkle* shows are renowned for their puns and dual-level humor. Some of this activity simply amuses the creators. More pointedly, however, television creators constantly capitalize on or recombine character types and concepts that have been successful before in an attempt to maximize commercial predictability.

[13]Self-reflexivity became a hallmark of Tex Avery's work. In the middle of the action a character might hold up a sign lettered, "Corny gag, ain't it?" (Scheib in Peary and Peary, 1980: 110-127).

[14]Sanders (1989) reports that cartoon characters are a common tattoo motif, especially Yosemite Sam or the Little Red Devil. From the tattooist's perspective, cartoons' distinct outlines make them readily adaptable to the new medium, their lack of complexity makes them quick to execute (raising income potential), and they require minimal artistic skill. From the consumer's perspective, cartoon characters possess personality characteristics with which the wearer identifies or sympathizes.

[15]Indecipherable wording.

Bibliography

Becker, H.S. (1973) Outsiders. New York: Free Press.

_____ (1982) Art Worlds. Berkeley: University of California Press.

Berenstain, S. and J. Berenstain (1981) "You Can't Animate a Plaid Shirt," Publisher's Weekly 219 (9): 99-100.

Brasch, W. (1983) Cartoon Monikers. Bowling Green, Ohio: Bowling Green University Popular Press.

Diamond, D. (1987) "Is the Toy Business Taking Over Kids' TV?" TV Guide 35 (24): 5-8.

Faulkner, R.R. (1983) Music on Demand: Composers and Careers in the Hollywood Film Industry. New Brunswick, N.J.: Transaction Press.

Goffman, E. (1963) Stigma Notes on the Management of Spoiled Identity. Englewood Cliffs, N.J.: Prentice-Hall.

Hirsch, P.M. (1972) "Processing Fads and Fashions: An Organization-Set Analysis of Cultural Industry Systems." American Journal of Sociology 77: 639-659.

Kealy, E. (1979) "From Craft to Art: The Case of Sound Mixers and Popular Music." Sociology of Work and Occupations 6: 3-29.

Keener, D. Telephone conversation, March 1987.

Klapp, O. (1956) "American Villain Types." American Sociological Review 21: 337-340.

_____ (1962) Heroes, Villains, and Fools. Englewood Cliffs, N.J.: Prentice-Hall.

Klein, I. (1980) "Origins of Mighty Mouse" pp. 171-177 in the American Animated Cartoon, ed. by G. Peary and D. Peary. New York: E.P. Dutton.

Lombroso, C. (1911) Crime. Its Cause and Remedies. trans. H.P. Horton. Boston: Little, Brown.

Lyon, E. (1974) "Work and Play: Resource Constraints in a Small Theater." Urban Life 3: 71-97.

Needelman, B. and N.L. Weiner (1976) "Heroes and Villains in Art." Society 14: 35-39.

Peterson, R.A. ed. (1976) The Production of Culture. Beverly Hills: Sage.

Sanders, C.R. (1989) Customizing the Body: The Art and Culture of Tattooing. Philadelphia: Temple University Press.

———— (1982) "Structural and Interactional Features of Popular Culture Production: An Introduction to the Production of Culture Perspective." Journal of Popular Culture 16: 66-74.

Scheib, R. (1980) "Tex Arcana: The Cartoons of Tex Avery," pp. 110-127 in The American Animated Cartoon, ed. by G. Peary and D. Peary. New York: E.P. Dutton.

Slafer, E. (1980) "A Conversation with Bill Hanna," pp. 255-260 in The American Animated Cartoon, ed. by G. Peary and D. Peary. New York: E.P. Dutton.

"Talk of the Town: Marketing." The New Yorker 63 (1): 28-29.

Webster's New World Dictionary, 2nd ed. (1970) s.v. "Azrael".

Young, J. (1973) "The Myth of the Drug Taker in the Mass Media," pp. 314-322 in The Manufacture of News, ed. by S. Cohen and J. Young. Beverly Hills, CA: Sage.

Cartoonography

Advertisement for The ThunderCats. Rankin-Bass. (9 November 1986) FOX. WFLD, Chicago.

"Antara the Terrible," Galtar and the Golden Lance. Hanna-Barbera Productions. FOX. WFLD, Chicago (9 November 1986).

"The Chase," Silverhawks. Rankin-Bass. FOX. WFLD, Chicago. (7 November 1986).

"Fractured Fairy Tales," Bullwinkle and Rocky Show. Jay Ward Productions. Independent. WPWR, Chicago. (16 November 1986).

"Not So Blind," He-Man. Filmation Associates. FOX. WFLD, Chicago. (7 November 1986).

"Something Old, Something New," She-Ra, Princess of Power. Filmation Associates, Inc. FOX. WFLD, Chicago. (7 November 1986).

"The Tragic Flute," The Ewoks. Lucasfilm. ABC. WLS, Chicago. (15 November 1986).

"Trash Can Derby," Potato Head Kids. Sunbow Productions. FOX. WFLD, Chicago. (10 November 1986).

Acting Like Cops:
The Social Reality of Crime and Law on TV Police Dramas

B. Keith Crew

Police dramas, a staple of network television entertainment since its earliest days, portray a strange world. It is a world inhabited by violent, psychopathic, predatory criminals, and heroic cops who use their guns more often in a single episode than the average real police officer does in a career. It is a world in which the legal system acts in mysterious, arbitrary ways, more often frustrating than fulfilling the need for orderly justice. It is unlikely that large numbers of viewers accept the social reality depicted on such shows as literally true; they are, after all, entertainment, fantasy, escape. Nevertheless, cop shows do contribute to the way in which the public thinks about crime and law enforcement (Gerbner and Gross, 1976; 1980; Schaefer, Vanderbok and Wisnoski, 1979). They do this not by creating whole new images of crime and criminals, but by exploiting current stereotypes of crime, which they intensify and repackage into standardized characters and plot devices. Specifically, the social reality of crime created in these shows has an ideological content that is almost inevitably conservative and reinforces passivity in the viewer.

This paper focuses on the social reality of crime as it is portrayed in network television series of recent vintage, particularly the popular series *Miami Vice.*. The analysis was guided by the thesis that the crime shows present the viewer with an ideological framework for interpreting crime and justice; one that Scheingold (1984) has labeled the "myth of crime and punishment." According to Scheingold, the myth of crime and punishment has as its core "a simple morality play that dramatizes the conflict between good and evil: because of bad people this is a dangerous and violent world" (Scheingold, 1984: 60). In this myth, the world is populated with violent, predatory strangers whose attacks on innocent persons threaten the very existence of society. Rooted in traditions of frontier vigilante justice, this myth suggests that such persons must be dealt with swiftly and punitively. It endorses swift and violent punishment as both a moral and practical approach to dealing with crime.

131

In the myth of crime and punishment, criminals are viewed as fundamentally different from law-abiding citizens. Consequently, although it does not completely denigrate the values of due process and rule of law, it reserves the commitment to legal rights for normal, non-criminal members of society. The image of hordes of predatory outsiders threatening to overrun society conjured up by this myth implies that society can not afford a full-fledged commitment to legality.

The myth of crime and punishment is resonant with conservative political ideology because it defines the problem of crime strictly as the effect of bad individuals rather than as a product of social and economic conditions. Moreover, it directs attention away from other social problems by using "crime" as a symbol for a wide range of threats to social order. The police shows examined in this study are not, however, simplistic exercises in propaganda for the status quo. They often portray political and business elites, as well as social institutions, in a negative way. In their efforts to be current and appeal to the audience's sense of sophistication, references to recent controversial news issues, such as the government's "secret" support of the Nicaraguan "contras." These references are often interpreted for the viewer in ways that are apparently critical of the existing social system. Nevertheless, these shows fail to provide viewers with interpretations of reality that are truly critical of existing social, political and economic arrangements. Hence, a secondary thesis of this study is that certain "formal features" (Gitlin, 1979) of television entertainment series function to contain and neutralize those negative interpretations. The very nature of TV crime dramas, in other words, causes them to reproduce the myth of crime and punishment at the expense of other "myths" with more critical and progressive orientations, while, at the same time, allowing viewers to vicariously express ambiguous and hostile feelings toward existing political and economic arrangements. The impact of these formal features on the ideological content of cop shows is examined through a comparison of how similar issues are used or interpreted in shows that differ in these formal features.

Format and Formula: We Know Who the Bad Guys Are, So Who Needs Due Process?

According to Blumberg (1985) the police come to view themselves as the best judges of criminal guilt, because they adopt a "crime control" orientation (Packer, 1968) to their work. Criminal status is conferred on a person as a result of competent police work. Thus, they may become frustrated with and cynical toward a judicial system based on a "due process" model (Packer, 1968) which emphasizes presumption of innocence, protection of suspects' rights, and rules of legal procedure. The distinction between factual and legal guilt is one of the more frustrating aspects of real police work. This tension is recreated for the viewer of cop shows because the audience is the best judge of guilt. Cop shows rarely adopt the form of the "whodunit" murder mystery used in shows such as *Perry Mason* and *Murder, She Wrote*. In most cop shows, the viewer knows who committed the illegal behavior: "the audience sees the crime committed or is privy to who did it" (Alley, 1979: 133).

This recurrent feature of cop shows is part of the "formula" that accompanies this "genre" (Gitlin, 1979). Specifically, cop shows focus on action; violent action. Unlike murder mysteries, where the case begins with the discovery of the body, cop shows often begin with the action of the crime. The notion of "genre" implies that types of shows (westerns, murder mysteries, cop shows) have more or less standardized conventions of plot, setting, and character. There are variations on themes and occasional surprises, but they tend to occur within the framework of these conventions.

The privileged position of the audience regarding the guilt of the bad guys makes it easy to share the frustration of due process requirements. Ever since the due process revolution of the Supreme Court in the early 1960s, the loss or potential loss of cases due to "legal technicalities" has been a favorite theme of cop shows (not to mention political campaigns and popular discussion). Empirical evidence indicates that less than one percent of felony arrests are "lost" due to the exclusionary rule (the rule that illegally obtained evidence can not be used in trial), and that most of those cases so "lost" are drug busts, not violent crimes (Currie, 1985: 66-67). TV cops, however, are in constant danger of having their hard work undone because of the sudden appearance of a "legal technicality." The dramatic and ironic potential of the police having to overcome the very legal system they are supposed to uphold is apparently irresistible to writers of cop shows. Such a plot device would not work in the murder mystery genre. It would be totally incongruous, for example, for Perry Mason or Matlock to get one of their clients "off" on a technicality; these sleuthing defense attorneys always prove the client's innocence, usually by discovering the real murderer.

The fact that the cop show audience knows the bad guys are guilty excuses illegal behavior on the part of the TV police. Several content analyses of police shows of the 1970s showed that the police consistently violated the constitutional rights of suspects, witnesses, and informants (Dominick, 1978; Arons and Katsh, 1977). The danger represented by allowing criminals to escape justice is typically shown as outweighing the benefits of due process rights. For example, Alley (1979: 138-139) describes an episode of *Kojak* (circa 1974) in which Kojak is chastised by a District Attorney for making an illegal arrest in order to cover up an illegal search. Kojak bitterly accuses the District Attorney of living in a "dream world." He asks him "whose side" he is on. Kojak's "realism" is, of course, vindicated when the released criminal commits several more crimes, including murder. The District Attorney's commitment to legality is shown to be naive, even if well-meant.

One ironic aspect of the "legal technicalities" theme is that, even though TV cops are usually portrayed as supercompetent—they solve almost all of their cases by the conclusion of each episode (Arcuri, 1977)—their frustration with due process implies that they cannot perform their job legally. In the *Kojak* episode described earlier, for example, the viewers are not presented with alternatives to the illegal search and arrest. Thus, the questionable tactic is presented as objectively necessary. Further, the format requirements of most cop shows do not allow much room for explanation and justification of due process requirements. The pace of the action must be kept up, the criminal must be apprehended or killed and all the "loose ends" of the plot tied up by the end of the sixty-minute episode. Legal alternatives to the illegal police tactics are likely to take "too much" time: at one level, because the criminal may strike again or get away; but at another level, because the case must be resolved within the standard sixty-minute episode. Hence, the legal "technicalities" appear as arbitrary; the rights of the accused are trivial compared to the danger they present.

How the conventions of the genre shape this interpretation of due process can be illustrated by a counter-example from a cop show that deviated significantly from the typical format and formula of the genre. *Hill Street Blues* was critically acclaimed precisely because of its breaks with traditional format and formula. There were usually several story lines developed at once, each lasting three or four episodes rather than being neatly resolved in one episode. Characters were allowed to develop and change over time, and their motives explained. The police did not always solve the crimes. Moreover, even though it had its share of action and violence, *Hill Street* relied more heavily on dialogue than visual action to advance its stories.

The example begins with the episode in which Officer Joe Coffey is killed. Coffey's partner, Sgt. Lucy Bates, gets a quick glimpse of Coffey's murderer. The audience sees only the same view of the killer as Sgt. Bates; the audience is not in this case "in on" the killer's identity. A suspect fitting the general description is brought into custody and put in a line-up, but Bates is unsure of her ability to make a positive identification. Lt. Buntz, a character whose appreciation of due process is, to put it mildly, somewhat questionable, tortures a confession out of the suspect. He knows the confession can not be used as evidence, but he uses it to tip off Bates that they do indeed have the right man. Bates almost gives in to the temptation to make a positive identification, but backs out at the line-up. Later, another officer illegally shows Bates other evidence linking the suspect to the crime (some clothes fitting Bates' general description of the suspect's attire at the time of the crime). Bates then decides to ask for another chance at the line-up. At about the same time, however, another suspect is brought in; he turns out to be Coffey's actual killer. This episode can be interpreted as a morality play for the rule of law, since the due process restraints placed on the police in fact prevented an innocent man from being punished. Compared to the Kojak episode described earlier, it provides a positive endorsement of due process.

The "legal technicalities" theme appeared frequently in *Hill Street Blues*, although not always in the positive light of the previous example. The cast of Hill Street included a capable advocate of due process, in the person of Public Defender Joyce Davenport. Her dialogues with Capt. Furillo (who was also her lover and later, husband) and with the prosecuting attorney provided a mechanism for explaining and justifying legal rules. The technicalities of due process, then, were given a logical context; they did not seem to spring out of thin air. Nevertheless, her role in the show often functioned to exaggerate the interference of due process with crime control. Armed with an uncanny instinct about police behavior, she apparently had the time to carefully examine every case she was assigned for constitutional infractions by the police. She almost never gave up the adversarial role of defense attorney, in spite of the fact that on *Hill Street*, as in the real world, most cases are decided by plea bargains. In reality, the institutionalization of plea-bargaining means that public defenders often behave in a cooperative rather than adversarial way toward prosecutors (Sudnow, 1965; Blumberg, 1967; Flemming, 1988).

Further, in spite of the sympathetic portrayal of Davenport's commitment to the rule of law, the sheer volume of social disorder shown on *Hill Street* threatened to overwhelm it. Indeed, her commitment to liberal values and legal rules was constantly tested, as when the killer of one of her colleagues was released on a technicality, or Davenport herself was attacked. Over and over the message is given that the police cannot protect society from criminals within the bounds of law. In the story described above, for example, when Officer Coffey's real killer is apprehended, the audience is encouraged to feel relieved that Davenport will not represent this suspect (she cannot, because she is already representing the first suspect). The second suspect, the actual killer, demands a public defender. One of the detectives gleefully informs him that he will "have to settle for some court-appointed shyster." On the surface, the comment is there to allow a sense of justice; it is gratifying to watch the bad guy's smugness turn to nervous squirming. Yet it also implies that the police cannot successfully bring the criminals to justice if defense attorneys insist on performing competently.

Hill Street Blues' deviations from the standard format allowed it to deal with some of the complexities of the conflicts between law enforcement and legal rights. *Miami Vice*, on the other hand, is a return to the action-oriented "you go after the crooks and nail them" format (Gitlin, 1983: 313). There is very little carryover from one episode to the next, except for occasional two-part stories. The stories are told primarily through action; the dialogue is minimalist. Visually, with the hip clothes, fast cars, and sparse but flashy ultramodern sets, the show resembles rock music videos. In fact, a large portion of the show's appeal lies in its use of rock music. Entire scenes are sometimes played out with no dialogue, only music on the soundtrack. In this fast-moving reality, there is no time for subtle debates about the conflicting demands of police work. Legal procedures have a reified, magical quality to them; they are there only to provide dramatic obstacles for the heroes to overcome in their pursuit of the criminals. Where in *Hill Street* the police occasionally commit technical violations because of the complex, confusing, and frustrating nature of the job, Sonny Crocket (Don Johnson) of *Miami Vice* often simply can not be bothered with cumbersome legal procedures. Besides, part of the fun of the show is having a hero who breaks the rules. When Crocket tells his partner Tubbs (Philip Michael Thomas) about teaching a younger cop rules and procedures, Tubbs responds, with mock surprise, "Rules? You taught rules?" Crocket replies, "Yeah. You gotta know the rules before you break 'em. Otherwise it's no fun." Among other things, Crocket often beats information out of petty criminals. Another favorite tactic is to threaten to harass people who ask for a search warrant: "If I have to go and get a search warrant, I'm going to clear my desk of all my other cases and make your life hell for the next six months." These actions are excused because they are directed at unsavory characters, and seen as necessary to get to the main criminals. They are, in other words, portrayed as good police work. While the vice cops seldom suffer consequences from these deliberate infractions, other legal technicalities appear out of the blue to destroy the products of good police work.

This theme is central to an episode involving a former Miami vice detective who had been forced to retire from the police department and admitted to a psychiatric hospital. He pesters the two main characters in the show, Tubbs and Crocket, with tips about gangland activity. His predictions are uncannily accurate, so much so that Tubbs and Crocket arrest him on the assumption that he must be involved. It is then that they discover that he is an ex-cop, obsessed with the notion that a notorious gangster named Arcaro is still alive and covertly running the largest drug-smuggling operations in Miami. Arcaro had been missing and presumed dead for several years. The ex-cop had worked on the Arcaro case for two years, only to see Arcaro released on a "technicality." It was shortly after his release that the gangster disappeared. Apparently, losing this case to a "technicality" drove the officer insane. In the concluding scene it is revealed that the ex-cop had killed Arcaro and hidden the body. Several interesting points are evident in this plot. The crazy detective was/is a good cop, extremely intelligent, maybe even better than the show's heroes, whom he outsmarts several times. Yet even the work of such an expert detective is undone by "legal technicalities." The "legal technicality" is introduced as a random, mysterious element in the story. The audience is not even told what it is: a faulty search warrant, an illegal search, failure to read the suspect his rights. The lack of context and information, coupled with the certainty of the officer's competence, forces the view of the law as dangerously arbitrary and capricious.

The main characters of the show are fatalistically and cynically resigned to such occurrences. In an early episode, Crocket and Tubbs arrest DeMarco, an enforcer for a gangster named Lombard. They force DeMarco to set up a meeting with Tubbs and Lombard; they place a "wire" on DeMarco to record Lombard incriminating himself. DeMarco panics at the meeting and ends up getting killed. Lombard is arrested, but sneers at the cops that he will be released "in time for my two o'clock racquetball game." In the final scene, Tubbs joins Crocket on his boat to lament the fact that Lombard is "probably already out." They simply accept as inevitable that their arrest will not hold up; Crocket suggests they go fishing as "sanity maintenance."

When the details of a legal technicality are revealed, the general rule seems to be: the more trivial the technical infraction of the police relative to the seriousness of the crimes, the greater the dramatic tension. For example, in one episode a case against an important drug dealer is lost because, in filling out the search warrant, one of the detectives typed an "M" instead of an "N" in the license number of the suspect's car. The sense of injustice created is even more intense when the loss of a case due to a technicality occurs because of the deliberate manipulation of a defense attorney. Defense attorneys are not often shown in a positive light on *Miami Vice*. Unlike the defendants on *Hill Street Blues*, the bad guys can afford private attorneys. Therefore, since these attorneys voluntarily associate with and indirectly profit from the criminals, their characters are tainted. They are often depicted as corrupt; one lawyer specializes in getting his drug-dealing clients off by bribing a judge who has a bad gambling habit. Another lawyer in a different episode steals his clients' drugs while the clients are in jail, and sells them himself.

This notion that lawyers who defend immoral clients must themselves be immoral resonates with a popular conception (or better, misconception) about law. A naive view of law, common in American culture, is that law is, or ought to be, equivalent to morality. This partially accounts for the impatience with the exclusionary rule, because common sense tells people that serious crimes like murder and robbery carry greater moral weight than the technical infractions of police. Criminals do not deserve the protection of legal rights. Sonny Crocket reinforces this point with his occasional scolding of defense attorneys, for example: "Does it matter to you that your little manipulations cut loose the guy that killed your best friend? What did you do, trade in your conscience when you passed the bar?" This particular lawyer eventually redeems his conscious by turning against his client. Again, the legal, moral and ethical dilemmas that would be implied by such an action in the real word are simplified in the TV reality by the overwhelming certainty of the client's past guilt and future criminal intentions.

Monsters, Freaks and Animals:
The Essentialization of Deviance and the threat to Social Order

It is frustrating in reality, and a source of dramatic tension in fiction, when "known" criminals exploit the very legal system that they violated in order to avoid their just deserts. These feelings are intensified on Miami Vice because the villains are depicted as almost superhumanly evil, and the legal system (except for the hero cops) is shown as helpless against their onslaught. Again, a comparison with *Hill Street Blues* is informative. On *Hill Street*, the behavior of the criminals, no matter how despicable, was placed in the context of the brutalizing conditions of life in a poor urban ghetto. The *Vice* villains appear to behave the way they do because of the kind of people they are. Hills (1980: 11) refers to this process as essentializing deviance. By exaggerating the deviant traits of a person, treating the deviant behavior as an essential quality of the person, they are defined as fundamentally different from normal people.

A *Miami Vice* story entitled "Viking Bikers from Hell" opens with the recently paroled leader of a motorcycle gang being greeted by his buddies. He announces his intentions to avenge the death of his best friend, a cocaine dealer killed by Crocket, by systematically executing all possible "suspects." To drive home the point that this is a bad man, he casually kills the newest member of the gang, because he does not want to ride as a passenger. Just in case any viewers miss the point, in a later scene a prison psychologist tells the detectives that "Reb" is a "classic psychopath, incapable of human emotions. He's crazy. The devil incarnate."

Repeatedly, the criminals on *Miami Vice* are shown to be not merely drug lords, arms smugglers or whatever, but essentially evil men. The following brief descriptions of an admittedly selective sample of *Miami Vice* bad guys demonstrate this device of essentializing evil. An arms smuggler played by Bruce Willis is also a wife-beater; when she tries to leave him, he hires thugs to rape her lawyer's wife and threaten his daughter. A murderous thief (Ted Nugent) uses his beautiful girlfriend to lure victims; he also beats her up, either to taunt Crocket (who is attracted to her) or to lure him into a meeting by playing on his sympathies for the woman. A drug kingpin is revealed to have forced his daughter into an incestuous relationship. A gang of modern pirates preying on expensive yachts, killing the passengers and stealing drugs, turns out to be a group of bored rich kids who commit violent crimes just because they enjoy it. The preceding examples are unusual, even for *Miami Vice*. The more typical villain is the leader of an organized crime ring, whose essential evil is shown by the way he coldly and casually murders, or orders the murder of, competitors, underlings, cops, and witnesses.

The sheer "otherness" of the villains contributes to the image of a threatening world contained in the myth of crime and punishment. As Crocket tells Tubbs, after the "Viking Bikers from Hell" have been eliminated, "They're out there—the monsters, the freaks, the animals. You think you know the streets, then you discover a whole new level." In constantly providing an interpretation of violent crime as the product of individuals who are fundamentally different from normal people, crime is stripped of its social context. The threat is externalized; it originates outside of society, or, at least, outside of the normal, respectable part of society. The only solution is swift, punitive action against the deviants. Extraordinary individual effort by the hero cops is necessary because social institutions such as the legal system are unprepared to deal with the threat. They can provide neither justice nor protection because they are out of touch with reality and compromised by politics.

In addition to the legal system, a favorite symbol of institutions that no longer meet the needs of society is the federal government, symbolized by federal law enforcement agents. In *Miami Vice*, federal agents of the FBI, CIA, or DEA (Drug Enforcement Administration) are frequently portrayed as incompetent, and occasionally as corrupt. They are the butts of many jokes, as when an obnoxious FBI agent encounters Crocket's pet alligator. Crocket and Tubbs needle the "Feds" for being poor shots, for being easily spotted when on surveillance, and for mistaking a middle-level drug dealer for a drug kingpin. When their investigations cross paths, they refuse to cooperate with the vice detectives, imperiously ordering Crocket and Tubbs to "turn over their files" (they never do). The main problem with the federal agents, according to Crocket and Tubbs, is that they robotically follow bureaucratic procedure, without understanding the "realities" of dealing with criminals. The Internal Affairs Division of their own department is portrayed similarly. Not surprisingly, Crocket and Tubbs are constantly investigated by Internal Affairs, but never for their actual infractions. The Internal Affairs investigator, not having Crocket and Tubbs' "street smarts," is easily fooled by criminals who "set up" the vice detectives.

The recurring theme of an incompetent federal government appeals to the average viewer's sense of alienation from the political structure and frustrations with bureaucratic institutions. Most viewers can readily identify with the experience of bureaucratic rules and regulations that interfere with the performance of a job. Further, when coupled with the failure of the courts to punish the criminals, it appeals to the traditions of vigilante justice (Scheingold, 1984). On the surface, at least, the police dramas do not actually endorse vigilantism. In fact, the TV police are constantly trying to prevent it, both in themselves and in "civilian" characters. The danger of vigilantism symbolizes the breakdown in social order that occurs when the state does not deal effectively with the "monsters, freaks, and animals."

A secondary plot in a three-part episode of *Hunter*, "City Under Siege," involves a crime wave occurring in a high school and the surrounding middle class neighborhood. Fed up with the failure of the police to protect them, some of the residents form citizen patrols, arming themselves with baseball bats. The leader of the vigilantes, a fireman played by former *Hill Street* regular James B. Sikking, kills a teenage boy who was apparently burglarizing an apartment. The local news media make the vigilante into a hero. The police want to charge him with manslaughter, but are prevented by an assistant chief who, because of his political aspirations, does not want to prosecute a hero. The police are portrayed not as incompetent, but as understaffed and paralyzed by the political manipulations of elites. The message is not that vigilantism is good, but that it is inevitable if the police are not allowed to do their job "properly," i.e., with all the force and technology necessary to strike back at the criminal element. Vigilantism is shown as dangerous because it is out of control, in contrast to the controlled use of force by the police.

In *Miami Vice*, this theme is more often played out at the personal level. In one show, a key informant named Rivers is murdered before he can testify against Mosca, an important crime boss. When Mosca is released because of a mistrial, Crocket and Tubbs barely prevent the Rivers' teenage son from shooting him. In another episode, they are not able to prevent a similar death. The wife-abusing arms dealer played by Bruce Willis is killed by the wife in the final scene, following his release. He was not let out on a technicality, but released because the CIA wanted to use him to sell arms to "certain parties" in Latin America, another instance of "politics" interfering with the dispensing of justice. For added visual symbolism, each of these two scenes take place literally on the steps of the courthouse.

Another recurrent theme is that the cops must control their own impulses to vigilantism. For example, there is an episode in which Detective Switek is tempted to conceal information that one drug dealer is planning to murder another because the intended victim is responsible for the murder of Switek's partner. At the last minute he relents, and the cops arrive just in time to participate in a three-way shoot-out with both gangs of drug dealers. Switek's sense of duty is rewarded, since he gets to personally shoot his partner's killer. In an earlier episode, when Tubbs appears too eager to get the drug dealer responsible for the death of his family, Crocket tells him to "get a hold on that vigilante impulse and start acting like a cop."

The phrase "act like a cop" crops up repeatedly in *Miami Vice* scripts. Usually it is heard in the context of situations where one or another of the detectives has, as in the previous two examples, gotten too personally involved in a case. In one instance Crocket repeats it to a detective (not one of the series regulars) who has fallen in love with a teenage prostitute. The series regulars repeatedly fall in love with characters involved in criminal activity. Inevitably, they straighten up and "act like a cop" in the final scene, sometimes killing or arresting the very person with whom they had earlier made love. Given the cynical attitude toward the law in this show, "act like a cop" apparently does not mean to place preeminent value on the law. Rather, it refers to a code of personal honor and loyalty to one's friends who form a type of surrogate family. The TV cops are there to dispense justice and uphold morality, not to enforce the law, as in the *Miami Vice* show where the producer of a pornographic "snuff" film has apparently gotten away with murder. Crocket goes to his studio and slaps him around, lecturing him about how violence is not pretty, glamorous, or artistic. As Crocket leaves, he casually steals a piece of ceramic art and hands it to a homeless man crouched in the alley. This small measure of justice may not balance out the failure of the system, but the vigilante impulses aroused by the story are safely absorbed and contained in the "cop" role.

Crime as Contamination:
The Maintenance of Self in a Corrupt World

Tradition recognizes that there is a danger associated with vigilante justice. The desire for vengeful justice, if unchecked, may reduce the enforcers of law to the moral level of the criminals, thus breeding further disorder. The ultimate challenge for these TV cops is to maintain a decent sense of self and commitment to the "private code" (Gitlin, 1983: 317) in a hostile world where justice can not be counted on to prevail and elites can not be trusted. The threat of crime to society is mirrored as a threat to self.

The 1988 season of *Miami Vice* featured an absurd two-part story in which Sonny Crocket suffers from amnesia. He takes on the identity of "Sonny Burnett," his undercover role. In a later episode, Crocket reluctantly agrees to a marathon session with a police psychologist. He explains to her that he is frightened at the recognition that he is a type of "junkie," addicted to the glamour and violence of undercover work. "You get to where you like your sewer," he confesses. Criminality is defined in these exchanges as a kind of disease that one might "catch" if one is exposed too often.

The heroes, of course, generally overcome the threat of contamination. Midway between the hero cops and the "monsters and animals," however, are characters who are basically good or normal, but are corrupted by the world of crime. Sometimes these are characters who are forced to cooperate with the "real" criminals, because of threats to themselves or to their families. A stock plot device is that of the "good cop gone bad." For example, during the investigation of a pornography ring, Crocket and Tubbs encounter an undercover FBI agent who apparently has "gone over to the other side" reveals Tubbs' and Crocket's true identities to the gang leader. In the end the FBI man "acts like a cop" by rescuing Tubbs and Crocket, but they receive word later that he killed himself during the investigation of his corrupt activities. In another episode a female DEA agent cooperates with a major drug dealer to stage phony arrests of other drug dealers, from whom they take money and drugs. She needs the money to cover the medical expenses of her husband, a wounded former DEA agent, and her son, who needs a kidney transplant. Like the FBI agent in the previous example, she partially recovers her "true self" by "acting like a cop" in the final scene.

The Bottom Line:
Reification and Individualization of Social Problems.

In addition to the theme of loss and redemption of self, the two examples in the previous section share another interesting feature. In each case, the "contamination" of the cop can be attributed to the failure of the institution for which he/she works. The FBI agent "went over to the other side" because he was left "under" too long. His superiors refused to pull him from the case when he asked. One might also wonder why, in the second case, the DEA did not provide adequate medical coverage for its agents, especially a hero wounded in action. This question is left unasked in the show; it is simply taken to be a fact of life that catastrophic medical needs can destroy a family and drive at least one of its members to crime. The failure to refer to this larger issue reduces the conflict to a matter of individual character.

This reduction of structural problems to individual problems serves to solidify and reify the myth of crime as purely a product of bad persons. For example, there is an episode of *Miami Vice* in which Tubbs is lured to an island by the family of Calderone, a drug dealer slain by Tubbs in a previous episode. He is stranded on the island, pursued by three gangsters determined to kill him. The islanders offer Tubbs no help, because the island used to be Calderone's major base of operations. In fact, they resent Tubbs because the island's economy was better off when Calderone was active. There is no time in an action show to adequately describe the ways the drug trade corrupts legitimate economies and exploits people in underdeveloped areas. Consequently, the issue is again presented as a simple moral choice for the islanders. The drug trade is a tempting reality in which individuals must summon the moral courage to "just say no."

By focusing on individual coping, even direct attacks on existing power structures in society are contained and neutralized. For example, in the Fall 1985 season premier of *Miami Vice*, Crocket and Tubbs discover that their efforts to bust a major Colombian drug ring have been thwarted by the behind-the-scenes manipulations of banking capitalists. In the final scene, they enter the darkened lair of a vampirish-looking corporate executive who explains economic "reality" to them. The "reality" is that powerful business interests have loaned enormous amounts of money to Colombia; the only export of Colombia likely to generate enough capital to pay off these loans is cocaine. Of course Crocket and Tubbs must "act like cops" and not like citizens of a democracy. They cannot use their primary means of taking action (arresting or shooting the criminal) because the capitalist is technically not a criminal. They have gained knowledge about the world with which they must deal, but they have no practical way of translating this knowledge into action.

Other critiques of cop shows have typically focused on their lack of realism. In particular, some authors have expressed concerns that cop shows will lead to exaggerated fears of crime (Gerbner and Gross, 1976) or to unrealistic expectations of the effectiveness of the police (Arcuri, 1977; Inciardi and Dee, 1987). The analysis presented here suggests that it does not really matter that shows like *Miami Vice* are often outrageously unrealistic in their portrayals of law enforcement because they are not really about crime. Rather, they are fantasies and fables about individual heroism in a confusing and corrupt world. That world itself appears on television, as it does in everyday life, as a reified reality, one that is beyond the ability of individuals to change.

Bibliography

Alley, R.S. (1979) "Television drama." In H. Newcomb (ed.) *Television: The Critical View*. New York: Oxford University Press.

Arcuri, A. (1977) "You can't take fingerprints off water: police officers' views toward 'cop' television shows." Human Relations 30, 3: 237-247.

Arons, S. and Katsh, E. (1977) "How TV cops flout the law." Saturday Review (March 19): 11-19.

Blumberg, A.S. (1967) "The practice of law as a confidence game." Law and Society Review 1: 15-39.

――― (1985) "The police and the social system: reflections and prospects." In A.S. Blumberg and E. Niederhoffer (eds.) *The Ambivalent Force*. New York: Holt, Rinehart and Winston.

Currie, E. (1985) *Confronting Crime*. New York: Pantheon.

Dominick, J.R. (1978) "Crime and law enforcement in the mass media." In C.W. Winick (ed.) *Deviance and Mass Media*. Beverly Hills, CA: Sage.

Flemming, R.B. (1988) "Client games: defense attorney perspectives on their relations with criminal clients." In G.F. Cole (ed.) *Criminal Justice: Law and Politics* (5th ed.). Pacific Grove, CA: Brooks/Cole.

Gerbner, G. and Gross, L. (1976) "Living with television: the violence profile." Journal of Communication 26, 2: 173-200.

Gerbner, G., Gross, L., Morgan M. and Signorielli (1980) "The mainstreaming of America: violence profile no. 11." Journal of Communication 30, 3: 13-45.

Gitlin, T. (1979) "Prime time ideology: the hegemonic process in television entertainment." Social Problems 26, 3: 251-266.

_____ (1983) *Inside Prime Time*. New York: Pantheon.

Hills, S.L. (1980) *Demystifying Social Deviance*. New York: McGraw-Hill.

Inciardi, J.A. and Dee, J.L. (1987) "From the keystone cops to *Miami Vice:* images of policing in popular culture." Journal of Popular Culture 21, 2: 84-102.

Mankiewicz, F. and Swerlow, J. (1978) *Remote Control*. New York: New York Times Books.

Schaefer, R., Vanderbok, W.G. and Wisnoski, E. (1979) "Television police shows and attitudes toward the police." Journal of Police Science and Administration 7, 1: 104-113.

Scheingold, S.A. (1984) *The Politics of Law and Order*. New York: Longman.

Media Murder and Mayhem:
Violence on Network Television

Eleanor Lyon

Violence in the media has been a public and social scientific concern for many years. Urban protests and increased reports of violent crime in the 1960s and 1970s led many observers to question the impact of widespread media violence. Numerous federal investigatory bodies have been created since that time to assess available evidence on connections between violence in the media and violent behavior.

The National Commission on the Causes and Prevention of Violence, formed in the late 1960s, devoted considerable attention to media violence generally (Baker and Ball, 1969). Shortly thereafter, concerns were focused on the effects of television violence on children, in particular (Surgeon General's Scientific Advisory Committee on Television and Social Behavior, 1971; Cater and Strickland, 1975). Many media critics have worried that television violence contributes to aggressive behavior among children who are heavy viewers, but research results have remained inconsistent (e.g. Eron, *et al.*, 1972; Feshbach and Singer, 1971; Heath, Kruttschnitt and Ward, 1986; Singer, Singer and Rapaczynski, 1984).

Similarly, researchers have studied media images of women. They have found that women are commonly shown to be dominated by men (Lemon, 1978) and are more likely to be victims of violence than they are to commit violent acts (Gerbner *et al.*, 1979). Feminists have argued that media depictions of sexual violence against women, in particular, encourage women's sexual and physical victimization (e.g. Lederer, 1980; Sommers and Check, 1987). These concerns have spawned numerous studies, a growing empirical literature, two federal investigatory commissions in less than twenty years, and increasingly heated debate (see, for example, Paletz, 1988; Linz and Donnerstein, 1988, and reply by Zillmann and Bryant, 1988; Einsiedel, 1988; Malamuth and Donnerstein, 1984; Bryant and Zillmann, 1986; Frost and Stauffer, 1988; Donnerstein and Berkowitz, 1981).

These studies of the impacts of media violence have examined potential effects of three major types. One is the effect on aggressive behavior by viewers—individually or collectively. Research in this area has investigated whether viewers learn violent behaviors from the media (a "modeling" effect), become less violent themselves by experiencing violence vicariously (a "cathartic" effect), or become stimulated to commit violent acts (an "arousal" effect).

Another type of impact is the effect on attitudes toward violence and its acceptability. Research in this area has focused primarily on whether the cumulative effect of exposure to repeated violence in the media "desensitizes" viewers, such that they regard violence as less harmful over time.

A third type of effect is on viewers' perceptions of "reality"—do those who are exposed to large amounts of media violence see their world differently than those who are not? Then, if their view is different, what effect does that have on their attitudes and behavior?

Research in the first two areas has achieved inconsistent results (Messner, 1986; Eysenck and Nias, 1978; Linz, Donnerstein, and Penrod, 1984; NIMH, 1982; Phillips and Hensley, 1984). There have been some inconsistent results in the third area, as well, but there is some agreement that repeated exposure to media violence is associated with heightened fear of personal victimization and the perception that the world is a dangerous place (Jaehnig, Weaver, and Fico, 1981; Gerbner, *et al.*, 1980; Comstock, 1977).

Although these effects can be found for different media, some researchers have argued that television may have the greatest impact, and is therefore especially important to study (Gerbner and Gross, 1976; Comstock, 1977). They point out that nearly everyone in American society has access to a television, that three quarters of the time spent with all media is spent with television, and that the average number of hours spent daily watching television ranks third behind work and sleep (Comstock, 1977: 321). Television is accessible in other ways, as well: it does not require an ability to read, many channels are available "free," it operates around the clock, and it is located within the home. For these reasons, television has become the medium shared by all groups in American society—regardless of age, race or ethnicity, social class, gender, or education (Gerbner and Gross, 1976: 176).

Gerbner and his associates have been studying violence on network television since 1967. They have looked at the frequency and types of violence shown, as well as who commits it, and against whom. They have also investigated "the conceptions of social reality that viewing cultivates in child and adult audiences" (Gerbner and Gross, 1976: 174), and found that heavy viewers sense greater danger in the world around them than do light viewers. The patterns in television content and the impact on viewers have remained relatively stable over time (Gerbner *et al.*, 1980). However, little has been reported on the content of television violence since 1980.

Television violence may be especially important for its ultimate effect on attitudes and perceptions which influence social policy. As Gerbner has stated, television functions "to demonstrate how power works in society and show who can get away with what" (Gerbner, 1977: 359). Further, violence on television "may cultivate exaggerated assumptions about the extent of threat and danger in the world and lead to demands for protection" (Gerbner and Gross, 1976: 194).

A small study was conducted recently which relates to these issues. It looked at violence in network television programming, and documented characteristics of violent episodes. A summary of relevant results follows, accompanied by a discussion of the accuracy of the images and their potential impact.

Violence on Network Television: 1988

Prime time week night and Saturday morning network television programs were studied for violent content in the fall of 1988.[1] Out of all 157 of the diverse programs shown during the weeks and times covered, at least one violent incident occurred in nearly two-thirds (65%). Further, violence appeared in 61% of the prime time fictional shows, but 79% of the Saturday morning children's programs. This represents a decline from the 70% for prime time reported for 1979 (Gerbner et al., 1980: 13).[2]

Of course, the appearance of violence varied with different types of programs[3] and the times at which they were shown. *All* of the "action" shows, for example, contained violence, compared to 80% of the cartoons, 79% of the "serious" (fiction) programs, 54% of the news/documentary shows, and 31% of the comedies. The "family viewing" hour (8 to 9 p.m. EST on week nights) remained the least violent, with 42% of the shows containing violence, perhaps because over half of these programs (58%) were comedies. In contrast, violence appeared in 67% of the 9 o'clock and 75% of the 10 o'clock shows.

The remainder of the results of this research will be reported for the fictional shows on week nights which contained violence—to describe the types of violence and their impact.[4] Although children's programming is also vitally important, the study results discussed here focus on adults.

Who Commits Violence on Television?

Over all, as seen in the sample programs, television remains predominantly white, middle class, and male.[5] These characteristics apply to most of the people shown initiating violence (the "violents"), as well. Of all the incidents recorded, 84% of the violents were male, 90% were White (while just 3% were Black and 3% were Latino), and 70% belonged to the middle class (or had "mixed" class characteristics). Notably, a larger proportion of the violents were upper class (19%) than were lower class (11%). In addition, 38% of the violents were "good" characters (primarily law enforcement personnel or adventure heroes), and 44% were "bad" (the remainder were "mixed").

A closer look at the way these characteristics were combined reveals some predictable patterns. For example, whether the violents were "good" or "bad" characters varied by sex and class. Female violents were more likely to be "good" (44% compared to 37% of the men) and less likely to be clearly "bad" (32%, compared to 46% of the men). Similarly, a larger percentage of upper class violents were "good" characters (43%) than was true for lower class violents (of whom 30% were "good"). A majority of the lower class violents were clearly "bad" characters (57%), while only 38% of those from the upper class were "bad." While the number of non-White violents was too small for this analysis, it is notable that there was *not one* "good" Latino violent in the sample. Finally, a larger percentage of female than male violents were upper class (35% compared to 16%).

These figures demonstrate some important points about depictions of violent characters on television. They are nearly as likely to be "good" characters as "bad". Although it is not a common occurrence, when women are violent, is it more likely to be socially approved (committed by "good" characters) than not; the same is true for upper class violents. Lower class violents are seen least often, but when they are, they are disproportionately male and their behavior is not socially approved (they are "bad").

Who Are the Victims of Violence on Television?

Television's victims of violence, as seen in the sample of programs, were even more unreflective of the general population than the initiators just described. A quarter of the victims were women, 93% were White (5% were Black, and there were *no* Latino victims), and 23% were upper class (64% were middle or "mixed" class, while just 13% were lower class). Further, over half (56%) of the victims were "good" characters, and only 22% were "bad".

As was true for the initiators of violence, the victims' combination of characteristics show interesting variations based on sex and class. A full 80% of the female victims were "good" characters, and only 4% were "bad", compared to 48% and 28% of the male victims, respectively. In addition, the women victims were twice as likely to be upper class (36% *vs.* 18% of the men) and less likely to be lower class (5% of the female victims, compared to 16% of the men). Nearly two-thirds (64%) of the upper class victims were "good" characters (and just 10% were "bad"), compared to only two-fifths of the lower class victims (of whom 43% were "bad"). Finally, again, there were no Latino victims, and just 5% were Black; of these, four-fifths were "good" characters, compared to 56% of the White victims.

Notably, there were few child victims in the sampled programs (they comprised 10% of the total), and less than one percent were elderly. The majority of victims were classified as "settled adults."

The data on victims reveals patterns in televised portrayals of who is most vulnerable and who most deserves violence. Women and upper class characters are disproportionately vulnerable to violence, especially upper class women (they are predominantly "good" or "innocent" victims). Both groups are also more likely to be victims than violents. Lower class characters (and men, to a lesser extent), in contrast, are more likely to be violents than victims, and to "deserve" violence because they are "bad".

What Is the Relationship between Violents and Victims?

Over all, relatively little family violence was shown in the sampled television programs. Just 7% of the incidents involved family members, compared to 49% in which the violent and victim were acquaintances, and 43% in which they were strangers. Most of the family violence occurred on "serious" shows, where it accounted for 12% of the incidents; over half (52%) of the violence on "action" shows occurred between strangers. Women were more likely than men to initiate violence against someone known to them: 15% of their victims were family members and 62% were acquaintances, compared to 5% and 47%, respectively, of the men's victims.

The violence also occurred most frequently between members of the same social class; it accounted for sixty-five percent of all the incidents in the sample. When violence was shown across classes, however, it was more likely to be initiated by lower class characters. Over a quarter (26%) of their victims were upper class, while only 10% of the victims of upper class violents were lower class.

Similarly, most of the violence shown was intraracial, but this was only because so few non-Whites were shown at all. Of all the violent incidents, 85% involved White violents and victims. However, *all* of the non-White violents victimized Whites, and *all* of the Black victims experienced violence at the hands of Whites. In other words, all of the violent incidents which involved non-White characters were interracial.

Additionally, most of the violent incidents (64%) occurred between men. About a fifth (21%) of the incidents involved women victimized by men, while the reverse was true in 11% of the cases. Just 5% of the incidents showed violence between women.

Finally, it was common to see violence initiated by "bad" characters against "good" ones; this was true for 29% of all of the incidents sampled. "Bad" violents directed 65% of their violence toward "good" victims, and 20% against other "bad" characters. The "good" violents, in contrast, directed violence at "good" characters just less than half of the time (49%), while 30% was aimed at "bad" characters.

What Type of Violence Is Shown?

For an incident to be recorded as "violence" (cf. Gerbner *et al.*, 1978: 179), it had to involve a clear physical act or a threat of death or physical injury. Violence, then, could occur through a variety of means. Of all the violent incidents recorded, hands or feet were the most common weapons (44%), followed by guns (26%), threats (7%) and knives (4%). All other weapons, such as clubs, whips, ropes, fire, and other objects, were used in a fifth of the incidents.

As might be expected, female violents were less likely to be shown using their hands or fists (26% of the time) than were men, who used their hands in 40% of the incidents in which they initiated the violence. In contrast, the women were more commonly shown using a gun (32%) or a knife (9%) than were the men (24% and 3%, respectively). A substantial proportion of the violence, then, involved men having fist fights with one another.

What Impact Does the Violence Have on the Victim?

Over all, the victim was killed in 18% of the sampled incidents, in 28% the victim was physically injured, and in 31% the victim was "coerced"— forced to do something to avoid death or injury. In the remainder of the cases the victim was able to escape from the situation through active resistance or flight and was not injured physically. The violence resulted in death most commonly on "action" shows (38% of the incidents), less in "serious" programs (8%), and least in comedies (6% of the incidents).

The impact of the violence on the victim varied substantially from one type of situation to another. Female violents, for example, were less likely to kill or injure their victims (36%) than were male violents (49%). The presence and type of weapons also made a difference in the impact on the victim. For example, the victim was killed in nearly half (48%) of the incidents involving a gun, and a quarter of the episodes where a knife was used. In contrast, the victim died in only 6% of the incidents involving hands and 13% where other weapons were used. Of all the victims killed, 65% were shot.

The impact of violence also varied by victim characteristics. For example, women were less likely than men to be killed (9%) or injured (13%) and more likely to be coerced (47%). In contrast, 22% of the men were killed, a third were injured, and just over a quarter (26%) were coerced. No children or adolescents were killed in the sampled shows, while nearly a quarter of the adults died in the violence. Further, the violence had a much more serious impact on lower class victims than on those from the upper class. Twelve percent of upper class victims were killed, and 38% were killed or injured, in contrast to 31% of lower class victims killed and 79% killed or injured.

Similarly, the consequences for "good" victims were much less serious than for "bad" victims. Of the former, 11% were killed, 29% were injured, and 34% were coerced. In contrast, a third of the "bad" victims were killed, 31% were injured, and 27% were coerced. In these cases, presumably, the viewer is supposed to believe that the victim "deserved" the outcome.

Finally, the relationship between the victim and the violent affected the outcome of the incident for the victim. In the cases where they were family members, the result was death 7% of the time and physical injury in 21% of the instances. Death occurred in 13% of the incidents between acquaintances, and injury in another quarter. Violence between strangers was the most dangerous: it resulted in death a quarter of the time and in physical injury in another 32% of the incidents.

Television Violence vs. "Real" Violence

The picture of violence drawn from the sample of programs in this study as well as others is distorted in important ways, compared to what is known about "real" violence.[6] First, the virtual absence on television of minority group members as both violents and victims is glaring. Drawing from the most recent government statistics on crime and crime victims (U.S. Department of Justice, 1988a and 1988b), for example, it is clear that Black males have the highest victimization rates of any group. Further, the overwhelming majority of violent crimes is intraracial.

Second, the preponderance of middle and upper class characters on television introduces distortions. Upper class people are not victimized by reported violent crime at anywhere near the rate they appeared in the sampled programs. Instead, the majority of known victims of violent crime come from the lower classes.

Third, family violence is pervasive; available evidence indicates that it can be found in at least half of American families, directed at adults and children (Straus and Gelles, 1988). Further, intrafamily homicides, with both adults and children as victims, account for over a quarter of the murders committed each year. The virtual absence of family violence seen in the sampled television programs, and the relatively minor consequences of that which was shown is a major departure from "reality."

Finally, with the exception of family violence, the incidents shown were unrealistically likely to end in the victim's death. Considering that the violent episodes recorded for the study included *threats* of imminent physical injury or death, having nearly one-fifth of them result in death may contribute to perceptions of violence as more dangerous than it is.

Discussion

It should be clear that the presentation of violence in fictionalized programs on network television is pervasive and departs in systematic ways from what is known about "real" violence. Despite the fact that these presentations are "fiction," the vivid imagery, dramatic impact, and sheer repetition influence public perceptions of violence.

A recent statewide random telephone survey[7] was conducted to investigate public understanding and awareness of crime and violence and to explore selected policy alternatives. Some of the poll's findings are directly pertinent to the impact of television portrayals.

First, it was notable that nearly a third of the respondents said that either "violence" or "murder" or "death" came to mind when they heard the word "crime." However, those who said they trusted television more than other sources of information were more likely to give the murder or death response than were other groups; further, those who offered this image cited television as the reason for their answer. The same pattern, distinguishing those who most trusted television compared to other information sources, held when respondents were asked what came to their mind when they heard the word "violence"—murder and death were their most frequent responses. Notably, those who trusted television were less likely than other groups to think of "domestic violence" in response to this question. Further, those who trusted television were more likely than others to maintain that most violence occurs in public places (instead of in the home). For this sample, then, there were systematic differences in general perceptions of crime and violence for those who trusted television.

The survey also found differences associated with fears of personal victimization. Those who reported increased concern about violence or for their personal safety, for example, cited television as the reason. Respondents who trusted television were also more likely than others to reveal that they thought they were likely to be mugged or harassed by street gangs within the next year, and to cite television as the reason. Their concern about being mugged was higher even though they had lower rates of mugging victimization than the other groups during the three years prior to the survey.

Finally, the poll found some differences in policy priorities for the group who most trusted television. They were more likely than others to be sympathetic toward crime victims and to stress the importance of supporting them. Respondents who trusted television were also more likely to advocate increases in police and to have difficulty conceiving of alternatives to jail in response to crime.

The differences found in the poll are sensible in the context of the frequency and patterns of violence in television programming revealed by the content analysis. Together, these two studies provide additional support for the years of research conducted by Gerbner and his associates, and for the concerns they raise:

Violence plays a key role in television's portrayal of the social order. It is the simplest and cheapest means to demonstrate who wins in the game of life and the rules by which the game is played. It tells us who are the aggressors and who are the victims. It demonstrates who has the power and who must acquiesce to that power. It tells us who should be feared...(Gerbner, *et al.*, 1979: 180)

[Televised violence] may cultivate exaggerated assumptions about the extent of threat and danger in the world and lead to demands for protection...A heightened sense of risk and insecurity (different for groups of varying power) is more likely to increase acquiescence to and dependence upon established authority, and to legitimize its use of force...(Gerbner and Gross, 1976: 194).

The available evidence from a variety of studies, then, indicates that violence on television affects public perceptions of violence, and these perceptions influence attitudes and preferences about related public policy. Although the prevalence of violence on television appears to be declining slowly, it still shows class, race, and gender biases and other distortions from known "reality." Upper class violents are "good" characters, lower class violents are "bad." Lower class victims are "bad," and are likely to be killed, while upper class people are vulnerable, but not consequentially so. Women are more likely to be victimized by violence than to commit it, but their victimization is relatively harmless. Black, Latino and other minority group members are infrequently seen in violent incidents, but are seen more frequently as violents than as victims, thus removing them from public view as among the victims deserving sympathy and support. Family violence is infrequent and, when it occurs, is relatively without impact. Finally, televised violence disproportionately leads to death.

Increased fear alone affects the quality of public life (Riedel, 1987; Ortega and Myles, 1987), and affects the relatively powerless more than the powerful. If public policy were based on the patterns just summarized, it could also be a frightening prospect. It could increase race and class divisions, take women's victimization less seriously, and reduce the already limited attention to pervasive violence in the family. Further reductions in fictionalized violence on television, coupled with educational programming on the "realities" of violence, might help to restore needed perspective.

Notes

[1]Data were collected from the three major networks during six weeks of fall, 1988. Programs which occurred between 8 and 11 week nights and between 8 and 11 Saturday mornings were coded from one network each week on an alternating basis. Data were collected on the type of show, major characters, and plot summary; in addition, a variety of information was collected on each violent incident. The definition of "violent episode" and the coding categories for many variables were the same as those used by Gerbner and his associates (see Gerbner *et al.*, 1980). The recorded characteristics of the violent incidents were selected from those used by Gerbner, with the addition of data on the relationship between the "violent" and the "victim", and incident impact categories beyond being "killed".

Data were gathered on a total of 157 programs which occurred during the designated time period. Some of these included news specials, documentaries, and variety entertainment programs, in addition to Saturday morning children's cartoons. As Gerbner has found, the cartoons contained more violence than other types of programs. Discussion here focuses on the 62 week night, non-cartoon, fictional programs which contained any violence.

[2]Gerbner and his associates reported that 92% of weekend children's programs contained violence in 1979, but his sample also included shows aired from 11 a.m. to 2 p.m. and on Sunday, so it is not fully comparable.

[3]"Action" shows included police and adventure series and movies; they accounted for 11% of the total sample. "Serious" shows consisted of fictional dramas, both series and movies; they made up 24% of the sample. The remaining categories are self-explanatory; 31% of the sample programs were comedies, 8% were news or documentary programs, and 26% were cartoons.

[4]News and documentaries were excluded because they are more subject to seasonal and other variations likely to distort the sample. The fall of 1988 included the Olympics and news specials devoted to the presidential election. This discussion focuses on programs aimed at "entertainment." As Gerbner and Gross have observed, "Entertainment is the most broadly effective educational fare in any culture" (1976: 177). Of the 62 fictional programs included here, 48% were "serious," 27% were "action" shows, and 24% were comedies.

[5]Up to four major characters were described for each program. Of the 566 characters recorded for the entire 157 shows in the sample, 375 (66%) were male.

[6]Of course, it is hard to know about actual violence with certainty because we rely on violent crime and victimization statistics and surveys.

[7]The telephone survey involved interviews with 600 adults, 18 years or older, throughout the state of Connecticut. It was conducted in January, 1988, by the Analysis Group, Inc., of New Haven, CT. Questions addressed perceptions and experiences associated with crime and violence, and sought public policy priorities in these areas.

Bibliography

Baker, R. and S. Ball (1969) *Mass Media and Violence,* staff report to the National Commission on the Causes and Prevention of Violence, Volume 9, Washington, D.C.: U.S. Government Printing Office.

Bryant, J. and D. Zillmann (eds.) (1986) *Perspectives on Media Effects,* Hillsdale, NJ: Lawrence Erlbaum.

Cater, D. and S. Strickland (1975) *T.V. Violence and the Child,* New York: Russell Sage.

Comstock, G. (1977) "The Effects of Television," in J. Fireman (ed.), *TV Book,* New York: Workman, pp. 321-324.

Donnerstein, E. and L. Berkowitz (1981) "Victim Reactions in Aggressive Erotic Films as a Factor in Violence Against Women," *Journal of Personality and Social Psychology* 41: 710-724.

Einsiedel, E. (1988) "The British, Canadian, and U.S. Pornography Commissions and Their Use of Social Science Research," *Journal of Communication* 38: 108-121.

Eron, L., L. Huesmann, M. Lefkowitz, and L. Walder (1972) "Does Television Violence Cause Aggression?" *American Psychologist* 27: 253-263.

Eysenck, H. and D. Nias (1978) *Sex, Violence, and the Media,* New York: Harper and Row.

Feshbach, S. and R. Singer (1971) *Television and Aggression,* San Francisco: Jossey-Bass.

Freedman, J. (1984) "Effect of Television Violence on Aggression," *Psychological Bulletin* 96: 227-246.

Frost, R. and J. Stauffer (1988) "The Effects of Social Class, Gender, and Personality on Physiological Responses to Filmed Violence," *Journal of Communication* 38: 29-45.

Gerbner, G., L. Gross, M. Morgan, and N. Signorelli (1980) "The 'Mainstreaming' of America: Violence Profile No. 11," *Journal of Communication* 30: 10-29.

Gerbner, G., L. Gross, N. Signorelli, M. Morgan, and M. Jackson-Beeck (1979) "The Demonstration of Power: Violence Profile No. 10," *Journal of Communication* 29: 177-196.

Gerbner, G. (1977) "The Real Threat of Television Violence," in J. Fireman (ed.), *TV Book,* New York: Workman, pp. 358-359.

Gerbner, G. and L. Gross (1976) "Living with Television: The Violence Profile," *Journal of Communication* 26: 173-199.

Heath, L., C. Kruttschnitt and D. Ward (1986) "Television and Violent Criminal Behavior: Beyond the Bobo Doll," *Violence and Victims* 1: 177-190.

Jaehnig, W., D. Weaver, and F. Fico (1981) "Reporting Crime and Fearing Crime in Three Communities," *Journal of Communication* 31: 88-96.

Lederer, L. (ed.) (1980) *Take Back the Night,* New York: William Morrow.

Lemon, J. (1978) "Dominant or Dominated? Women on Prime-Time Television," in G. Tuchman, A. Daniels, and J. Benet (eds), *Hearth and Home: Images of Women in the Mass Media,* New York: Oxford University Press, pp. 51-68.

Linz, D., E. Donnerstein, and S. Penrod (1984) "The Effects of Multiple Exposures to Filmed Violence Against Women," *Journal of Communication* 34: 130-147.

Linz, D. and E. Donnerstein (1988) "The Methods and Merits of Pornography Research," *Journal of Communication* 38: 122-126.

Malamuth, N. and E. Donnerstein (eds.) (1984) *Pornography and Sexual Aggression,* Orlando, Fla: Academic Press.

Messner, S. (1986) "Television Violence and Violent Crime: An Aggregate Analysis," *Social Problems* 33: 218-235.

National Institute of Mental Health (1982) *Television and Behavior: Ten Years of Scientific Progress and Implications for the Eighties,* Washington, D.C.: U.S. Government Printing Office.

Ortega, S. and J. Myles (1987) "Race and Gender Effects on Fear of Crime: An Interactive Model with Age," *Criminology* 25: 133-152.

Paletz, D. (1988) "Pornography, Politics, and the Press: The U.S. Attorney General's Commission on Pornography," *Journal of Communication* 38: 92-106.

Phillips, D. and J. Hensley (1984) "When Violence is Rewarded or Punished: The Impact of Mass Media Stories on Homicide," *Journal of Communication* 34: 101-116.

Riedel, M. (1987) "Stranger Violence: Perspectives, Issues, and Problems," *Journal of Criminal Law and Criminology* 78: 223-258.

Singer, J., D. Singer, and W. Rapaczynski (1984) "Family Patterns and Television Viewing as Predictors of Children's Beliefs and Aggression," *Journal of Communication* 34: 73-89.

Sommers, E. and J. Check (1987) "An Empirical Investigation of the Role of Pornography in the Verbal and Physical Abuse of Women," *Violence and Victims* 2: 189-209.

Straus, M. and R. Gelles (1988) *Intimate Violence,* New York: Simon and Schuster.

Surgeon General's Scientific Advisory Committee on Television and Social Behavior (1971) *Television and Growing Up: The Impact of Televised Violence,* report to the Surgeon General of the United States, Washington, D.C.: U.S. Government Printing Office.

U.S. Department of Justice (1988a) *Criminal Victimization in the United States, 1986,* Bureau of Justice Statistics, Washington, D.C.: U.S. Government Printing Office.

U.S. Department of Justice (1988b) *Uniform Crime Report of the United States, 1987,* Federal Bureau of Investigation, Washington, D.C.: U.S. Government Printing Office.

Zillmann, D. and J. Bryant (1988) "Response to Linz and Donnerstein," *Journal of Communication* 38: 127-134.

Moralizing Resentment:
The Morton Downey, Jr. Show and
Conservative Populism

Jon D. Cruz

"Mort! Mort! Mort! Mort!..." If this were the death chant of an ancient
Roman audience, the object of attention would be doomed. But this is the
enlivening welcome given nightly to television talk-show host, Morton
Downey, Jr. Launched for national syndication in May 1988, *The Morton
Downey, Jr. Show* found its way into most major urban cable television
markets in the country. In a rather short period, Morton Downey, Jr. became
something of a celebrity. The popular press (*Newsweek, Time, People
Magazine*), the "pop" press (*Rolling Stone*), film and television industry
trade publications (*Variety, Broadcasting*), and some hard news enterprises
(*New York Times, Wall Street Journal*) presented stories, editorials and think-
pieces on Downey's show. Television, too, paid him attention. Serious in-
depth news programs such as *The MacNeil/Lehrer News Hour, West 57th*,
and *Nightline* took up the case of Morton Downey, Jr. Merchandising his
celebrity, Downey has written a horn-tooting book,[1] and is promoting a
game ("Loudmouth") based on the talk-show.[2] In early 1989, Downey was
also a guest on *Saturday Night Live*, an indicator that he had acquired
some of the cultural capital required to appear on "hip" television.

The rapid success of *The Morton Downey, Jr. Show* left television
observers disturbed. Signaling distress, commentators rallied around key
themes—the digression of protocol, the violation of acceptable boundaries
of talk-show standards, the celebrated dismissal of public civility. What was
particularly aggravating was what the show represented in its production
values and its *manner* of delivery. Downey claimed to be providing an
"information-generating" show. Critics saw, instead, the transformation of
discourse into irrational verbal bludgeoning. Intentionally obnoxious and
rude, Downey was selling.[3]

The *Downey Show* has since become television history. By fall of 1989,
most stations had dropped the program due to lack of *sponsor* support.
His disappearance should not be equated with the disappearance of an
important cultural sensibility. Downey's show coincided with the rise of
what some in the television industry call "reality programming." While
Downey himself is no longer a nightly feature, he was a significant part

of the rise of reality programming which, as a cultural form, has since flourished. What follows is an attempt to illuminate some important aspects of the political culture and the larger socio-cultural context which helped to make possible a program like the Downey show.

While most commentators have framed Downey as deviant and his style as aberrant, he is actually quite consistent with conservative strands within contemporary American popular *political* culture, especially in the way his treatment of social issues feeds from, and back into, conservative views. He is more populist than deviant, something he and his production company recognize. As Bob Pittman, the producer of *The Morton Downey, Jr. Show* (Pittman also produced and launched *Music Television Video*) notes,

[T]he element that makes Mort work is that he is truly not a conservative; he is a populist. If you watch him, he is sometimes on the liberal side of the issue. He bounces around. What he's really interested in is the *little man's opinion: that's really what he is representing*....[H]e makes a great argument and does it with what I think works best on TV—emotion and passion. Downey doesn't take an intellectual approach to things, but an emotional approach.[4]

If we were to dwell on talk show host persona, then Downey stands out with a screaming presence. But if we consider the broader cultural context, and in particular the success of the New Right and the neo-conservatives[5] to seize certain topics of the public agenda, and to portray the crisis of select social issues by rooting them in the asserted failure of democratic liberalism, then Downey is merely an amplifier of already existing and somewhat mainstream sensibilities. Labelling him "deviant," a "media crank," obscures his cultural fit with sensibilities that may very well be found in the mainstream. Since he has become something of a national spectacle, he signifies a cultural phenomenon that deserves attention.

To be sure, Downey's show is a nightly demonstration of how to violate traditional television talk show protocol. With his highly opinionated and knee-jerk responses to both his guests and the issues, Downey staked out new territory. He became quickly known for his trademarks—a no-emotions-or-expletives-barred format designed to crescendo beyond argument to sheer hollering matches, and a flaunted and brazen disregard for the ordinary, tamed civil language of talk-show chatter. Downey begins each program with a monologue that simultaneously opens up and closes around the topic: in thirty seconds he sets the agenda, signals a serious crisis, frames the issues, and, in the process, suggests how to think. The show proceeds with Downey probing and editorializing along every micro-step in the discussion, always ready for the pounce, the expected emotional tirade.

Downey's show is also a quasi-collective event which aspires toward achieving a mini-spectacle. As a modern-day moral entrepreneur Downey always comes complete with an audience that provides Greek-chorus amplification to his condemnations as it hoots on cue to second his emotional discharges. As Downey makes his routine verbal pounce upon guests, he is cheered on by his studio audience which consists mostly of young, white males.[6] From beginning to end it is staged dialogue stylized around brash confrontation and touted as "advocacy," with Downey jockeying to position his topics and guests in order to verbally demolish some of them. When the curve of emotion reaches the appropriate vitriolic height, the "public" is allowed to make its move, while Downey directs the emotional traffic. With Downey having drawn the first blood, the show proceeds with selected members of the audience who come forward from the American "majority" and position themselves behind a podium on which is painted a "loud mouth," the show's official logo. Here, Downey tells us, we get to hear the "real America" express itself.

While the show is always topical and, like other talk shows, provides a forum for "information," *The Morton Downey, Jr. Show* takes a significantly different emotional turn. The stage and studio audience are soon enveloped in a distinctively vengeful mood that seems part witch-hunt, part carnival. As the hour progresses, what unfolds is something akin to a morality play held in a theatre of resentment. Indeed, resentment is what makes Downey's show so unlike other talk-shows. Other hosts may have resentful guests on their show, but the hosts themselves do not incarnate that particular emotion. Downey, however, does. And so does his audience. Resentment is legitimated and licensed. Downey calls this "advocacy."

Crawling From the Wreckage

In the classical narrative of the morality play we are presented with individuals in a state of innocence. Soon enough they are made vulnerable by some kind of internal flaw or external circumstance which leads to a fall. Redemption, however, comes around to right things. On Downey's show, the first two stages are usually absent; but if present, they are quickly dismissed. Innocence has already been violated; the fall is presumed to have occurred; power has already perverted. Victims and culprits are present and fully formed. There is no need to guess. Downey can move immediately into cultural crises. But there is an ultimate context: America—especially "middle America"—is threatened by a host of social evils already rampant and wreaking havoc. The litany of popularized problems is familiar: terrorism, nuclear energy, support for anti-communist covert operations, foreign aid, and so on are juxtaposed with domestic concerns such as welfare, housing, the homeless, the poor, capital punishment, victim's rights, lawyers on the take, racial problems, affirmative action, the women's movement, prostitution, and homosexuality. From global issues to the scrutiny of micro-behavior, the list is sprawling.

Virtually all of these topics are part of the landscape of tension-ridden issues that have configured contemporary American populism. American populism is sufficiently broad and wide-ranging enough to be of service to more specific and politically focused ideologies. As Jim Hightower put it:

...the great center of American politics is not square dab in the middle of the spectrum, equal distance from conservatism and liberalism. Rather, the true center is in populism. Which is rooted in that realization that too few people control all the money and power, leaving very little for the rest of us. And they use that money and power to gain more for themselves. Populism is propelled politically by the simmering desire of the mass of people to upend that arrangement. [Hightower, 1986: 241]

Populism cannot be reduced to a liberal versus conservative framework. "Liberal" and "conservative" postures are politically selective appropriations of much more nebulous political cultures which encompass populism.

Resentment toward bureaucracy, bigness, power, monopolization, and ostentatious wealth has a long tradition in American popular politics. Downey frequently acknowledges these strains of American popular political sensibilities as he alludes to "fat cats" and "the rich" hovering like vultures over the rest of us. Trotting out America's troubles before a national audience, Downey plays off this deep cultural sensibility of powerlessness. Downey, however, exercises a heavy hand on the issues and unabashedly steers discussions toward a distinctly conservative scenario. He rallies free-floating frustration, grants legitimacy to the articulation of hostility, and points popular tensions toward their target, which he also identifies as their source: the Liberal State.

Appeals to rugged individualism—that peculiarly American resource that seems perpetually renewable—are made: individuals must regain control over government. Individualism may appear as a romanticized atomistic baseline for social action; but individualism politicized points toward a collective re-action that Downey extols as the solution to the brazen carelessness and bureaucratic insularity of "Big Government." His scenario reenacts the maxim: think global, act local. For Downey, "global" means "liberalism," and "local" means the mobilization of resentment against whatever locally *represents* the evils of liberalism, manifested in "pabulum-puking liberals" (clearly, there is a lot of play here). In this regard, Downey's ability to frame social issues in ways consistent with a distinctly conservative agenda lends itself to a much larger cultural and political stage.

Taking the Stage and Charting the (Dis)Course

The show is about to begin. The camera peeks beyond the corner of the studio bleachers. Out trots Downey, waving to a cheering audience. He's cool, confident, appears chummy, but also a bit cocky. He passes by the front row where he demonstrates a bit of male bravado, exchanging hard hand slaps with a few select males, the kind athletes give one another on the basketball court or football field. Having signified solidarity and resolve in the face of impending challenge, he moves along to kiss and hug some of the women. Free from any traces of performance anxiety, Morton has bonded with his audience. Later, some will get to come forward and say their piece at the Loud Mouth podium.

It is on to the studio stage. There, Mort shakes the hand of his guest(s), and turns to face the camera. He begins his introductory monologue with a "hey, we're all just folks" appeal as he delivers the privileged lowdown. As he talks, the camera zooms in until his preamble coincides with an earnest close-up:

> Used to be if you lived in Los Angeles and wanted a taste of old Mexico, baby, you hopped on the freeway and headed south, alright.
>
> Now with the recent wave of legal and illegal immigrations, you get all the way down there, what good does it do you. You got the Mexican culture right in L.A. You'll never have to leave your community. Just go into the bathroom, open the door, everything's written in Spanish. Is there anything wrong with that? Are we still the great melting pot? Are we inviting economic and social disaster by allowing foreigners to flood our borders when we can't take care of our own people? Integration or disintegration? You decide...

So opened a show on immigration. This introduction is typical: the issue is posed, the agenda is not so hidden, and conclusions are contained in the premises. "You decide...", says Downey, flattering the audience and viewers with an invitation to pseudo-participation.

But a subtle decision has already been smuggled into the preamble which laments that fact that "Mexican culture" was something you could once visit by leaving your L.A. home and embarking as a tourist seeking a foreign experience. Now, to live in L.A. is to be overwhelmed and overrun by a once foreign and distant culture. The message is not subtle: there is something very wrong and undesirable with this scenario; something is out of control. As to be expected from this preamble, the key issues presented by Downey's favored guests and audience members are "border control" and the social harm brought upon Americans by "aliens."

Reducing social and historical complexity to the surface features of multi-cultural antagonism illustrates how historical memory in America suffers from amnesia.[7] The result is a combination of historical ignorance and hysterical amazement: Now, there's Mexican culture in L.A.! and "everything's written in Spanish." In the Mexican-American War of 1846-48, Mexico lost one-third of its territory, and the United States gained the areas that became the vast "Southwest," including the whole of California. Los Angeles was once part of Mexico. As a recent Bureau of Census pamphlet entitled "We, the Mexican Americans" noted, from a Mexican-American perspective "The United States Came to Us."[8] Some of the "foreigners" who, much to Downey's distress read and speak Spanish, are likely to have ancestors who lived in the region prior to its being annexed through conquest. But none of this history is relevant to the new-founded horizon of post-1970 resurgent ethnic and racial resentment that Downey exploits.

The rest of the show proceeds toward the conclusion that the borders should be closed to "foreigners" since legitimate Americans at home now have acute problems that need attending. The litany is presented: "Foreign culture" overwhelming "American" (Los Angeles) culture; "illegal" and "legal immigration" (both equally problematic); "aliens" who "take away jobs from Americans;" an equally alien government that cares more for the "rights" of *groups* (read "race") that have dubious status as illegitimate, undeserving, and/or hyphenated-Americans; and the cries for an "English-only" policy. The withdrawal of civil rights based on English language proficiency is even raised: If they can't read, write, and speak English "reasonably well," then, citizenship or not, "they shouldn't vote."

We have seen this logic put into practice before. Coupled with sanctioned violence, it motivated the wide-spread use of literacy tests designed to prevent African-American citizens from exercising their franchise in the post-bellum south. The insidious similarity between the two cases does not even surface in the program. The overriding theme is the suffering of working, middle class Americans whose problems are exacerbated by "the recent wave of legal and illegal immigration." The show was televised in the WWOR New Jersey studio with an almost all-white audience. One wonders what kind of audience response his racially significant framing strategies would elicit if it were taped in Los Angeles before an audience that was reflective of the racial composition of the location.

Throughout the show, the issue of race looms in the background as if it were the dark slate upon which these various problems are sketched. And, as with most of Downey's shows, the particular list of grievances is transformed into examples that define and demonstrate the heart of conservative social critique: the failure of an overly permissive Liberal Welfare State.

Deviant or Mainstream?

"I am not a talk show host. I am an advocate... I think television should reflect life's realities and possibilities."

—Morton Downey[9]

"I don't think [capital punishment is] cruel and unusual enough. I'm sick and tired of hearing about defendant's rights and prisoner's rights! How about the rights of the people being murdered everyday?...Murderers and drug pushers...hang the creeps by their testicles!"

—Morton Downey
(closing comments on a program on the death penalty)

Clearly, Morton Downey, Jr. has become newsworthy. He and the show are important to the commentators. He is getting talked about, he certainly is being watched, he is getting a lot of circulation. Downey *has*—or *is*—or *represents*—some kind of cultural capital. Downey is significant; but what is his *significance?*

In scanning the popular print and broadcast coverage, one is left with the impression that Downey represents some kind of "violation." Most of the popular press's dismay and dismissal of Downey has focused on his belligerent and acerbic style. He screams, spits, swears, chain-smokes, belittles, and ambushes his guests as he uses their perspectives as springboards for his own platform. Downey trades dialogue for demagoguery by smuggling in his own highly politicized interpretations of social problems as if they were the common sensical positions that all Americans accept. Recalcitrant views held by guests are met with Downey's grimaces and groans which usually elicits the audience's howl of confirmation. Downey's sneers serve as visual connotations that recognize the twisted logic of his guests who remained mired in their liberal or other additionally deviant views. Altogether, Downey performs—in an hour's televised work—a feat in great demand: he reduces complex social, political, economic, and historically bequeathed concerns into very simple descriptions which harbor even more simplistic solutions. Even the most erudite lack the wherewithal to do this.

As his producers are keen to point out, part of Downey's attraction and success depends upon his theatrical deployment of *emotion:* Morton Downey "cares"—so much that he has to resort to end-of-his-wits anger when confronted with the intractable, wrong-headed, often liberal, views of one of his foils. But this helps him and the perspective he articulates to imperially seize the moral high ground. Anger, frustration, even rage translate into the perception of *genuine authenticity* (a most rare attribute in mass society). As the critics point out, all of this is unbecoming of both broadcast entertainment and news, and Downey blurs the two. News and so-called objective journalism, however, are not neutral enterprises; they are steeped in institutional routines that are contingent upon the unavoidable pressures of social and cultural forces. Nevertheless, part of the alarm around the Downey show leaves the impression that this blurring of news and entertainment is new.

But much of prime-time television entertainment programming—from situation comedies, to dramas, to made-for-TV movies—draws upon (and certainly distorts) social events (Gitlin, 1983). The linkage between fiction and the real is necessary if entertainment is to be intelligible within culturally specific contexts. While many insist that news and entertainment are mutually exclusive enterprises, the blurring of the two actually has been a central feature on prime-time television for some time. Witness the long-term success of *Sixty Minutes*, one of CBS's major information-programming staples since 1968.[10] There are a host of national and local "magazine" programs in which journalism, travel narratives, and voyeurism ooze together to offer viewers the privileged peek behind the walls of the "rich and famous." America's fascination with celebrity, however, is not all that new. In a study of popular magazines, sociologist Leo Lowenthal (Lowenthal, 1944) noted some time ago that a shift in American culture, from the celebration of "idols of production" to "idols of consumption," had begun to take place as early as the 1920s and was firmly established by the late 1940s.[11] Given our commercially oriented society, we should not be surprised with the conflation of news and entertainment. After all, commercial television is an industry with markets driven by viewer ratings; these are *the* unavoidable parameters within which both news and entertainment must compete.

What Downey does, however, has been criticized as the worst possible combination of news and entertainment. Television programming, as a highly routinized and institutionalized enterprise, has and will continue to have its ranges of stability and predictability, its accepted and pragmatically-driven conventions. Conventions measure the margins, the exceptions, the deviations, the Morton Downey's.[12]

While critics see Downey as deviant, and view his show with a jaundiced eye, Downey claims he's more normal than most of the fanfare on television. As he sees it, the loudness, the brash talk, the yelling—all of these behaviors are mainstream American. Go into most families and this is what you witness, claims Downey. Downey may be deviant in terms of established talk show norms, but he sees his own conduct as totally compatible with American family life.

Obnoxious and unconventional, Downey stands out. If he were just a media crank, we might as well tune out all of the hoopla and go to sleep. We can count on the television industry's adeptness at repetition and cloning to routinize novelty. Audiences would get used to him as his wildly negative charisma became predictable and eventually boring. In a culture in which the "new" must make space for the "newer," or even succumb to planned obsolescence, Downey would eventually run out of steam.

Anti-Liberalism and Populist Vengeance

But the kind of criticism I have noted rests on misplaced concreteness. By focusing on persona and the violation of television convention we are likely to miss something of greater importance. The question is not about Downey himself, or the distinctions to be made and maintained between news and information. Rather, we should be concerned about the broader popular politics that inform as well as refract the sentiments and sensibilities that he helps to articulate each week night on America's television screens. Downey's antics, his concocted and emotionally mimetic audience, the slants that he puts on issues—all of this should concern us as questions about *popular cultural forms and discourses*.

We need a *symptomatic* assessment of this particular *form* of entertainment and its linkage to other social dimensions. Indeed I would like to argue that Downey's stylized interpretation of populism, and the angles with which he helps deliver a televisual "view" of social concerns, are merely the veneer of a cultural frustration that goes hand in glove with a conservative populism that runs much broader and deeper than what the critics thus far have highlighted. Framing Downey as deviant within the narrow parameters of programming conventions prevents us from seeing how he might also represent more mainstream American sensibilities.

In the critic's scramble for the right labels, we have perhaps proceeded on the wrong footing. We read and we hear that what he does is not up to established standards: what he does is "tabloid tv," "trash tv," "sleaze tv," "confrontainment." He has been called a "bully," a "racist," a "sexist," and even a "fascist." While these terms and labels are not simply misnomers, they fail to link Downey's entertaining machinations with the New Right and the neo-conservative strands within American populism. And that is precisely where Downey's socio-cultural significance must be grounded.

In the early 1980s Richard Viguerie, a key strategist for the emerging New Right, spoke of a "new populism" which was anti-intellectual, anti-statist, and, above all, hostile to political liberalism (Viguerie, 1981; 1983).[13] While leaders of the "New Christian Right" might find Downey's foul language and practiced media hooliganism distasteful, *The Morton Downey, Jr. Show* represents the transformation of Viguerie's observations into an entertainment format that works in tandem with the mobilization of anti-modernist impulses that fuel, in part, the New Right's sense of malaise. Many of the show's themes and the angle from which they are rendered "meaningful" serve much of the same agenda proposed by the New Right and neo-conservatives. What Downey is particularly good at is tapping the raw emotions and frustrations of "middle Americans" who do perceive the limits and frailty of their social and economic status. Most importantly, however, is Downey's ability to link populist sensibilities with a larger right-wing ideological framework that focuses the source of social problems on democratic liberalism. With liberalism identified as the source of violation, moral outrage is given a concrete target—the numerous "social issues" which rally the New Right and the Neo-Conservatives. As Durkheim pointed out,[14] moral outrage and a sense of solidarity go hand in hand.

No doubt there is an abundance of social crises; hence plenty of raw material for the packaging of talk-show topics. Over the last couple of years, talk shows have become increasingly emboldened in their probes into the scandalous, deviant, politically charged, and culturally repressed. Much of the fanfare titillates voyeurism, and there has been a shift toward what industry insiders and commentators call "reality programming." Talk-shows hosted by Phil Donahue, Oprah Winfrey, Geraldo Rivera, Sally Jessie Raphael, and Morton Downey overlap somewhat with a growing group of "reality" programs such as *The Reporters, A Current Affair, Inside Edition, America's Most Wanted, On Trial, Unsolved Mysteries, 911, Hard Copy, Crimewatch Tonight* and *Cops*. These feature re-enactments of real events, or presentations of actual (as opposed to acted) events. In a way, these shows take the common media stock human interest story to its outer reaches of civility where things have turned sour, tragic, ugly, brutal, and even barbarous.

But before we adopt the underlying thesis that there is something really new here, we should not forget that television has long drawn on "reality" which is recast as fiction on prime-time dramas. This has been going on for decades, and, more recently, has been the basis for numerous "serious" "made-for-TV" movies. Writers and producers routinely survey (selectively, to be sure) the "real world" for script material. Marx once wrote, sardonically, that history can repeat itself—first as tragedy, then as farce. What actually happens, happens again, is re-presented, as culturally brokered and institutionally constructed narratives on prime-time television.

Much of popular culture taps, reflects, and refracts aspects of everyday life and feeds into and out of the cultural construction of identities. Because social identities in a segmented and fragmented society are often lived out as social conflict, popular culture is *political* in a very general sense. But *The Morton Downey, Jr. Show*, while serving simultaneously as entertainment, is *overtly political*. In his own televised words, he is an avowed "right-winger" and "conservative." This makes the show a cultural spectacle whose importance we should not slight. Aimed at an errant liberalism, Downey's choreography of frustration into rage delivers emotional slices of populist resentment in an entertainment format. Downey's show offers us insights into some of the popular ways in which deep and underlying resentment and frustration are translated into virtuous and self-righteous belligerence, and how particular narrow interests are transformed into general moral indignation bent on increasingly universal—that is, hegemonic—suasion.

Regardless of the evaluation given to Downey's theatrics of outrage, his tirade (as well as that of a growing segment of the American population) against liberalism is not simply a howl in the wilderness where marginalized malcontents might congregate. Sensibilities have histories and are connected to social structures (which, of course, change).[15] As Michael Omi and Howard Winant have noted, during the last two decades a great social and political transformation took place. This coincided with the "collapse of the 'American Dream'—the apolitical, perpetually prosperous, militarily invincible and deeply self-absorbed and self-righteous 'mainstream' American culture [has been]...shaken to its foundations by developments over this period. Commonly held concepts of nation, community and family were transformed, and no new principle of cohesion, no new cultural center, emerged to replace them" (Omi and Winant, 1986: 118-119). Much of Downey's conservatism makes sense against this background as a *competing articulation* of social and cultural battles over how to define social crises.

With rampant deindustrialization and deficit spending, a myriad of seemingly insurmountable problems have emerged. Americans are plagued by the erosion of economic stability brought about by structural and global changes in world-system economies which impact the domestic dimension of social relations (Braverman, 1974; Bluestone and Harrison, 1982; Gordon, *et al.*, 1982). As Daniel Bell noted in his pioneering work on post-industrialism (Bell, 1973), the shift toward a service economy has been underway for more than two decades. There are related consequences: traditional family patterns and gender roles have unravelled and have been transformed; amenities that make modern life the good life (in terms of liberal democratic capitalist consumer society)—like education, affordable and comfortable housing, and accessible as well as reasonably priced health care (in addition to the extra creature comforts)—are being placed out of reach by skyrocketing costs; growing needs for social services have increased in inverse proportion to the diminishing capacities of local economies, especially those once dependent upon manufacture; while the number of jobs has increased in the decade of the 1980s, real earning power, take home wages, has dropped; underemployment, deskilling, and unemployment threaten to deliver individuals and families into growing pools of poverty and homelessness.

It is against this backdrop—of social change and the conservative mobilization around social issues—that Downey's crisis-ridden televised theatrics take on their socio-cultural and historical importance. There is, then, an underlying tragedy behind many of the issues Downey "covers." For many Americans, things are not "ok." Americans today have had to come to grips with major social, economic, and political transformations which have affected the whole cultural terrain of everyday life.

In order for social frustrations to develop into conscious social actions, they must be named, labeled, and explained within the popularly available schemas of comprehension. In constructing popular agendas, conservative political architects have been quite effective in linking liberalism with the failure to achieve the American Dream. The *simplification* of complex and emotionally charged issues must be intelligible, believable, and meaningful to cultural constituents. But simplification can often—in the name of common sense argument—launch the sometimes hostile takeover of argumentation and can truncate logical assessment. As Stuart Hall puts it:

Labels are important, especially when applied to dramatic public events. They not only place and identify those events; they assign events to a context. Thereafter the use of the label is likely to mobilise *this whole referential context*, with all its associated meanings and connotations (Hall, *et al.*, 1978: 16).

This kind of cultural nexus achieved great importance during the 1988 presidential election with the powerful and overdetermining significance commanded by the notorious "L-word"—the Republican party's euphemism for "liberalism"—employed so effectively in the Bush campaign strategy. Buoyed by the rise of the New Right, the Christian fundamentalist resurgence, and the neo-conservatives, the Republican party, from the early Reagan years on, was able to parlay the wide-spread populist frustration identified with "social issues"—abortion, school prayer, busing, welfare, housing, affirmative action, etc.—into a critique of political liberalism. It was "liberalism" in general—and the Democratic party in particular—that was to blame for all of the erroneous social engineering that ran amok as it meddled in the lives of individuals and communities. And it was the American people who carried the burdens of a liberal government that was thematized on countless occasions as being "out of control."

Translated to the institutional level, frustration was collectivized and transformed into resentment toward "Big Government"—the code word for "liberal" control over the State and society within the broader referential context of an American society in crisis. Take, for example, Downey's introduction to a show on housing segregation:

How's this grab you gang?...The City of Yonkers, NY has just spent over $10 million in legal fees, pitted neighbor against neighbor, raised the ugly prospect of racial conflict, all because the government decided it wanted 800 units of low income housing deposited in a middle class neighborhood. And here we go again. Some bubble head bureaucrat is in Washington telling people where they should live and with whom. It didn't work with busing. It won't work with housing. Yonkers...Next on the Morton Downey Show.

From this preamble one can get the impression that intervention was simply hatched in Washington; by logical annexation, "big government" becomes a source of social conflict and racial antagonism. Despite the fact that the Yonkers ruling, in response to pervasive racial segregation, was implemented by the Federal Government under a Republican administration, liberals are nevertheless behind this because, by definition, it involves an externally imposed political power. This is part of the conservative mystique about the nature of the State: a genuinely conservative State (at least in its "ideal" manifestation) does not intervene in private affairs.

Virtually every week night during the last few months of the 1988 presidential campaign, Downey, as a self-proclaimed "right-winger," echoed the same theme: Liberal bureaucrats are on the loose; and protected by huckstering democrats they are busy pilferaging the public purse, operating "at the taxpayer's expense." With *The Morton Downey, Jr. Show* demonstrating its presidential elective affinities, the Republican presidential campaign planners could not have engineered a more populist-oriented, hour-long, loud-mouthed sound bite. There could not have been a better partisan fit with popular culture.

Demagogy of the Repressed

What matters now [for the demagogue] is to preserve (or restore) that what we have had and what is....And this enforcement normalizes, and renders legitimate a good deal of the violence which the agitator illegitimately invokes...But legitimate force must not appear as violence...."The verbal fury of the agitator is only a rehearsal of real fury."

—Herbert Marcuse[16]

Dershowitz: Now you have said some things about gay people, I remember on one of your shows. You described the anus as an exit and not an entrance... How would you feel if as the result of watching your show, some crazy guy out there, saw a gay guy sitting in the streets somewhere, or making a speech, and assaulted him.

Downey: I wouldn't like that at all. I am not in favor of physical violence as a way of settling debates or disputes. [Later, Downey looks into the camera, talking louder)...And if you...can't use the right part, then you deserve whatever happens to you.

Dershowitz: By whose standards are parts determined to be right?

Downey: I'm not a doctor, nor am I a theologian. *I would like to consider myself a very logical individual.*

—from interview on Alan Dershowitz's
On the Record

As Downey argues, the "typical American" is deeply frustrated and has not been given the chance to express those frustrations. The show, claims Downey, provides that opportunity. He is simply an "advocate" for the "little guy." But the "little guy"—like "middle America," the frequently imputed collective counterpart—is more a rhetorical device for Downey's agenda. Through his sheer aggressive style he makes it clear that it is *his* show (he occasionally has to remind particularly contrary guests of this fact), and the issues are ultimately framed by him. Downey has agendas, and he makes no pretense to the contrary. Guests as well as the audience members often appear to be props, raw material, the stuff he draws upon to articulate his own conservative populist agenda. Bob Pittman, Downey's producer, may be correct when he notes that Downey *is* the agenda: "There's a whole other way to do a show. You don't have to do talk-show-host-as-moderator; you can do talk-show-host-as-advocate. Instead of trying to draw things out of very special guests, you can *make the host the star and make the show about extreme versus extreme.*[17]

While marketing Downey's abrasive and triumphant resentment as star-making charisma is plausible, it is only a piece of the explanation. The program has substance; it's topics, mobilized sentiments, and the parade of social problems have social and political objects which are figured against the background of an errant liberalism.

Downey's advocacy is actually an attempt to *evoke*. As a *pseudo-public sphere*, the show draws some of its peculiar, evocative meanings from Downey's manipulation of selected public fears, frustrations, and anxieties organized through intense emotional exchanges.[18] The show's trademark volatility and post-civil public discourse would not take place if he did not prod dialogue toward the populist resentment he has knowingly assembled in his audience of "real Americans." Consider the heavy-handed steering displayed by Downey on a program on racism with an African-American guest, Dr. Charles King, representing the Urban Crisis Center:

King: Let's find out what the people in the audience really think. How far have we really come?
Downey: Good. (Addressing the audience) Let's be perfectly candid alright. Don't be afraid to say you hate the black race, or the Hispanic race...
King: You setting them up, now...
Downey: ...or the Oriental race...
King: ...Don't set them up...
Downey: I'm not setting them up. You said to be honest...
King: ...Don't set them up...
Downey: You said be honest...

As Aristotle once surmised, the individual is like the nation. Downey is no Aristolelian. On the contrary, he seems to reverse Aristotle's view: the nation should be like him, his self-interests should be the nation's interests. Covered in a storm of emotional display of advocacy is the transformation of Downey's *presentation of self* into the *representation of nation*. With interpretive frames already in place, Downey guides, conducts, drives, even hijacks the emotions that he has rallied and tapped. The merger between Downey and audience is based on his own assumptions about *his* experience and its universalizing credibility. On Alan Dershowitz's show, *On the Record*, Downey was queried about his audience. His response is more telling of his underlying assumptions which give him license to evoke what is presumably present but repressed.

Dershowitz: How can you get on television and appeal to this frustrated mass of people? Downey: Because I was frustrated most of my life....I'm able to come out there and present *my frustration* which I now recognize are the frustrations that *every American* goes through at one time or another in their life. (emphasis added)

He is hyper-American, an ideal type, a synthesis of all the smaller parts that can be found among the "little men" out there. As a master narrator, and a universalizer of particulars, he speaks with authority gleaned from personal recognition of the emotional reality of "every American." This recognition is self-legitimizing; it enables him to leap from personal to mass public representation.

Prophet of Deceit or Profits from Deceit?

"America, Kick Ass!"
—Morton Downey
(phrase frequently used to close show)

These two guys wouldn't have been killed if they hadn't been cruising the streets picking up teenage boys....I don't care much for queers cruising the streets.
—Judge Hampton, Dallas, Texas commenting (12/18/88) on the murder of two gays

With this convenient and self-serving slide between self and society, Downey's agenda is America's agenda and vice versa. There is no difference or distance between his immediate frustrations (and his explanations for them) and those of the larger majority. In this regard, Downey provides the convenient closure around all of the social issues that are opened for assessment on his program. His apparent brazenness is justified by identifying his own perspective with that of the larger American population. How he frames things is thus never a problem in itself; he merely reflects, refracts, and mediates the sentiments and will of "the people." By drawing upon the audience who give testimony to the basic soundness of the issues as framed by Downey, the frequent retreat to raw and imperial emotion enables Downey to equate self-advocacy with civic advocacy, personal identity with public identity, self-interests with the national interest. As Lowenthal and Guterman point out, the agitator

...directly reflects the audience's predisposition. [He] does not confront his audience from the outside; he seems rather like someone arising from its midst to express its innermost thoughts. He works, so to speak, from inside the audience, stirring up what lies dormant there. (Lowenthal and Guterman, 1970:5)

Downey imputes the frustrations, values and aspirations of the "real America"—present as audience—in which he is proudly submerged. Again, an excerpt from his interview with Alan Dershowitz:

Dershowitz: Would you be happy if 25 years from now Americans were what you are?
Downey: Oh, you bet!
Dershowitz: Would you like an America which was like your audiences?
Downey: ...*America is like my audience.* My audience finally has an opportunity to express the frustration that they've been feeling. My audience is loaded with wonderful people.
Dershowitz: Your audiences...uh...they bring out in some respects the worst of the group they represent. I mean, this is not the image that group of Americans would be proud of, is it?
Downey: Oh, I think they should be proud of it. I think they should be proud that they're concerned, proud that they're venting their frustration, proud that they're doing it in a vocal way, alright, not necessarily a way with guns and knives and fists.

[And a bit later in the interview]

Dershowitz: You're not a talk-show host, you're an advocate. What's your philosophy?
Downey: ...Very succinctly, it's I'm tired of the government running the people. I want the people to run the government.
Dershowitz: And you think the people out there that you appeal to are capable of running a government?
Downey: You bet your life they are. Much more capable than the government has indicated they are capable of.
Dershowitz: What kind of government would we have if your people ran it?
Downey: You'd have a government that was *sympathetic.* (emphasis added)

It all sounds so simple, so spiritually and correctly American, so fundamentally democratic. Government by "the people." Sympathetic government—who doesn't want that?

In this enlightened moment the clouds darken. The German government was "sympathetic" the evenings of November 9-10, 1938 (also known as *kristaalnacht,* or "night of broken glass"), when soldiers and civilians throughout Germany destroyed Jewish homes, businesses, and synagogues. The rampage was, in part, an act of mobilized populism rooted in resentment and animosity which was allowed to turn into a national spasm of anti-semitic vengeance. And as an act of state-sponsored hooliganism ok'd from above, it opened the curtain for the Jewish holocaust.

The holocaust may seem distant and foreign for Americans who are not of Jewish descent. But in the American context there too is a long tradition of "sympathetic" state support with regard to nativistic racism. In the

American context, the early colonial government was sympathetic to slavery. As the nation developed and progressed, sympathies were extended to the race wars with Native American tribes which led to systematic confiscation of lands from indigenous peoples and, eventually, their almost total annihilation; from the late 19th century well up into the mid-twentieth century, there were laws that excluded Asians ("resident aliens") from owning property, testifying in U.S. courts, or being eligible for citizenship; the state supported the massive transference of land ownership from Mexicans to Anglos in the southwest after the Mexican-American war (the U.S. government did not recognize the "legal" claims of the land's indigenous inhabitants to land possession); there was the long-standing practices of Jim Crow politics and the tolerated "folkways" of segregation and systematic violence in the South which lasted for more than a century after emancipation in some areas; and approximately 110,000 Japanese-Americans (but not German- or Italian-Americans) were incarcerated during World War II. It was only with the very recent reversal of this traditional sympathy of siding with deeply institutionalized racism, when civil rights legislation was finally enacted in the 1960s, that the Government actually took steps to protect the democratic rights of minority citizens.

Yet, it is important to recognize that the broadened extension of civil rights in the mid-1960s took hold at a peculiar historical juncture, precisely at the time the specter of *deindustrialization* was transforming the social and economic landscape.[19] Just as the State began to take a new *cultural* direction by recognizing and protecting "civil rights," *structural-economic* changes began to erode the seemingly solid post-war economic surplus which gave many white middle-class Americans a sense of affluence and security. Liberal agendas during the 1970s were compromised, and in the decade of the 1980s pruned back as a growing recognition of fiscal constraint emerged. The populist resentment toward the "women's movement," feminism, and broader concerns regarding civil rights illustrates the existence of a *post-civil rights* sentiment articulated in many of Downey's views. The women's movement and other programs aimed at correcting discrimination are now themselves forms of injustice. Here is how he wrapped up a show on "men's rights:"

> There's no question: the women's movement was a cause who's time had come, alright. But like most zealots, the women are now guilty of inflicting the many injustices that they seek to resolve. Well, we men aren't going to take it lying down anymore. Stand up for your rights..."

This closure characterizes Downey's summaries on many social problems that have a "rights" dimension. Here, one could simply substitute for "women's movement" any of the social issues which have been *racialized* in the popular imagination (e.g., racial struggles against inequality, housing and educational desegregation, busing, affirmative action, etc.). Downey's message is that "real Americans" of the "mainstream" are now up against the wall, and are being victimized by the liberal intellectuals profiting from their own social problems industry.[20] Under the protection of the Liberal State, women and minorities in particular have gone too far, are exerting more power than they are entitled to, and this must be arrested.[21]

Violence can regenerate a threatened and eroding sense of solidarity (Durkheim, 1984 [1893], Girard, 1977; Slotkin, 1973; Drinnon, 1980; Jordan, 1968; Blauner, 1972; and Fanon, 1963). In 1982 Vincent Chin, a young Chinese American, was brutally killed on the streets of Detroit. He was bludgeoned with a baseball bat wielded by two white unemployed auto workers. To them, Vincent was a "Jap." For years, Japan has been popularized in the mass media as an "unfair trading partner," and the popularity of Japanese autos among American consumers was, in part, seen as responsible for domestic unemployment in the auto industry. Vincent had no real connection to the frustration felt by his killers. But, on the other hand, his *race* provided a symbolic connection. Vincent signified their problems, and his immediate existence was enough to complete the psychic wiring needed to ground their floating frustration. Of course, neither Vincent nor Japan were responsible for the corporate decisions made decades ago to not reinvest in the aging steel mills of America's industrial centers; and the attractive, non-unionized, and less costly labor markets abroad have helped funnel American capital out of the country. Historical and structural conditions—deindustrialization at home and capital investment (or "capital flight") abroad—helped to set the context for the tragic collision of history and biography leading to acts of violence and private fate. That Vincent was present at the wrong moment is beside the point; it could have been another Asian, perhaps an African-American, or a Hispanic. Violence, in this case, is anger and resentment *grounded*. The resentment and frustration that often finds *race* as a short-circuiting signifier for status erosion (and *racialized* social issues like immigration, welfare, affirmative action, etc.) could have just as easily produced another casualty.

Vincent Chin's death should not be seen in isolation. There have been other cases of assault and violence linked to racial antagonism in recent years. Some of these incidents—such as the widely praised and romanticized view of Bernard Geotz who was popularized as a "subway vigilante" for his shooting of several blacks, the killing at Howard Beach, Tawana Brawley's claim to have been assaulted by a group of men (one alleged to be a police officer), and the murder of a young Ethiopian immigrant by several skin head gang members of the East Side White Pride in Portland, Oregon— have been treated on national media. And add to this the "gay bashing" and the flurry of racial incidents on college and university campuses across the country. Even the 1988 Presidential campaign was marred by allegations that Vice-President Bush's campaign strategy recognized and massaged racial sentiments and fears when it ran political ads featuring Willie Horton, a black convict who committed a violent crime while on furlough from a Massachusetts prison.[22] Brought into the heart of the campaign (and on *The Morton Downey, Jr. Show* as well), this tragedy and other politicized associations helped the Bush campaign link presidential candidate Michael Dukakis and the whole Democratic Party to the catch-all slogan of "liberal"— the ultimate dirty "L-word".

From Cultural Forum to Cultural Form

What Downey does so well is to tap the sentiment of resentment, give it a narrative, a grammar, and a manner of articulation, and parlay it into populist vengeance. Resentment is beckoned, stroked, coddled, pandered to, and ultimately granted moral approval. Thus Downey can end his show, as he frequently does, with a rallying exhortation: "America—kick ass!" This rally to turn rantings into viewer ratings has a definite and tragic cultural echo. One can't help but think that this was part of what the individuals who dispensed the fatal violence in Detroit, Howard Beach, and Portland thought they were doing—kicking ass. And there was the February 1989 election of David Duke (Ku Klux Klan-affiliated leader of the National Association for the Advancement of White People) to the Louisiana State Legislature on the Republican ticket. Downey had Duke on his program in 1988, when Duke was running for President as a Democrat. Downey did his best to distance himself from the racist views of Duke and like-minded neo-nazis and skinheads. Yet his show simultaneously panders to the kind of status erosion and resentment that characterizes the perceptions of many who find race, welfare, and feminist issues a convenient arena for blame. The kind of frustration and resentment massaged by Downey's strategy to highlight a talk show around conservative populism is compatible with the racially coded political rhetoric championed by David Duke.

Downey's show is a logical extension of many of the cultural and economic crises present in contemporary American society. There are individuals, groups, and whole communities looking for something or someone to blame. Capital flight, deindustrialization, the shift from a manufacturing to a communication and service based economy—these are enormously difficult abstractions to grasp. Their reality, for some, is manifested only as an erosion of personal security and lifestyle. Especially for the young with limited resources, who see—perhaps accurately—a future that promises diminishing returns, the challenge is to figure things out *locally*, within the context of personal/familial immediacy, and against the background of everyday life.

Unfortunately, in the last half-decade, this local "understanding" has occurred too frequently as racist and anti-feminist backlash. Downey's show feeds upon and extends social crises. This is not because social crises are sponsored and promoted by right and neo-conservative rhetoric. Rather, in the wake of shrinking expectations, the sentiments of erosion felt by lower, middle, and working class Americans, and the rhetoric against liberal society, meld into a hostile, resentful, and vengeance-bent morality—summed up in a cry for "fairness"—that regenerates, on the fringes, its own sense of virtue through intolerance and violence, with the majority standing in silent complicity. Thus affirmative action is reduced to a criticism of "set asides" (e.g., certain percentages of federal, state, or municipal-sponsored spending earmarked, for example, for minority contractors). In the vengeance-bent politics of the new clamor for "fairness," this means that the considerations for minorities and women be themselves *set aside*. Downey's micro-management of emotions and frustrations *processes* some of these sentiments, while he—and the cultural form his show represents—is simultaneously a *cultural product* of social circumstances.

While noted for all of its rough edges, *The Morton Downey, Jr. Show* is a cultural phenomenon that has a rather smooth fit in contemporary society. We should avoid reducing him to a pop-political narcissist or an opportunistic huckster (though he contains ample elements of both). Indeed, his guest appearance on *Saturday Night Live*—where, in skit, he "acted" his trash-tv talk-show host persona—could easily give shrewd and jaded viewers the impression that Downey is all act, a put-on, just another guy with a gimmick, laughing on his way to the bank. These notions are certainly plausible.

But this quick take on Downey captures the surfaces, and leaves the cultural depths unfathomed. The cynical dismissal of Downey—and, more importantly, what he represents—is an indication of analytic exhaustion. In this regard, cynicism is not a road to explanation, but a path in retreat. The cynical view undercuts the sociological dimension which must be accounted for in the program's *success*—not just Downey's success as a culturally commodified figure on television, but the success of the whole compressed and culturally complicated profile of the show's form and content within the context of contemporary social crises out of which the show emerges and to which it must speak. Downey's show, and its broad range of ideological packaging, rests on the grounds of conservative populism which allow Downey a place in the contemporary cultural arena where struggles over the *popular interpretation* of social issues take place. Cynical dismissal is cultural dismissal.

The dismissal of Downey—as shrill wacko or smooth show-biz huckster—is simultaneously a dismissal of *cultural forms*. While warranted, the view of Downey as huckster is too simple for two general reasons. First, it represents a withdrawal from the underlying context of social relations that are stamped by specific historical and cultural contexts. Secondly, it reduces the show's content down to the sheer power of persona, hype, and cynicism. Downey is not a fluke or a freak; his persona and style, the show's content, and its ability to find a significant and growing audience do not exist in a cultural vacuum. He is not just an opportunistic operator engaged in issue distortion and social mis-construction of reality. Downey does with American middle and working-class angst what the Sex Pistol's manager, Malcolm McLaren, claimed he was doing with late 1970s British working-class Punk music: producing "cash from chaos." Working-class British Punk was spectacle—explosive, malcontent, raw, angry, hostile and nihilistic. But it was also self-righteously perceptive (as so much of the Sex Pistol's and the Clash's music demonstrates). Punk comprehended the dismal future for its working-class constituents, but its vision could not overcome; it offered insight, but no way out. Like Punk, Downey gives his viewers the quick summary of America's problems. In the process, dialogue is transformed into diatribe, historical complexity into hysterical simplicity. Rage coming from society is returned back to it. But this is precisely part of the show's drawing power. Downey taps mainstream conservative populist thinking, perhaps even more directly and effectively than, say, the writings of a Richard Viguerie.

Even if we adopted the totally cynically view that he is no different from the classic snake-oil salesman passing through our electronic communities long enough for he and his production company to profit from their therapeutic deceit, this would still not diminish his cultural relevance. What Downey represents is a mobilization and expansion of the *conservative annexation of populist frustrations*, televised every week night on cable television. Downey is a conservative populist cultural broker: he takes the resentment that stems from the feelings of powerlessness, gives it a so-called forum, translates sentiment and emotion into animosity, and provides resentment with a negative epistemology: political liberalism and its strangle-hold on the people is stupid and wrong, and a rekindled conservatism will right things. In this regard, Downey illustrates one important way in which populist sensibilities are being grounded within contemporary American society.

* * *

Downey has run out of time. The show—this one on terrorism—is about to end. He looks into the camera as he begins his wrap-up. The camera zooms in until Downey's face dominates the viewer's screen. Downey must exert his own ideological determination in the last instance. He's ready for closure. This time, the loud mouth is Downey's, not the audience's. "What does America want?" The mood being enhanced comes through loud and clear as his fist strikes the air and his hostile face emits the holler: "Revenge! Revenge! Revenge!" The predominantly white, young, male crowd howls righteously as if somewhere in this choreographed rage they have been given an important promise.

Downey's audience—the supposedly down-troddened, bureaucratically brow-beaten, ordinarily silenced "real Americans," fighting off the Liberal Moloch State—is temporarily enthralled in its own pseudo-empowerment. And as Downey exits, the audience watches the last traces of its own image fade on the studio monitors. They end much as they began: "Mort, Mort, Mort, Mort, Mort..."

Acknowledgements

My thanks to Dan Clawson, Tess Boley Cruz, Gene Fischer, Todd Gitlin, Gerald Platt, Denise Scott, and Randall Stokes for helpful comments.

Notes

[1]Morton Downey, Jr. (with William Hoffer), *Mort! Mort! Mort!: No Place to Hide.* New York: Delacourt Press/Bantam Doubleday Dell Publishing Group, 1988.

[2]*New York Times,* 12/18/88, pp. 1, 38.

[3]On the surprising and rapid success of the show in its early months of syndication, see "MCA's 'Downey' Rates Strong in National Syndication Debut," *Variety,* June 8, 1988, p. 43.

[4]Quoted in an interview in *Broadcasting,* May 16, 1988, p. 44.

[5]There are important distinctions between "conservative," "neo-conservative," "new right," and "far right." I use the terms loosely in this essay because the social groups, political sensibilities, and agendas to which they refer overlap on one key point: they oppose democratic liberalism. The reader might compare conservative political analyst Kevin Phillips (Phillips, 1982) with new right populist Richard Viguerie (Viguerie, 1981; 1983). For a discussion on these distinctions, see Omi and Winant, 1986: 109-135 and Crawford, 1980.

[6]My observations of the show are based entirely on watching it during telecast hours and viewing video tapes. Since its initial syndication in May 1988, I have videotaped approximately 3 episodes per week. Most shows have an audience that is predominantly white and male. But there are episodes with topics that are specifically about "race relations," and on these shows the audience usually has more African Americans (as when the guest is the Reverend Al Sharpton, known most recently by his association with the Tawana Brawley case), but (insofar as racial distinctions can be ascertained televisually) the African American audience composition rarely exceeds 5 percent. Asians and Hispanics are seldom present. With regard to African Americans, there are occasional exceptions. For example, during the last week of December 1987 (before Downey was nationally syndicated), the show was broadcasted from New York's famed Apollo Theatre, and approximately a year later Downey taped a week's worth of shows in Detroit with several episodes addressing race relations in the "Motor City." In both of these contexts, the audience was predominantly African American.

Downey's home-based studio (WWOR, Secaucus, New Jersey) is where the bulk of the taping occurs, and the show's audience is almost entirely white and predominantly male. This is significant because it is the primary representation seen nationally. Over the many months since syndication, however, I have noticed an increase in the number of women in the audience.

[7]Television's commercially driven perpetual rush into the present cannot help but contribute to the dehistoricization of historical awareness. As Bill Moyers put it, "I worry that my own business...helps to make this an anxious age of agitated amnesiacs... We Americans seem to know everything about the last twenty-four hours but very little of the last sixty centuries or the last sixty years" (quoted in Postman, 1985: 137). In an industry that perceives its best market strategies in the packaging of contemporary anxieties, historical reflection is the first and most unfortunate casualty.

[8]Cf. Edward Simmen, editor. *Pain and Promise: The Chicano Today.* New York and Scarborough, Ont.: 1972, p. 46.

[9]*New York Times,* 5/16/88, section C, p. 15.

[10]TV talk show precedents, to some extent, can be found in the acerbic *Joe Pine Show*, or the pompous and snobbish affect displayed by conservative William F. Buckley on his *Firing Line*, or California's *Wally George Show*. "Talk radio," where Morton Downey, Jr. got his start in media, helped prepare the ground.

[11]Cultural analyses of advertising fit centrally within the transition to a consumer society. On the transformation of cultural imagery in advertising and its links to social and historical change, cf. Ewen, 1977; 1988; Leiss, *et al.*, 1986; Schudson, 1984; and Lears, 1983.

[12]Cable television has evolved into a major competitive force for network television, and the latter's conventions have been impacted as a result. It is interesting to note that the major networks (CBS, NBC and ABC) have begun to diminish the powers of internal monitoring of "standards and practices"—in essence, less censorship to meet the challenge of the less censored programming on cable television.

[13]Viguerie's first book contains an introduction written by the Reverend Jerry Falwell, founder and leader of the Moral Majority, and is an indication of the link between formal conservative politics and the new religious right. See also Rusher, 1984. For data on patterns of religious transformation and the emergence of the "new religious right", see Roof and McKinney, 1987.

[14]Durkheim's (Durkheim, 1984 [1893]) classic theory of solidarity and the functional importance of moral outrage presents rich theoretical ground and is worth considering here.

[15]Indeed, the negative populist resentment and animosity aimed at specific social issues (such as busing, welfare, affirmative action, women's rights, abortion, etc.) and their linkage to democratic liberalism represent a cultural logic that has a history. See Block, *et al.*, 1987; Ehrenreich, 1987. For an interesting sociological work which points out deeper dimensions to the underlying antimodernism that take the form of right-wing populism, cf. the essays in Bell, 1963.

[16]From Marcuse's foreword to Lowenthal and Guterman, 1970: vii.

[17]*Broadcasting*, 5/16/88, p. 44.

[18]From the producer's point of view, the exchange of emotions (which gives the show its market-based exchange-value, e.g. ratings for advertising fees) help make the show work. Pittman's theory of emotional experience as audience desire was apparently developed with his early success in launching MTV, of which he said: "People don't watch these clips to find out what's going to happen. They watch to *feel* a certain way. It's a *"mood enhancer"* (quoted in Frith, 1988: 209, emphasis added).

[19]From a perspective of American racial history and its inextricable ties to post-WWII economic development and the ensuing decades of decline effecting the middle class, we are able to see how civil rights legislation launched by a *liberal* policy toward race relations in the 1960s could come to *represent* one of the major developments that mars the conservative longing for more traditional patterns of local control within civil society, (a sentiment homologous to the cries for "states rights" in the south) when Jim Crow laws were actually in the stages of being dismantled. Ironically the presidential campaign of George Wallace represented a last stand of this sentiment associated with the South. But the Wallace campaign was simultaneously a sign of a new beginning of a resurgent conservative wing headed by Barry Goldwater. Wallace and Goldwater were bellwether politicians who heralded the gradual republicanization of the southern blue-collar as well as industrial democrats.

In the contemporary era of diminishing promises (and withering returns), the State, once hailed as progressive, is seen from the conservative perspective as having gone too far along the path of democratic liberalism. The expansion of "rights" is now costly in ways unperceived in the earlier decades of affluence. The antimodernist sentiments raised by the New Right and neo-conservatives call for various strategies to "rollback" legislation which is seen as too interventionist. In the sphere of conservative populism, part of this "rollback" is manifested in a *post*-civil rights sentiment, a politics of resentment, which is aimed upward toward Liberal "Big Government," and below toward minorities clustered at the poverty line, waiting for their break into the great scramble for the American Dream. Mainstream and "real" Americans (i.e. white—effectively melted-in-the-melting-pot—ethnics who deserve a better shake in the cornucopia of modern democratic capitalism) have come to resent the liberal protections extended to minorities and women, since the expansion of rights has actually increased the competitive reality effecting white working and middle class males who, in the earlier periods of economic formation, did not have to contend with these racial and gendered marginalized sectors.

On American nativism, see Higham, 1981. See also Slotkin, 1973; Rogin, 1975; Takaki, 1979; 1982; Jordan, 1968; Montajano, 1988; Barrera, 1979; and McWilliams, 1944. See also Edelman, 1988: 66-89 for an illustrative discussion on the "displacement of targets" and the "cognitive structuring" that takes place through the "construction of enemies."

[20]Richard Viguerie has stressed this in his work which cites Hoover Institute conservative Thomas Sewell who has argued that liberal intellectuals have profited by creating a government-subsidized industry around "social problems" (one of the conservative's favorite indictments of the "Welfare State" and the institutional weight of eastern intellectuals): "To be blunt, the poor are a gold mine. By the time they are studied, advised, experimented with, and administered, the poor have helped many a middle-class liberal to achieve affluence with government money" (quoted in Viguerie, 1981: 145).

From this view, those programs that have attempted to assist and alleviate the hardships of the poor are themselves the problem. Aside from the profound cynicism that underlies this criticism, there is a fuzzy-headed assumption about the virtues of free-market logic and its capacity to solve structural inequality. It reads something like this: If only the liberals would go away, so too would the poor. Because, after all, there is a transcendental, quasi-religious notion of the withering away of the State to make room for Nature's "Invisible Hand", *the marketplace*, which will eventually solve social problems. And if the market cannot solve them, then such social problems must be *natural*, part of nature, part of the order of things, all of which is governed by the greatest of hidden hands. For an excellent overview of the ideological deep structure as well as the notions of natural law that inform the moral as well as epistemological foundations of utilitarianism see Halevy, 1972.

[21]Part of the rights backlash has taken the form of an "ethnic revival" among white Americans which emerged in the late 1960s. There are debates as to whether this is an ethnic or a class-based formation. Drawing upon the advantages demonstrated by the Black Power movement, empowerment became an issue equally attractive to white ethnics, especially those of working class status and who were Catholic, Jewish, and East European. In the late 1960s, this ethnic resurgence took on a political dimension. Many white ethnics saw the gains made by blacks as setbacks for them: black gains would come at the expense of the white ethnic working class. On these issues cf. Novak, 1971; Goering, 1971; Ransford, 1972; and Murray, 1984. On white ethnic resistance to affirmative action cf. Kluegel and Smith, 1986; Patterson, 1977; and Stasz, 1981.

[22]See "Horton Ad's Creators Claim Quiet Backing of Bush Staff," *New York Times*, November 3, 1988, p. 1. The association between "liberalism" and race is acknowledged by William Krystyniak, a Chicago Alderman who also ran as a Democrat for an Illinois Senate seat. According to Krystyniak, "To my constituents, *a liberal is a person who supports the blacks, plain and simple . . .* Quite frankly, that's why Dukakis is having such a hard time attracting support in my neighborhood." See "The L-word's Dirty Little Secret" by Salim Muwakkil, *In These Times*, Oct. 26-Nov. 1, 1988, p. 2, emphasis added.

Bibliography

Barrera, M. (1979) *Race and Class in the Southwest: a Theory of Inequality.* Notre Dame: University of Notre Dame Press.

Bell, D. (1973) *The Coming of Post-Industrial Society: A Venture in Social Forecasting.* New York: Basic Books.

——— (ed.) (1963) *The Radical Right.* Garden City, New York: Doubleday and Co.

Blauner, R. (1972) *Racial Oppression in America.* New York: Harper and Row.

Block, F., R. Cloward, B. Ehrenreich and F. Piven. (1987) *The Mean Season: The Attack on the Welfare State.* New York: Pantheon.

Bluestone, B. and B. Harrison. (1982) *The Deindustrialization of America: Plant Closings, Community Abandonment, and the Dismantling of Basic Industry.* New York: Basic Books.

Braverman, H. (1974) *Labor and Monopoly Capital: The Degradation of Work in the Twentieth Century.* New York: Monthly Review Press.

Broadcasting, May 16, 1988, p. 44.

Crawford, A. (1980) *Thunder on the Right: The "New Right" and the Politics of Resentment.* New York: Pantheon Books.

Drinnon, R. (1980) *Facing West: the Metaphysics of Indian-Hating and Empire-Building.* New York: Meridian/New American Library.

Durkheim, E. (1984) [1893] *The Division of Labor in Society.* New York: The Free Press.

Edelman, M. (1988) *Constructing the Political Spectacle.* Chicago: University of Chicago.

Ehrenreich, B. (1987) "The new right attack on social welfare," pp. 161-195 in F. Block, *et al.*, *The Mean Season: The Attack on the Welfare State.* New York: Pantheon.

Ewen, S. (1977) *Captains of Consciousness: Advertising and the Social Roots of the Consumer Society.* New York: McGraw-Hill.

——— (1988) *All Consuming Images: The Politics of Style in Contemporary Culture.* New York: Basic Books.

Fanon, F. (1963) *The Wretched of the Earth.* New York: Grove Press.

Frith, S. (1988) *Music for Pleasure.* New York: Routledge.

Girard, R. (1977) *Violence and the Sacred.* Baltimore: John Hopkins University Press.

Gitlin, T. (1983) *Inside Prime-Time.* New York: Pantheon.

Goering, J. (1971) "The emergence of ethnic interests: a case of serendipity." *Social Forces* 49: 379-384.

Gordon, D., R. Edwards and M. Reich. (1982) *Segmented Work, Divided Work: The Historical Transformation of Labor in the United States.* Cambridge: Cambridge University Press.

Halevy, E. (1972) *The Growth of Philosophic Radicalism.* Clifton, N.J.: Augustus M. Kelley Publishers.

Hall, S., C. Critcher, T. Jefferson, J. Clarke and B. Roberts. (1978) *Policing the Crisis: Mugging, the State, and Law and Order.* London: MacMillan.

Higham, J. (1981) *Stranger in the Land: Patterns of American Nativism 1860-1925.* New York: Atheneum.

Hightower, J. (1986) "Kick-ass populism: a speech to the national press club," pp. 240-251 in H. Boyte and F. Riessman (eds.) *The New Populism: The Politics of Empowerment.* Philadelphia: Temple University Press.

Jordan, W. (1968) *White Over Black.* Chapel Hill: University of North Carolina.

Kluegel, J. and E. Smith. (1986) *Beliefs about Inequality: American Views of What Is and What Ought to Be.* Hawthorn, N.Y.: Aldine de Gruyter.

Lears, T.J. (1983) "From salvation to self-realization: advertising and the therapeutic roots of the consumer culture, 1880-1930," pp. 3-38 in R.W. Fox and T.J. Jackson Lears (eds.) *The Culture of Consumption.* New York: Pantheon.

Leiss, W., S. Kline and S. Jhally. (1986) *Social Communication in Advertising: Persons, Products, and Images of Well-Being.* New York: Methuen.

Lowenthal, L. (1944) "Biographies in Popular Magazines" in P.F. Lazarsfeld and F. Stanton (eds.) *Radio Research: 1942-1943.* New York: Duell, Sloan and Pearce. Reprinted as Chapter 4 in L. Lowenthal, *Literature, Popular Culture, and Society.* Palo Alto: Pacific Books, 1961.

––––––– and H. Guterman. (1970) [1949] *Prophets of Deceit.* Palo Alto: Pacifica.

McWilliams, C. (1944) *Prejudice: Japanese-Americans: Symbol of Racial Intolerance.* Boston: Little, Brown and Company.

Montajano, D. (1987) *Anglos and Mexicans in the Making of Texas. 1836-1986.* Austin: University of Texas.

Murray, C. (1984) *Losing Ground: American Social Policy 1950-1980* New York: Basic Books.

Muwakkil, S. (1988) "The L-word's dirty little secret." *In These Times,* Oct. 26-Nov. 1, 1988, p. 2.

New York Times, 12/18/88, pp. 1, 38.

––––––– 5/16/88, section C, p. 15.

––––––– November 3, 1988, p. 1.

Novak, M. (1971) *The Rise of the Unmeltable Ethnics.* New York: MacMillan.

Omi, M. and H. Winant. (1986) *Racial Formation in the United States from the 1960s to the 1980s.* New York: Routledge & Kegan Paul.

Patterson, O. (1977) *Ethnic Chauvinism: The Reactionary Impulse.* New York: Stein and Day.

Phillips, K. (1982) *Post-Conservative America: People, Politics and Ideology in a Time of Crisis.* New York: Random House.

Postman, N. (1985) *Amusing Ourselves to Death: Public Discourse in the Age of Show Business.* New York: Viking Penguin, Inc.

Ransford, H.E. (1972) "Blue-collar anger: reactions to student and black protest." *American Sociological Review* 37: 333-346.

Rogin, M. (1975) *Fathers and Children: Andrew Jackson and the Subjugation of the American Indian.* New York: Alford A. Knopf.

Roof, W.C. and W. McKinney. (1987) *American Mainline Religion: Its Changing Shape and Future.* New Brunswick: Rutgers University Press.

Rusher, W. (1984) *The Rise of the Right.* New York: William Morrow & Co.

Schudson, M. (1984) *Advertising, the Uneasy Persuasion.* New York: Basic Books.

Simmen, E. editor. (1972) *Pain and Promise: The Chicano Today.* New York and Scarborough, Ontario.

Slotkin, R. (1973) *Regeneration through Violence: The Mythology of the American Frontier.* Middletown, Conn.: Wesleyan University Press.

Stasz, C. (1981) *The American Nightmare: Why Inequality Persists* New York: Schocken.

Takaki, R. (1979) *Iron Cages: Race and Culture in 19th-Century America.* New York: Alfred A. Knopf.

_____ (1982) "Reflections on racial patterns in America: an historical perspective." *Ethnicity and Public Policy*, 1: 1-23.

Viguerie, R. (1981) *The New Right: We're Ready to Lead.* Falls Church, VA: The Viguerie Company.

_____ (1983) *The Establishment vs. the People: Is a New Populist Revolt on the Way?* Chicago: Regnery Gateway, Inc.

Contributors

Rod Carveth is currently an Assistant Professor in the Communication Department at the University of Hartford. He holds a B.A. in Sociology from Yale University, and an M.A. and Ph.D. in Communication from the University of Massachusetts-Amherst. His research interests include the impact of daytime serials on viewers and depictions of AIDS in popular culture. He is currently president of the Northeast Popular Culture Association.

B. Keith Crew received his Ph.D. in Sociology from the University of Kentucky in 1987. His main research interests are in legal processing and interpersonal violence. He is currently at the University of Northern Iowa, where he teaches courses in the Sociology of Law, Sociology of Policing, and criminological theory. He also watches far too much television.

Jon Cruz received his Ph.D in Sociology from the University of California, Berkeley and teaches sociology at the University of Massachusetts at Amherst. He is completing a book which examines the ways in which social fractions within the dominant society discover and attempt to gain access to minority popular culture, and how minority popular cultural practices serve in the formation of public spheres. He is currently studying television's new "reality programming" and the links between social crisis and images of race.

Russell F. Farnen is Director of the University of Connecticut at Hartford and Professor of Political Science. His academic areas of specialization include mass media and politics, national defense, and cross national political socialization. He previously co-authored two American government texts, *Civic Education in Ten Countries: An Empirical Study* (Wiley, 1976), and "War, Presidents, and the Constitution" in *Presidential Studies Quarterly* (summer 1988). He has also contributed a piece on cross national impacts of television news to the International Studies in Political Science and Political Education series published by Peter Lang Verlag (N.Y. and Frankfurt/Main 1988) and is author of volume 4 in the same series on *Integrating Political Science, Education and Public Policy: International Perspectives on Decision-Making, Systems Theory, and Socialization Research* (1990). The financial and technical assistance provided by the University of Connecticut Research Foundation is gratefully acknowledged.

Bruce K. Friesen is a Ph.D. candidate in Sociology at the University of Calgary in Alberta, Canada. He obtained a Bachelor of Religious Education (psychology minor) from Hillcrest College (Medicine Hat, Alberta) in 1980; a Bachelor of Arts (History) from the University of Waterloo (Waterloo, Ontario) in 1983; and a Master of Arts in Sociology from the University of Calgary in 1986. His current research interests involve the politicization of problems concerning children and youth, and he has focused his dissertation on the political aspects of the child day care issue.

Jerry M. Lewis is a professor of sociology at Kent State University where he has been a member of the faculty since 1966. His Ph.D. is from the University of Illinois (Urbana). His research interests are in the areas of collective behavior, popular culture, and sociology of sport. His film watching tends to run to comedies, spy movies, and anything with Jane Fonda in it.

Eleanor Lyon is currently a research associate at Child and Family Services in Hartford, CT. Her most recent research has focused on homicide, incest, female offenders, and family violence. She also teaches courses on sociological perspectives on women, interpersonal violence, and the family at the Hartford campus of the University of Connecticut.

Stephen L. Markson: In 1971, as I was about to graduate from S.U.N.Y. Buffalo with a B.A. in Sociology, some officious "real adult world" types tried to burst my psychic bubble with an unsettling pronouncement of truth. I was informed that with my degree would come the inevitable end to days spent on a college campus, listening to rock and roll, and criticizing government policies. Thankfully, they were wrong. Eighteen years later, having completed a Ph.D. in Sociology at the University of Massachusetts and now teaching and conducting research on popular culture at the University of Hartford, I spend my days on a college campus, listening to rock and roll, and criticizing government policies.

Marek Payerhin, a Ph.D. candidate in the department of Political Science, University of Connecticut, Storrs, Connecticut, has written a master's thesis on media and terrorism and published articles on this subject in Poland, where he permanently resides.

Linda Powell graduated from Kent State in 1976 with a B.A. (summa cum laude) in Corrections.

Clinton R. Sanders is an associate professor of sociology at the Greater Hartford Campus of the University of Connecticut. His areas of specialization include deviant behavior, cultural production, and qualitative research methods. His most recent study focused on the social world surrounding tattooing. He is currently involved in investigating the development of relationships between humans and companion animals.

Barbara Stenross is a Lecturer in the Department of Sociology, University of North Carolina at Chapel Hill. Her research interests include occupational and leisure subcultures, including the link between work and pleasure in "business hobbies." She has recently published (with Sherryl Kleinman), "The Highs and Lows of Emotional Labor: Detectives' Encounters with Criminals and Victims" *(Journal of Contemporary Ethnography,* January 1989).

Carrie Stern is currently completing her Ph.D. in New York University's Department of Performance Studies. A professional choreographer, performer and teacher, Ms. Stern has experience with a wide variety of western and non-western dance forms including both the theatrical and the vernacular. In addition to her ongoing studies as a modern dancer, her current focus is on the various types of social dancing in the United States, as well as parades and festivals.

Priscilla K. Warner died suddenly on August 7, 1989. At the time of her death she was on the faculty of the department of Sociology and Anthropology at the University of Northern Iowa. Her research involved the animation market, animators' careers, and the work routines of creative personnel.